A Boy's Own

OILY

Adventure

by

Brian Page

PlashMill Press

Published in Scotland and the United Kingdom in 2009 by
PlashMill Press

First Edition

All characters in this publication are based on real people but have been modified and names have been changed to protect the identities of those concerned. All events described in the book are based on real events. No responsibility or liability whatsoever will be accepted by the publisher or the author for damage or injury caused by attempts to replicate them.

A CIP catalogue record for this book is available from the British Library.

ISBN 978-0-9554535-9-5

PlashMill Press
The Plash Mill
Friockheim
Angus DD11 4SH
Scotland.

Printed and bound by Robertson Printers, Forfar

This book, as with all the others, is dedicated to my family, Bobbie, Susie, Julie and Martin, without whom these tales would be meaningless.

Brian Page

In memory of our good friend Abb' Littlejohn
June 1918 – September 2009

'My formula for success is to rise early, work late and strike oil.'

Paul Getty

Contents

Section 1
Offshore Again

Section 2
Onshore Activities

Contents

Section 3
Foreign Parts

Acknowledgements

To my Editor, Rod Fleming, who still believes I can remember things and has faith enough to publish the result.

To John Cramond and Bill Taylor, whose collective memories came to my rescue and reminded me of yet more true adventures; thanks chaps.

To Alex, who tried to convince me I would enjoy working in strange places.

To Gianpaolo, a good friend who introduced me to the Italian way of life.

And last but not least to George—for buying a Liverpool scarf.

INTRODUCTION

This book is by way of a follow-up to that best selling tale of daring-do and self sacrifice entitled *A Boy's Own Offshore Adventure.* "How can this be? I hear you ask" (I've been hearing voices lately.) Well it came about as a result of a discussion with my Editor, who wondered whether I could write a block-busting detective novel, in the manner, he said, of your hero Ian Rankin. Having quickly realised the futility of such a request, he suggested, in another unguarded moment, that I might like to write a sequel to the Boy's Own Offshore saga. In order, he said, to share with my loyal readers, some further adventures in a career dedicated to providing the populace with oil and gas.

So, without further ado, be prepared to meet once again those unsung heroes of Book One—Liam, Bert, Sid, Andy, Allan, and Vince. All of whom were around at the same time as me during the rush for oil in the 1970's.

Then, having said all I can remember about life offshore, you will be given a unique insight as to why Italians are superior to us in many ways, how we adapted to life without television in Kazakhstan and why Africa is no place for a pale, spectacle-wearing Anglo-Saxon.

As ever, on these occasions, I have to say that should any eagle-eyed reader spot a technical or chronological error, they should just move on to the next section where—you never know—things might turn out to be more accurate.

Section One

Offshore Again

1. A Heroic Rescue

It was a dark and stormy night. Well not dark exactly, more a bit dull if I'm honest. In fact, it wasn't very stormy either, but there was definitely a bit of a drizzle. However, we need to set the correct dramatic tone for what happened next—so to speak.

Liam and Bert were arguing—as usual. The substance of the disagreement seemed to be centred around whose turn it was to crawl to the top of the flare boom in order to make sure all was well, prior to burning off a considerable amount more gas than we had been doing up until now. Fortunately for us, Mr Benn, the well-known diarist, pipe smoker and esteemed Secretary of State for Energy, hadn't yet cottoned on to the fact that we were intent on burning lots of his lovely energy. However, as we were about to increase production, it fell to one of us Maintenance chaps to clamber up the boom, stare meaningfully at the nozzles, make a highly technical pronouncement along the lines of, 'it looks okay to me' and clamber back down again.

Being fearless offshore tigers, the current discussion between Liam and Bert was littered with pithy statements such as, "I went last time, it's your turn." "I can't go, it's raining and I can't find me waterproof jacket." "It'll be pitch black up there and my torch is on the blink."

Once again finding myself in the role of arbitrator in our happy, close-knit team, I suggested we toss a coin to see who should undertake this onerous task, especially as the film was about to start in the next half-hour. I reckoned that should do the trick, as we'd been promised an uncut copy of the original version of 'The Hound of the Baskervilles,' a rare treat, as most of us had only seen it three or four times before. So, in the time honoured fashion and to avoid any further recriminations, I tossed a coin and as you do, they both called 'heads.' However, on the third flip, Bert lost the toss and in an attempt to convince us he was pleased with the outcome, said, "I don't mind missing the start of the film, as the last time it was shown, I could answer Watson's questions before Basil

Rathbone could."

You don't get self-sacrifice like that every day.

So, having found our waterproof gear and a torch with batteries, off we went to the base of the flare-boom, the end of which disappeared into the darkness.

"Well don't just stand there, get yourself up the boom and let's be getting back in the warm," said Liam, coming over all masterful.

"Sod off," replied Bert as he started the long trek upwards.

Now, for those unfamiliar with the offshore scene; a word of explanation. When the oil comes out of the well it contains an awful lot of gas, which we didn't know what to do with. So, in the early days, we used to dispose of it by flaring, which is a technical term for setting fire to it. This meant we had to have something to carry the gas pipe away from the platform, hence the need for a boom. Picture a giant crane with growing problems, a walkway up the side, a gas pipe running up the middle and fixed to the end of the platform with an upward slope of about thirty degrees. Ours was about 110 feet long and as the bottom end was forty feet above the water, by the time you arrived at the top you were probably about eighty feet over the sea. The other interesting thing was that being a cantilever, it moved up and down as you made your way along, so that by the time you arrived at the top, the damn thing was leaping about with the sole intention of throwing you into the sea.

Anyway, having flashed his torch on and off several times and with nothing more than the odd curse, Bert had set off on the long climb, while Liam and I bravely defied the rain and awaited the return of our mate.

"It's taking him a bloody long time," said Liam by way of conversation.

"Give him a chance," I said, "I can see his light waving about in the gloom; he shouldn't be long, all he has to do is climb onto the nozzle, lean out over the end, shine his torch into the innards and check there are no bits missing."

Mind you, after another five or ten minutes had gone by and there was still no sign of Bert, we began to fear the worst.

"I'll bet the daft sod's found something wrong and we'll be up all night trying to fix it," said Liam. However, just as we were reconciling ourselves to missing the big picture, we saw Bert's torch waving about as he descended. "At bloody last," said Liam, continuing to maintain a positive attitude.

"What did you find that took you so long," I asked, before Liam could launch further into critical mode.

"There's a bloke up there."

"Up where?"

"Where the bloody hell do you think, he's up there at the top of the flare."

"Well, what's he doing up there?"

"How the hell do I know what he's doing up there, he's just sodding well up there. How many more times do I have to tell you?"

"Hang on Bert," I said, "Didn't you ask him what he was doing on the top of the flare boom at this time of night, in the pouring rain?"

"And anyway," said Liam, chipping in, "Who is the daft sod?"

Bert, staring at us with something approaching hatred, said, "All I know is that when I got to the top, I got the fright of my bloody life to hear a sort of low moaning sound, which became even more frightening when I shone my light on the tip, to find one of the production technicians kneeling on a cross member and clinging for dear life to the ignition pipe."

"Yes, that's all very well," said Liam, "But why doesn't he just bloody well come down and let us finish the job."

"Because," said Bert, with enforced patience, "The poor bastard's suffering from vertigo. He's terrified and says he can't move either up or down."

"It would be quicker all round if he could just move up a bit more,' said Liam, "We could then fish him out of the sea."

"Well one thing's for sure, we can't just leave him there," I said, in what I thought was a fair summary. After all, I was supposed to be in charge and therefore capable of quickly grasping the essentials.

Bert said, "We're getting nowhere. Why don't we send for Andy? He's the Medic, he should know all about vertigo."

"Aye, that'll be right," said Liam, "We'll then be in the delightful situation where there are two idiots trapped at the top of the boom. If you've any more bright ideas like that, the place will start to get crowded."

Reluctantly I said, "You're right Liam, the only thing we can do is for you and me to go up to the top and between us we'll have to help him down. In the meantime, Bert could get Andy to the base here, so as he can check him over on arrival."

I thought this was a masterly plan and was somewhat surprised to find that Liam was less than enchanted with the idea.

"Oh bloody right," he said, "That's all I need, some idiot clinging to the pipework, two of us jammed on a single walkway at the top and just to make it more interesting, it's pitch black and it's pissing down."

Bert said, "You're just miffed because the film's about to start."

"Come on," I said, "Otherwise we'll be here all night and the poor devil will end up falling off anyway."

So, after checking Bert's torch once more, Liam and I set off one behind the other, until we were almost at the top of the boom. Did I mention the fact that by the time you arrived, the end of the boom would be moving? Well with two of us clumping up the slope the thing went into overdrive, even Liam and I had to hang on with both hands as we arrived at the top.

Ever one to get to the root of a problem, Liam shone his torch on our victim and said, "Bloody hell I know who it is—it's Billy! What are you bloody playing at, you daft sod?"

Now as an opening gambit, designed to provide reassurance and comfort, I felt Liam's approach lacked a certain degree of care and understanding—so I decided to have a try.

"Billy, let go of the sodding pipe, turn around and come down with us before we all get blown off the blasted boom." This approach, I felt, struck just the right note of urgency, clarity of purpose and care. So I was somewhat surprised to find that Billy, far from being consoled, let out a further selection of curses and for the first time, a reasonably coherent explanation.

"I can't come down, I can't move and I sure as hell can't let go of the bloody pipe! I'm telling you, it's no use—I'm stuck, me legs won't move and I'm bloody freezing." And with that concise resume of his situation, he gripped the pipe even harder and started to moan again.

Looking back, I think we must have based our reassurance patter on one of those films where the hero climbs out onto the top ledge of a skyscraper and calmly prevents a would-be suicide from jumping to his death. Well, in our case, we must have missed a crucial bit of the film because, despite our efforts at reassurance, Billy continued to moan with increasing volume. It also became noticeable that the moaning was now interspersed with an enviable selection of curses, which seemed to coincide with the oscillations of the boom.

Liam and I looked at one another and I think at that moment, we both decided to abandon any further attempts to implement a 'trained negotiator' strategy. Not least because we obviously knew nothing about it, we were soaked, it was dark, the wind was increasing and the film had now started.

Liam said, "Right, let's get the idiot down." With that, he grabbed Billy's wrists, twisted them off the pipe, pushed them onto my shoulders and said, "Right, move it, you two." So, with me at the front and Liam at the back holding onto Billy's overalls, we tentatively made our way down the boom.

After what seemed like a lifetime we reached the base, to be met by Bert and Andy.

"Well, that took you two some bloody time," said Bert—with what might be construed as insensitivity. Reeling from this display of gross ingratitude, we inadvertently let go of Billy, who promptly fell on the deck. Then, as one, we turned on Bert and as ever, it was Liam who spoke for the pair of us.

"Listen Bert, the next bloody time you find some daft sod up a boom, down a hole, along a pipe or hanging from the crane—don't sodding tell me—just leave them to it." So, still muttering, the three of us left Billy in the tender care of Andy and, sustained by a strong brew and a sticky bun, we agreed that if any of us saw someone in dire straits in future, we would pretend we hadn't seen them, especially if it occurred near to the start of a film. Then, nodding in agreement, Bert said, "If we're quick, we'll still be in time to catch the last reel of the Hound of the Baskervilles." Perfect.

2. A Word of Explanation

In the early 1970's I was in what was laughingly known as a 'professional occupation.' I was a Lecturer in Mining Engineering at a College in Lancashire and had a briefcase, a sports jacket with leather patches and a salary instead of wages. The only problem was I couldn't for the life of me see me doing this for the next thirty years. (This concern, as it turned out, was fortuitous, because in the 1980's a caring Government decided to do away with the Mining Industry.) Anyway, after a number of false starts, I entered the previously unknown world of Oil Exploration and Production, at a time when the UK offshore adventure was just gathering pace. During the next nine years I was involved in the development and installation of three major Production Platforms in the North Sea. As a result of which I met with a great bunch of guys, many of whom seemed to be slightly mad, but with diverse skills in Design, Construction, Commissioning, Operations, Maintenance and various supporting roles.

During those early days I got to play with real man-sized plant and equipment, there were giant cranes to be driven, pumps to be started and stopped, helicopters to fly, tankers to moor, radios to operate and lifeboats to sail.

In an act of abject cowardice you will find that names have been changed to protect reputations and avoid libel action. However, I would add that all of the recollections are true and in the main unembellished. As they say about many of the things that happen in life, 'you couldn't make it up.'

Although there were a great many bodies on board during the final stages of construction, I worked mainly within a self-appointed exclusive club. The main players were Liam and Bert, who were both Maintenance Technicians. We were ably supported by Sid, the OIM; Andy, the Medic; Ken the Radio Operator; Allan, the on-site Helicopter Pilot and Vince the Project Manager.

Later on, having been sent out into the wide world to fend for myself, I was asked to take on a three week assignment for a Project in Kazakhstan, which lasted some eight years. It was there I learned a good deal about the cultural differences between the Brits and the Italians—with the Italians winning hands down. But more of that later.

3. Overtime and the Sociologist

Sid, our esteemed Installation Manager, called me into his office one afternoon. Slightly puzzled but reassured to see his favourite cardigan was in place, slippers were firmly on the feet and the Times was open at the crossword, I asked him what was up.

"I need your help," he said, "some genius in Personnel onshore has come up with a brilliant idea of hiring a University to carry out a survey on offshore working hours and we've been chosen for interview. They're a bunch of bloody idiots—it's asking for trouble."

Now as this was 1975, Human Resources hadn't yet been invented and instead we were in the tender care of a bunch of people known as the Personnel Department. I have to say they tried hard to support us offshore malcontents and the ladies in particular were unfailingly helpful, even though half the time they must have been appalled at our futile attempts to be 'big oil and gas men' - as portrayed by John Wayne in that unforgettable saga 'Hellfighters' in which our hero single-handedly douses oilfield fires. (As ever with JW films, the clue lies in the title.)

Anyway, as we were all very much in favour of overtime, I began to see snags in the proposal. After all, I reasoned, if you've already worked for twelve hours, another two or three is no real hardship, and besides, the snooker table was waiting for a new cover and the films were generally of the 'oh no—not again' variety.

"What makes them think it's a good idea?" I asked.

"I'll tell you what," said Sid, beginning to warm to his theme. "Some bloody idiot in a university with nothing better to do, has been casting around for a subject which might get a nice, easy PhD in Sociology. They've approached our company and some lunatic onshore has been sold on the idea of getting lots of free information regarding the lads' overtime. You mark my words, it'll be some wet behind the ears spotty students, who've never done a day's work in their lives, inflicting themselves on us and asking a lot of damn-fool questions."

Once again, I found myself in awe of Sid; here was a man who could spot a 'con' from fifty yards and provide a lucid, unbiased appraisal of the situation. However, I reasoned whom should I believe—Sid, who had worked for the company all around the world, had been a prisoner of war and escaped on numerous occasions (but sadly, captured each time,) was completely unflappable and had a wonderful world-weary cynicism. Or—some fourteen year old in the office who, without considering the awful consequences, thought 'gosh this is a good idea' and even more alarmingly—had convinced someone higher-up to accept the offer.

Hoping for the best, but fearing the worst, I said, "What do you want me to do?"

"Do? I'll tell you what I want you to do. We're into damage limitation here; I need you to get some of your more sane guys together, brief them on the proposal and then meet with the idiots and answer their questions, but—" and here he emphasised the point — "For god's sake don't let the lads give them the wrong impression."

As I had no idea what the wrong impression might be—and didn't want to ask—I nodded and went off in search of the lads. My main worry being that Sid had specified they were to be reasonably sane.

Using the simple but unfailing ploy of offering to fetch mugs of tea and a sticky bun each, I managed to collar Liam, Bert and Allan and explained as best I could that they'd all volunteered to be part of an important research programme by some clever academics.

Having stared at me for what seemed to be a long time, questions were asked, what was it all about, why us, is there money in it, would there be time off? These and other pertinent queries were fired at me, but, as I'd no idea what the answers were, I fell back on the time honoured tactic of lying and said there was bound to be a reward somewhere from a grateful company.

I don't think they were convinced for a second, but it sounded better than spending a freezing afternoon mooring tankers on the remote buoy.

Reporting back to Sid, I asked him just what it was a sociologist did for a living. Sid said, "Good question. I wasn't sure myself, so I asked a mate of mine and he said that in the main they studied things like the meaning of life, identity and embodiment, the social self and modernity and social theory."

I must have looked stunned, because he went on, "Don't look at me like that, I had to write the sodding stuff down when he told me."

"Yes, but what the hell does it mean and what's it got to do with us?"

"Not a bloody clue," said Sid, "But for god's sake, don't let the lads know that we don't know, if you see what I mean. Anyway we'll find out soon enough; they're due out on a round trip tomorrow."

The following day found us crammed in Sid's office where we were introduced to our researchers. One was a girl who looked about twelve; the other was a lad who looked like her younger brother while the third member was Gary, a representative from Personnel, who looked uncomfortable.

Introductions over, Sid said, "Okay, I'll leave it to you folks now," and with that, the cowardly sod nipped out.

The girl, who turned out to be the senior partner, then looked nervously about her and set the scene.

"The sociology people in our university are carrying out a study into the mental and physical effects of working long hours. We understand that offshore people, such as you, are in this category and we would like to obtain some statistical information for our research. We also believe that working such long hours may have a detrimental effect on personal relationships."

"So what are you saying?" asked Liam.

"Well, our early conclusions are that you should all work shorter hours and be given more relaxed recreational facilities."

At this, I noticed the lads had begun to nod in agreement, while Gary had begun to shift uneasily in his seat.

"What hours do you think we should work?" asked Bert, coming over all interested.

"It's difficult to be concise, but we think eight hours in a day in such a harsh environment is sufficient for a healthy outlook."

By now the lads were positively beaming, as Liam remarked, "Bloody hell, at present we're doing a twelve hour shift, with another two or three hours on top if anything goes wrong. Eight hours sounds great to me." There were more nods from the lads and it was fast becoming a mutual admiration society until, that is, Allan spoke for the first time.

"Presumably," he said, "If we adopt your recommendations, we'll be paid for eight hours instead of twelve and there wouldn't be any overtime payments?"

On hearing this, several things happened at once — the girl and boy looked at one another in some alarm, Gary began to whistle tunelessly and the lads' demeanour changed from admiration to consternation.

"Just a cotton pickin' minute," said Bert, who recently had been watching a number of films set in the Deep South. "Let me get this straight. Are you telling me I'm expected to leave home for a week, fly a hundred miles out in the North Sea, share a cabin with three other hairy idiots, put up with lumpy custard, test lifeboats and get covered in oil, all so that you lot can reduce my wages by at least a third and, by way of compensation, expect me to play snooker on a crappy table for the remaining eight hours every day?"

There was what might be termed 'a pregnant silence' and then we all started nodding again, only this time it was directed at Bert. The sociologists looked crestfallen and not a little fearful, obviously never having been on the receiving end of a man suffering from strong emotions. Then Gary cleared his throat and said, 'Well thanks everyone. I think we've achieved all we're going to, so we'd best be getting back onshore."

"Aye," said Liam, "I think that's the best thing to do, after all, I suppose you've lots of other platforms to visit."

"We'll need to have a review meeting when we get ashore and then we can decide what to do next,' said Gary, who by now had stopped whistling.

Liam said, "I'd be careful though, because you lot have just caused me more mental anguish than working long hours ever will. I'm off for a cup of tea."

Some time later and having tried desperately to calm the lads down, I found Sid earnestly studying the Times crossword. I reported on the substance of the meeting. "Bloody fools," he muttered, "They really should keep these academic children away from the real world. I didn't think the lads would be keen to swap money for some bloody mystical feeling of wellbeing."

We'd just started one of Sid's weekly safety meetings on our next shift and as I was about to read the previous minutes, Liam said, "Never mind all that rubbish, what we all want to know is—what's the outcome of the working-hours research?"

Sid, who'd obviously been expecting this to crop up at some time, said, 'I had a word with one of the more senior Personnel ladies and mentioned the distinct possibility that implementing such a hare-brained scheme would probably bring the North Sea to a standstill. I heard from her yesterday and apparently, the Company have reviewed the proposal and concluded that as their offshore workforce were subjected to regular medical examinations and pronounced physically fit —they intended to call off the research for the time being."

"That's a victory for common sense," I said.

"I guess you could say that," said Sid, "But I noticed she made no mention of mental fitness."

4. How Can You Lose Two Spaniards?

It was Sunday and once again Sid had decreed we should have a lifeboat drill before dinner. As he said, it would give everyone an appetite and the thought of missing a nice bit of fillet would concentrate the mind and prevent time-wasting.

Muster Stations were located around the accommodation and Liam, being in the wrong place at the wrong time, was appointed Muster Checker for the station, which was mainly allocated to visitors. This meant that he had to contend with a random selection of guys, most of whom had a couple of things in common—they had never set foot on a platform before and were, in general, apt to react nervously each time an alarm sounded. These minor problems meant that Liam had to take on a number of additional roles, that of nursemaid, mentor, father-figure and confidence booster; especially as his group could see the regulars milling about and chatting happily with their respective checkers.

Due to their prevailing nervousness and being anxious not to miss a word he said, the visitors clustered around Liam who had to make doubly sure that everyone on his list had turned up, were adequately equipped and knew the whereabouts of their lifeboat and - even more importantly— they knew how to get there.

On this particular occasion, everyone was accounted for; the checkers had confirmed the status to Sid, who, being in command mode, was ensconced in the radio room with a Motorola radio clutched to his ear. Then, having received the good news, he initiated Part Two of the drill and pressed the signal to 'go to lifeboats.'

Now, we had six lifeboats, one at each corner and one in the middle of each of the longest sides and it was at one such boat that Bert and I played our part in the saga. I was the appointed lifeboat and lifejacket checker, whilst Bert opened up the boat and prepared to make sure everyone was seated in some sort of order.

To get to your appointed boat from the Muster Stations meant going down three flights of stairs and travelling around the perimeter walkway until you arrived. Simple really, until that is, you began to see the same people, all going in different directions, pass you for about the fourth time.

In the meantime, I was confirming that the new arrivals were at the correct boat station, getting them to fit their life-jackets (an epic tale of endurance in itself) ticking them off on my list and passing them into the caring hands of Bert, who with a considerable amount of pushing, shoving and cursing, got them seated in the boat.

By now Liam had arrived and Sid was happily on the radio, checking that all was well and that my numbers tallied with Liam's Muster list. It was looking good and fillet steak would be soon on the plate until, that is, we noticed a distinct absence of further arrivals and Bert said "Okay, they're all in."

I said, "There's still two missing."

"What?" shouted my two cohorts in unison.

"I'm afraid so, I've still got two names not ticked off."

"Who the hell are they?" said Liam, "I made doubly sure everyone was present at the muster and I saw them all move off towards the stairs."

"Well, at a wild guess I'd say they were Spanish, one's called Santos and the other's Escobar."

"I remember them," said Liam, "they're on board to check the installation of their company's isolation valves. They only arrived this morning and their english isn't very good, but I spent some time showing them where their boat was located and the signals they would hear telling them what to do."

"And a right bloody cock-up you've made of it," said Bert, "As neither of them has arrived." Sometimes life seemed simple to Bert, especially if in his mind, he could convince himself that all our mishaps were Liam's fault.

"Never mind that," I said, coming over all managerial, "We're going to have to locate them as quick as we can because any minute now, Sid's going to call me on the radio to confirm that we have a full complement."

Sure enough, at that moment my radio burst into life and the dulcet tones of Sid could be heard asking the fateful question, "Boat 6, report in please, are all your people present and correct?"

Unfortunately, as far as Sid was concerned, this was a rhetorical question, as he believed he already had an affirmative answer, which simply required confirmation from me. The other minor embarrassment was the fact that the other five lifeboats could hear the conversation.

"Er, not quite Sid," I said, in what I fondly believed to be a commanding voice.

"What the bloody hell do you mean—'not quite'—is everyone there, or aren't they? What are you lot playing at? I've got everyone on the

Installation accounted for and now you tell me there's a problem, bloody hell."

We looked at one another, this was Sid at his wrathful best and excuses weren't going to placate him, especially as we all knew he just hated being late for his dinner.

"The problem is we've got two guys missing. I think they're Spanish. Their names are Santos and Escobar. Liam's convinced they were at the muster station and when the signal to go to lifeboats sounded, he definitely saw them make their way out, and since then there's been no sign of them."

I could see Liam staring at me, "What's all this crap about me being definite? They were just part of a group milling about when the signal went."

"We need to sound confident," I said, "Otherwise Sid will throw a fit if he thinks we lost them at the muster." Then, just as we all feared, Sid's patience snapped.

"What the bloody hell are you three playing at? It's not the biggest Installation in the world! How can you lose two sodding Spaniards between the accommodation and the lifeboat? You don't think the daft sods have fallen overboard, do you?"

Being unsure how or indeed whether to answer Sid's tirade, I suggested he double check with the other boats.

"Right," said Sid, "Boat 1—have you got any stray Spaniards with you?"

"No."

"Boat 2, have you got any with you?"

"No."

Then, just as the situation was becoming even more fraught, Bert said, "Hang on, who's this coming down the stairs?"

Liam said, "Bloody hell, it's the missing Spaniards! Where the hell have they been?"

Somewhat tentatively I said, "Hang on Sid, I think we've found them."

Then, as they got nearer, we began see the reason for the delay. Both were dressed in their going-home clothes, suits, shiny slip-on shoes, an overcoat each slung over one arm, but what completed the surreal scene was the fact that they were also dragging fully packed suitcases, a briefcase apiece and a folder full of documents. Slowly, and completely oblivious of the stir they were causing, they stopped at the lifejacket box, put down the suitcases, smiled at the three of us, said "Buenos tardes Senor" to Liam, and waited for further instructions.

"Never mind bloody Buenos wotsisname, where the hell have you two been until now?" demanded Liam, "You've had half the platform searching for you! I can't understand it, I saw you go out of the muster station, where did you go?"

Bert said, "I think it's sodding obvious, they've gone back to their cabin, got changed, gathered up their belongings and turned up here ready to abandon the Platform."

Throughout this exchange, our Iberian friends looked at one another, looked at us and looked puzzled. Then one said, "Is a problem?"

"Well, yes there is," I said with what I fondly thought of as dignified understatement. "You should have come straight to the boat from the muster. You didn't need to get changed and bring all your gear with you—all we're going to do is put you in the boat—then when everyone is accounted for, we cancel the exercise and return to the accommodation for our dinner."

There was what might be called a puzzled silence as our latecomers absorbed the information. Then, after a while, one of them said, "Scuse, senor, aren't we going to sail away in the lifeboats?"

"No, we're bloody well not," said Liam, "All we do is tick your name, put on a lifejacket and climb into the boat. We don't go anywhere in the blasted thing. Besides, it's probably the worst way in the world of getting off this heap of iron."

At this point, realising they would never understand what we were on about, they shrugged and said, "Scuse, we should get into the boat now," and with that, they grabbed a lifejacket apiece, gathered up the suitcases and staggered towards the boat's entrance. This evinced a cry from Bert who yelled, "Not sodding likely! You two just stay where you are, there's no way I'm going to try and get you and all your bloody accoutrements into the blasted boat. Let's just call it quits and we can get back in the warm for some dinner."

Just as Liam and I nodded in agreement, one of the Spaniards said, "Quits?—please what is quits?"

"Never mind what it is, lads," said Liam, "Just you two stand there for a minute, then once we're clear you can sod off back to your cabin."

"Please senor, what is sod off?"

Just then, before Liam became even more tight-lipped, Sid finally gave the all clear over the tannoy and we all sodded off for dinner.

5. Never Yield to Pressure

This might well have been Sid's favourite mantra and became increasingly apparent during the course of our somewhat futile, but generally enjoyable Staff Committee meetings. When I first got to know Sid he was probably in his late fifties and had been a Toolpusher for many years, but despite this, I found him to be great company. He was our first Offshore Installation Manager and this was the culmination of a long and varied career which had been anything but average. He had extensive experience of drilling in many countries, notably the Middle and Far East and just before the outbreak of hostilities, had been involved in sabotaging oil wells in Sarawak in order to foil the Japanese. (They'd obviously realised that Hitler wasn't all he was cracked up to be and so, starting with the Far East, had decided to take over the world themselves.)

Later on, he was involved in some Special Service activities in Europe during the Second World War, during which he was taken prisoner. This situation didn't suit Sid and he made something like eighteen failed attempts to escape from various prison camps.

After all this, managing a disparate bunch of workers during construction, commissioning, drilling and plant operation—whilst wearing carpet slippers—presented no real problems.

One day, Sid received an edict from 'Onshore' that he should hold regular staff meetings. These were were the brainchild of the Personnel Department who, as they explained to Sid, thought it would be a good idea to 'take soundings' with regard to issues of a recreational nature. This view wasn't shared by Sid, who believed that you could have too much democracy and that allowing the proletariat a means of airing their views was asking for trouble.

Initially, he was reluctant to comply and muttered all week about interference and bureaucracy. He told all and sundry that if anyone had a problem, they only had to tell him and he would do his best to solve it. This latter statement turned out to be a load of rubbish, but we were still very naive and consequently were impressed for a short time.

However, being an 'old hand' and recognising the futility of protest, he inaugurated a series of meetings and, without bothering to ask, 'volunteered' me to be his Secretary. Commenting at the time that he wasn't about to go it alone and besides, he said, 'it would provide me with good experience in man-management.'

The committee consisted of representatives from Production, Drilling and Catering, Sid's idea was to pick the most amenable people but, as we shall see, either he was rubbish at picking the right people, or they became power mad on being given the opportunity to raise their favourite grievances.

In the main and due in no small part to Sid's ability as a chairman, the meetings made a welcome break from work, except when they landed me with a number of challenges regarding appropriate (but not necessarily truthful) wording of the minutes.

As secretary, my job was to translate Sid's tendency to treat each issue as though it was singularly unimportant, into crucial sounding text, which vaguely identified actions to be taken.

This required me to use what is known as 'creative' wording and, as Sid was generally the only person who had the authority to provide solutions, I had to be doubly careful not to make him the 'action party' for everything.

And just to make things even more interesting, the minutes also had to convince our masters onshore that not only did we have an awesome grasp of critical issues, but at a stroke, were able to provide solutions.

Unfortunately for me, Sid tended to display a cavalier attitude towards the need for urgent action. Juggling with the facts required me to tread a fine line between flippancy (not treating things with due reverence) and sycophancy (treating Sid as our saviour.)

I also quickly realised that, whenever he was challenged about an item in the minutes, he had no compunction in asserting that the secretary must have failed to reflect what he had actually said. This was despite the fact that the draft minutes were approved by him prior to issue. I think it's called a 'learning curve.'

The continuing need for caution was brought home to me one day when Liam said to Sid, "That last meeting was a waste of time. You promised to get the guy out to re-cover the snooker table and so far there's been no sign of him."

Sid said, "I definitely don't recall making any such promise. Obviously me bloody secretary must have made a mistake when he took the minutes. Honestly, you can't trust anyone these days to do a simple job." I began to realise that Sid's idea of truth and veracity was largely dependent on whether he was expected to assume responsibility for carrying out his own rash promises. Still, I suppose if you had successfully lied your way out of several Stalags during the war, a little thing like failing to order a new snooker cloth wouldn't seem overly important.

I won't dwell again on the old favourite gripes—films, newspapers and the laundry—enough has been said about them already. However, it would be remiss of me, as a faithful scribe, not to mention a number of other, perhaps less well documented problems that beset the lives of a newly minted bunch of 'big oil and gas men' (as the Americans were wont to call themselves.)

There was, for instance, the thorny problem surrounding video tapes. Remember, this was 1975 and the taping of programmes was something of an adventure. Someone, generally from the Personnel Department, who was affluent enough to own a video cassette recorder would take home a tape and record a number of programmes. This had certain drawbacks. If, for instance, the recorder was enamoured with the ongoing real-life drama in Coronation Street, there was a tendency to neglect other, perhaps more intellectually stimulating fare such as The Sweeney or Game for a Laugh. Having successfully recorded something, the 'taper' would dutifully label the video, take it to the office and pop it in a mailbag destined for the platform. This system, although reliable, had a couple of flaws; as many of the lads worked one week on and one week off, it wasn't unusual to find that by the time the tape arrived, it was already a week old. This meant that the lucky viewers, having peeled their oranges, unwrapped their sweeties and settled down for a good viewing; found that they'd seen the damn thing during their previous off-duty. Still, seeing it for the second time had to be better than seeing the current film for the fourth time, so they pressed on. Witness, therefore, the cries of delight when they found that, having come to the end of the particular Coronation Street episode, the kindly recorder had let the tape run into the following programme. Witness even more delight when our viewers realised it was an episode of Danger Man, which they hadn't seen. Witness the sense of utter devastation when—having arrived at the part where the baddie is just about to be caught by our hero—the tape stopped. Suddenly the oranges turned sour, sweeties were choked on—there was only one thing for it — this callous neglect of people's feelings had to be raised, as a matter of urgency, at the next committee meeting.

Sid received the complaint with his usual distain for all things entertainment. He didn't play either snooker or darts and the thought of having to watch an old episode of Coronation Street filled him with dread. Sid's idea of relaxation heaven was a copy of the Times or Telegraph folded open at the crossword, a mug of tea and a plateful of those shiny plastic topped cakes. It was something of a surprise, therefore, to find he had, in fact, followed up the complaint and offered an explanation at the next meeting.

"Apparently," he said, "The person copying the programme had let it run on for a while, as she felt it would be very frustrating to find the last five minutes missing. She wasn't, therefore, aware of the trauma caused by the idiots on board believing there was another programme on the tape, especially when her label clearly specified there was only one."

Now whilst the explanation had the benefit of logic it did little to satisfy the complainants, especially when Sid reminded them that when on leave, they mostly occupied their spare time by playing golf or boozing and not by watching 'soaps' on television.

A couple of trips later Sid sent for me and coming straight to the point said, "What the bloody hell's this?"

'This' turned out to be the agenda for the next committee meeting and the bit causing Sid some annoyance was, Item 3 — Video Problems.

"It's no good shouting at me," I said, "I only put down the topics the members want to discuss."

"I thought we'd resolved all the problems with the damned thing; what's bothering them now?"

"Apparently," I said, choosing my words carefully, because it wasn't unusual for Sid to blame me for allowing what he called 'flippant' issues to be raised. "There's a new problem with the video itself; it seems that when a tape is being played, there's a lot of interference which makes it difficult to follow the plot, so to speak."

"Plot, plot, what bloody plot? Most of the programmes don't have any plot! Give me strength."

This was Sid at his obtuse best and I knew I'd have a job to convince him of the seriousness of the situation. After all, no self-respecting hairy offshore tiger could be expected to give of his best knowing that all he could watch by way for relaxation was a blurred video. I tried again.

"Sid, as you know, the video recorder is kept in the radio room and when anyone wants to watch a tape, they take it to Kenny and he puts it in the machine."

"I know all that, so what's the problem?"

"Well, it seems that Kenny has had some new electronic wizardry installed and, according to him, it's not screened or something and is obviously causing the new stuff to interfere with video reception."

"Then the answer's simple," said Sid, "Let's just move the sodding machine out of the radio room and put it in the corner of the recreation area. That way, no one needs to bother Kenny any more and it should be far enough away from the source of the interference."

I had to say, this sounded to be the answer, until I had another thought. "Yes, but Sid, if we leave the setting up of the videos to every Tom, Dick and Harry, the machine's bound to get damaged. I can see the tapes being jammed and people poking knives or pencils into the works trying to free the thing. It'll be ruined within the week."

"Exactly," replied Sid.

And then we had a request for a toilet to be located somewhere on the plant. The production representative made this plea at one of our meetings, citing the fact that it was a hell of a long trek back up into the accommodation should anyone get an urgent call of nature, so to speak. (These weren't his exact words, but as I had to send copies of the minutes to our boss's secretary onshore, I needed to paraphrase on occasions.)

For some reason, this plea seemed to cause Sid a good deal of amusement and most unusually, he offered several proposals, none of which, as it turned out, had the benefit of either comfort or practicality. One such suggestion was to locate the unit at the south end of the platform in close proximity to the flare. "This," he said, "Would keep people warm whilst they went about their business," however, he acknowledged, "There was always the risk of second degree burns to the nether regions should they linger too long." With that, he gave another throaty chuckle and the members began to realise that he wasn't perhaps taking the matter as seriously as they believed was required.

Sid's attempt at humour was also beginning to give me a problem regarding the minutes when Liam said, "It's all very well you lot wanting crappers all over the place, but have any of you considered the difficulties of connecting them to the sewage unit which is on the same level as your proposed locations? If we have no force of gravity to move the stuff along, it's just going to lie in the pipe until it overflows. There's one thing for sure, I'm not getting involved in maintaining such a half-arsed system."

This highly technical outburst from Liam brought about a twofold reaction; the members looked disconsolate and Sid beamed at Liam, with what he incorrectly thought of as approval. Then, just as I was wrestling once more with wording for the minutes, Bert said, "Don't talk to me about sewage; I want nothing to do with it, I'm still getting over the sodding mess we had to shift from under the accommodation a while ago."

At this revelation, we all leaned forward and even Sid, who by now was usually half out of the door, stopped and said, "Mess? What bloody mess? I don't remember anything going wrong."

Bert said, "No you won't, it was before your time and it was horrible."

Liam said, "Well are you going to tell us, or is it some sort of secret?"

Bert gave Liam one of his long-distance stares he usually reserved for requests to help in changing crane ropes and said, "Well, as you know, when I first came out the platform wasn't fully built and we used to stay at night on the crane barge, which brought out the modules ready to assemble on the steel jacket. The accommodation module was one of the biggest units and while it was on the deck of the barge, the construction gang finished coupling up the pipework and electric cables.

"Anyway, the day came when the weather was calm, the work was finished and the crane lifted the accommodation onto the platform. The lads then set to work to make it habitable, with power, heating and ventilation to the galley so we could have chips. I then came on board and began to check everything was okay before we could use the facilities.

"All went well for a couple of weeks, until people began to complain of a terrible smell coming from somewhere under the accommodation. Even with a strong northerly gale, the smell percolated though the cabins and it was so bad it put people off their pudding. We checked all the toilets but they were clear and when we put hoses down the water ran away all right - but despite all this, the awful smell was still there.

"In the end, there was nothing for it but to crawl under the accommodation and try to find out where the hell it was coming from. Now, the gap between the base and the deck is very small and obviously it's dark, so we got flat on our stomachs and pushed our way under. I then shone my torch on the most horrible, nasty, smelly sight I've ever seen. The whole of the space underneath was a sea of sewage, slopping gently to and fro with the motion of the deck. I couldn't get out of there fast enough. And it was then we realised the awful truth—the bastards had forgotten to couple up the sewage pipework when the accommodation was lifted into place. So instead of all the hobgoblins being transported to the sewage plant, the bloody stuff was going no further than the space underneath where we lived."

Then, just as Bert paused for breath and we were contemplating the horror of it all, the catering representative asked a damnfool question.

"How did you get rid of the crap?"

"Well there's one thing for sure," said Bert. "We didn't swab the bloody stuff up with your mop and buckets. We waited for a strong north-easterly and then turned three fire hoses on the congealed muck. After about ten minutes of high pressure spraying, the whole lot finally broke loose and as it emerged from under the accommodation, we had a sort of horrible smelly cloud of liquid brown crap being caught by the gale, before most of it flew over the side of the platform. Although I have to admit that on its way, a good deal of the stuff was caught on the rails and walkway, which took some getting rid of. By then, I didn't give a damn where it was going, as long I didn't get downwind of the sodding cloud as it billowed out from under the deck.

"So all I'm saying is—don't think you can get me involved in any more hare-brained bog extension schemes—just count me out." And with that Bert stared at the members as if daring them to contradict him.

Sid, who had been listening to the awful tale with growing unease, realised he had a golden opportunity to close out yet another item with which he had no sympathy. So, before the committee had a chance to recover from the saga, he favoured Bert with a big smile and said, "Well gentlemen, I don't think we'll be hearing any more foolish talk about extra toilets, will we."

6. Some Like It Hot

You may be fooled into thinking that as an oilfield is pretty big, you could just float out your new platform, look around a bit and say, 'this is near enough—we'll plonk it down about here.' You couldn't be more wrong—remember we're engineers and accuracy is our byword.

No;—calculations are made, errors are eliminated, risks are assessed, weather windows are identified, sea-bed soil is analysed, programmes are refined, reservoir experts are consulted, the media is notified, champagne is on hand and a name is chosen. After which, we tow the platform out and at a given moment we say — 'this looks about right, we'll drop it here.'

While all of the foregoing activities are important, there is one overriding calculation we have to be sure of, that's the orientation of the platform. This is vital because we will —if the reservoir people have got their sums right and there is oil somewhere underneath —be burning lots of gas. Therefore, if we're to avoid having a giant blow-lamp pointing at us, we need to have the flare boom located so that the prevailing wind blows the gas away from the platform and not towards it. I suppose our theme song might have been that one about Marilyn Monroe called 'A Candle in the Wind,' except for the fact that the strange little lad with the big glasses hadn't written it at the time.

Now, even though we were engineers and could use slide-rules, the decision regarding orientation was deemed too important to leave to us and so we called in the experts.

This was clearly a case for the meteorological people, so we rang the BBC and asked if they had a weatherman at a loose end. What we needed was for someone to calculate the most effective direction in which to place the platform, using nautical things like points of the compass. This of course meant that records would need to be consulted, words like — isobars, depressions, precipitation, veering, backing, cyclones, outlook, Beaufort scale, heat index, squall line, wind chill, velocity, inversion, jet stream, occluded front, relative humidity, trough and ridge — would all be freely used to baffle us during the course of numerous presentations and the production of copious reports.

Sadly, despite the proliferation of data, there turned out to be little worthwhile or reliable information available regarding the best place to set up shop. Despite the Met boffins having carried out complex calculations, made predictions and consulted old charts; we were convinced they'd ultimately been reduced to asking some Trawler Skippers in what direction the wind was blowing, when they were fishing in the vicinity.

After considerable deliberation and having translated the skippers' pronouncements from Doric into something loosely resembling English—the word came back—place the platform so that the flare boom faced south.

So, having cadged a compass, we took their advice and set the platform in place with the accommodation facing north and the flare facing south—perfect.

Unfortunately, one relatively important thing missing throughout all this brilliant planning was any valid knowledge of what the wind would actually do. It's all right thinking, 'Oh yes—that Michael Fish and his men certainly know a lot about weather,' and indeed that may be so when they're asked if it'll rain at Lord's on a Monday. But providing an accurate prediction for a speck of water in the middle of the North Sea, one hundred miles out from Aberdeen, was a different matter. As we were about to find out.

So there we were, 'in situ' as they say, facing the right way and, after some months consisting mainly of banging and hammering, we went into production. This meant we now had lots of gas that we didn't know what to do with — so we lit it. I know this sounds simple, but in the early days, lighting the flare required Sid to leave the safety of his office and fire a Very pistol into the gas cloud. (For those of a curious nature, a full account of the rationale behind this madness can be found in 'A Boy's Own Offshore Adventure,' in which, due to Liam's repeated failure to achieve ignition with oily rags, Sid becomes a reluctant sharp-shooter.)

How then, having consulted widely and followed recommendations to the letter, could anything possibly go wrong?

Well to be honest, for a start, nothing did go wrong, but then, as if on a whim one day, the wind changed direction and decided to blow from the south. Now, as we've seen, clever people had assured us that something called the 'prevailing wind' would be from the north and being of a trusting nature - we'd believed them. So not only were we now facing the wrong way as far as the flare was concerned, we'd also installed another small but crucial piece of kit, in what was now the wrong place. I refer to the accommodation air-conditioning intakes.

Being engineers (I keep repeating this just to remind you) and therefore, able to apply logic, we thought the best place for the conditioning unit would be facing south, the rationale being that if it faced due north it would draw in extremely cold air throughout the winter. It would, therefore, be a clever wheeze to site it where we could get the best of both worlds - not too cold and not too hot. So far so good, until that is, the blasted wind changed direction and we need now to talk about a thing called 'radiant heat.'

Imagine it's a freezing cold evening and you've dropped in to your Local for a nice pint accompanied by steak pie (complete with removable crust) and chips. While your drink is being poured, you notice a blazing fire in the grate. Moving swiftly over, you turn your back and standing as close as you dare without setting fire to your anorak, you begin to feel lovely and warm. That's it—radiant heat in all its glory.

Our flare behaved in much the same way as the pub fire, in that it transmitted radiant heat, but on a rather different scale. We were flaring several million cubic feet of gas each day, which, as I'm sure you can imagine, beats the average gas cooker hands down and produces an awful lot of heat and light.

On a cold day, when the wind was blowing the flare in the correct direction, you could stand on the south walkway and bask in its warmth. In fact, it also became a nice little stop-off for all sorts of birds. You could just imagine some migrants sitting on a rail, with feathers all puffed up and saying to one another, 'Why don't we give Africa a miss this year,? This'll do for me.' Until, as I mentioned earlier, the wind thought, 'I wonder what it's like blowing the other way—make a nice change that will.'

Suddenly, instead of the flare being blown in a southerly direction away from the platform, it found itself battling against a freshening Force 5 on the Beaufort scale. Now, while the wind couldn't completely change the flare's direction, it could, and did, bend the flame somewhat and redirect all that lovely heat back towards us. The result of which was to make those birds that weren't immediately incinerated think, 'to hell with this, I'm off, it's cooler in Africa.' People started avoiding the south end of the platform and extremely hot air was now being drawn into the air-conditioning intakes. In the meantime, our radiant heat friend was intent on warming up the handrails, welders' gas bottles, the cold food store, aluminium safety helmets and the metal clad walls of the accommodation. The laundry, which already had six dryers going full blast, now reached a temperature of about 90 degrees Fahrenheit.

Now what you have to remember is that we're 100 miles out in the North Sea and when we joined, clever people told us in no uncertain terms not to fall in. If you were careless, they said, the water is so cold it would freeze your eye and other associated balls in about five minutes and you would then sink gently beneath the waves —as they say. However, as we were now experiencing temperatures generally to be found in the Gobi desert, the thought of a little gently induced hypothermia was becoming increasingly attractive. There was only one thing for it — strong representation had to be made at the next committee meeting.

Inevitably, on this occasion, the small matter of excess heat was uppermost in the delegates' minds at the next meeting. As time wore on, I could see Sid's interest in the proceedings waning and I have to say he didn't exactly help matters when, in a futile attempt to downplay the situation, he said, "Look, I know it's a bit warm at the moment, but...." He got no further, as there was uproar and the taking of minutes became impossible.

"A bit bloody warm? I'll say it's a bit bloody warm! Our cabin is like a sodding sauna, I haven't slept for three nights, the sheets are soaking wet with sweat, we can hardly breathe, you daren't lean against the bulkhead and you could make bloody tea with the cold tap water. Aye, it's a bit bloody warm alright and what are you going to do about it, that's what I want to know?"

This tirade came from the production representative, who was normally a mild-mannered sort, given, when off duty, to studying bird life around the platform. As he sagged back, obviously in the grip of some strong emotion, there were mutterings of support from the other members, each bidding to outdo the others in recounting tales of heat induced hardship and discomfort. There was considerable support for the drilling representative's contention that his people were suffering from heat exhaustion, which was unusual, as under normal circumstances, nobody cared a toss for the drilling guys, due primarily to their tendency to cover everything in mud. However, on this occasion, their discomfort could well be used to bolster the general concern. I think its called opportunism.

Words were now being bandied about such as nausea, fatigue, weakness, headache, muscle cramps and dizziness. Again, there were nods of agreement all round, until that is, Sid realised he was about to be lumbered with trying to solve an impossible situation.

Glaring at the delegates, he said, "What a bunch of sissies! Another ten minutes and you'd all be telling me that people are suffering from hallucinations, rapid pulse, strange behaviour and disorientation. It's a bloody good job you lot hadn't been employed in the middle of Australia just after the war—talk about heat—we didn't have nice cabins, a cool breeze, lots of water to drink, salt bloody tablets or salad for tea." This was Sid at his attacking best and slowly the mutterings died down and I started to regain control of the minutes, although what the hell I could record was, at that moment, beyond me.

"Now," said Sid, "Are there any problems to do with actual work which are affected by the heat?"

There was a lengthy silence as the delegates pondered on the possible repercussions which might ensue if they overstated their work grievances, when Steve, the petroleum engineer gingerly raised a hand.

"Well," said Sid, "What's your problem?"

"Well Sid as you know, I have a window in my office which faces the drilling rig. I need to be able to see what's happening so that I can observe progress and revise my calculations regarding depth, mud weight and drilling progress. The problem is the flare has made the window red hot and I wondered whether a sort of transparent buffer could be rigged up just in front of the window to deflect the heat."

Sid, never one to miss an opportunity to divert attention from the real problem, said, "No problem, I'll get the Maintenance lads to knock something up for you. After all, we can't have you working blind."

With that he beamed all round and before anyone else had a chance to raise more heat related points, declared the meeting closed.

It was about a week later and thankfully the wind had decided to revert back to what was laughingly called 'prevailing,' when Steve poked his head around Sid's door.

Now it was generally understood, but never acknowledged, that the P.E, as he was commonly known, was probably the most intelligent chap on the Platform. He knew a great deal about things we could barely pronounce, let alone understand. If you were in the vicinity of his desk at any time, it wasn't unusual to hear words such as interfacial phenomena, fluid flow through porous media, multiphase flow, applied mass transfer, principles of surfactant flooding and most exciting of all — the algebraic and numerical application of thermodynamic theory applied to reservoir fluids.

All this learning meant that the poor guy inevitably had an uneasy relationship with his boss, the toolpusher. Our early toolpushers were of the old school, hire and fire mentality and most had never actually come into direct contact with a P.E, let alone owned one. One of our saner toolpushers actually confessed to me that he felt very uneasy having a youngster like Steve tell him things about the reservoir which, previously, he had made either a considered guess, if he was lucky or, a wild guess—if he wasn't.

Sid, on the other hand, found Steve to be very useful when stumped with crucial issues such as 10 across, 7 letters, in the Times crossword. So, having diffidently poked his head around the door, Sid welcomed the lad into his lair and insisted he take a seat. This invitation to relax used to cause Steve some further nervousness, as he was terrified the Toolpusher would spot him thus ensconced, when he should be making esoteric calculations on his slide-rule. Sid, seeing the lad's discomfort, tried to reassure him by saying, "Never mind that mad bastard, how can I help?"

"Well," said Steve, "You remember the other week I asked if I could have a transparent barrier in front of my window?"

"Certainly, and what's more I gave clear instructions to the maintenance mob that one should be made forthwith." This last pronouncement was accompanied by a meaningful glance at me.

"No, no, that's not the problem," said Steve quickly, "The barrier was built in record time just before I went off the platform."

"Well then, what's the problem?"

Steve drew a deep breath and said, "The problem is that when I try to look through it, everything on the drill deck is distorted."

Liam, who had been listening quietly up to then, said, "That's the best way to see a drilling rig in my opinion."

"Never mind what you think," said Sid, obviously becoming worried that this setback might impinge on continuing access to Steve's intellectual prowess. "What do you mean, everything's distorted?"

Steve ploughed on, "Well, the transparent element seems to have been made of some sort of translucent roofing sheet and because it's shaped in a sort of box profile, the outcome is similar to looking in one of those distorting mirrors you see in a fairground."

"Bloody hell," said Sid, "What a bloody fiasco, can't you lot be trusted to do a simple job properly?"

Liam said, "I'll find out."

"Aye, and while your doing so, take the sodding thing down."

Steve then made things worse by saying, "I'm sorry to be a nuisance."

"Nuisance," shouted Sid, "It's not you that's the nuisance; it's the incompetent bastard who, with his obviously limited intellect, thought that a sodding roofing sheet would be the ideal thing to make a window you can see through—give me bloody strength."

I decided it was time to try and defuse the situation.

"I think the cakes have just arrived."

Fortunately, it did the trick. Sid looked at me and said, "Are there any of those with the pink icing on top? I'm rather partial to them, come on, let's get a brew."

Sometimes I find, it's just a matter of knowing the right diplomatic buttons to press and in Sid's case, those shiny, plastic-topped cakes would do it every time.

7. A Couple of Nice Days Out

We were just finishing one of Sid's afternoon meetings when he waved a telex at me and said, "I think it's time you and your cohorts went on a course; it's all fixed, you're to travel up a day early and come out a couple of days late. I think you'll all enjoy the change." With that, he gave a sort of sinister smile and sat back.

As Sid wasn't renowned for being left understaffed, especially with regard to maintenance, I was somewhat stunned and it rather belatedly occurred to me to ask what type of course we'd been volunteered for.

Another sinister smile, followed by, "As you three are fond of swanning about in helicopters and lifeboats, I thought it would be good for you to do the survival and fire-fighting courses. I understand they're very realistic and you should all learn a lot, especially if you don't get burned or drowned."

I stared at our worthy Installation Manager with something approaching hatred and said, "Bloody hell, Sid, have you told Liam and Bert about your grand plan?"

"Me? No, I thought it would be better coming from you. After all you're in charge and I like to observe line management protocol."

"Sid, you know and I know that's a load of rubbish; all you're afraid of is being lynched by the lads."

"Really, I don't know where you get these wild ideas from! It's not a problem, just tell them they're off for a couple of days' jollies."

Realising I had once more been well and truly conned; I waited until we were tucking in to our evening steak and chips (followed by spotted dick and custard) before broaching the subject of training. Sadly, it was just as I'd predicted, they both stared at me and once again I had a feeling that it's better to receive than to give. However, just as I was about to deliver a spirited, but no doubt, futile attempt to sell what was obviously going to be several days of pain and discomfort, Bert jumped to the wrong conclusion, based, I imagine, on wish fulfilment and said, "I guess we're going to the United States to see the new Gas Compressors; great stuff, I've always wanted to see New York."

Liam, latching on to this totally erroneous premise, joined in, "It's about time we had a nice jolly, when do we go, where are we flying to, how long can we stay, will we get lots of time off?"

Slowly and inexorably, I could see that what little amount of control I had was slipping away. How the hell could I convince them that being alternately soaked and blistered in Aberdeen was vastly superior to a trip across the Atlantic? The short answer was—I couldn't, but you have to try.

So, waiting until consumption of the spotted dick was well under way, I said, "Now listen you two, nobody's mentioned the sodding USA; what I'm trying to tell you is that Sid has booked us on two survival courses."

At this disclosure, there was a disconcerting metallic sound as the pudding spoons clattered onto the Formica table-top and two pairs of distinctly unfriendly eyes turned in my direction.

"What?"

"What do you mean— 'what?' I've just explained."

"What we mean,' said Liam with heavy emphasis, "Is what the bloody hell happened to our trip to the States, that's what. And furthermore, whose bright idea was it to think we would want to give up our days off to mess about in water?"

"I keep telling you, a trip to the States is a figment of your overheated imaginations; no one's said anything about the bloody States, how many times do I have to spell it out — we're off to the baths, followed by some pyrotechnic maniacs trying to singe your eyebrows."

Then, just as I thought things couldn't get any worse, Sid arrived at the table. "I see you've given them the good news then." This was accompanied by what Sid erroneously thought of as a friendly grin, but which would be more accurately described as a sort of leer.

"I don't know what all the fuss is about. It's just a couple of courses, you ought to think yourselves lucky the Company believes so highly in your welfare."

"Sod off, Sid," said Liam with some feeling, "I don't see your name on the list, the least you could do is set an example."

"Ah," replied Sid, "normally nothing would keep me away, but as I'm the Installation Manager, I can't leave my post. As you know it's a legal requirement and I'm powerless to change it."

And with another rictus smile, he sauntered off in search of some cake.

"How the hell we're supposed to trust a guy who fastens his cardigan one hole out of sequence, beats me," said Bert, "Still I suppose we'll have to go on the blasted course, if he's arranged it."

Now I don't know just how familiar the average person is with regard to the so-called 'survival' courses, but let me tell you straight away, they've been designed with a considerable amount of sadistic enjoyment on the part of the organisers. It's the old story, if you take an expert in anything physical; they consider it their sworn duty, when passing on some useless expertise, to inject as much pain and discomfort as possible. This diabolic approach to the learning process is generally dressed up as an integral part of the experience and is to be avoided at all costs — if you don't believe me, try white-water rafting.

You've seen it on television, a bright summers day, eight or nine people on a big inflatable raft, careering down a fast-running river, shouts of laughter, splashes of water and a man in charge who's job it is to keep everyone safe. So, filled with a desire to partake in such a fun-packed event, you wait for a nice warm day and turn up at the rafting venue to enrol.

Only it doesn't work like that. The man behind the desk is somewhat evasive, he smiles a lot, takes your name, address, age, weight and rather worryingly, your next of kin. Then, just as you feel he's ready to usher you into a raft, he drops the first bombshell.

"Unfortunately we can't go rafting today; we'll be in touch with a date when conditions are perfect, as obviously our aim is to give you the best possible experience." This latter statement is verified by his silent cohort, who, although dressed in some kind of one-piece rubber suit, nods approvingly at the wisdom of his mate's assessment of the situation.

"I thought we could go now; why do we have to wait?"

Another smile. "Well sadly, we've not had enough rain lately and as a consequence the river is a bit too low for a good rafting session."

As he says this, you just happen to glance out of the window onto what appears to be a raging torrent. In your mind, it's distinctly reminiscent of that film 'The River Wild' where Meryl Streep goes white-water rafting and very soon people are being shot at and flung overboard.

What you were hoping for was a nice wee boat ride, accompanied by the odd splash of water on your shirt, just to prove you'd faced untold danger and lived to tell the tale.

Well I have to tell you that the sadists running the survival course have also been brought up in the'let's scare the living daylights out of this lot, while pretending it's in their best interests'school of thought.

This is brought home to you in no uncertain terms when you turn up at the Venue on the first morning and the sadist in charge greets you with the following pack of lies.

"Now lads, gather round and I'll explain what the course is all about. We've designed it for your benefit and our aim is for you all to get the best out of the day."

As he says this, we're all we're standing on the side of a swimming pool, dressed in a pair of swimming trunks and ill-fitting overalls. But what's really the focus of our attention is the fact that suspended above our heads is what looks like the sawn-off section of a helicopter cabin. And then, just as we're trying to concentrate on what our instructor is on about, you notice out of the corner of your eye, three or four guys dressed in frogman's outfits slip quietly into the pool.

Bert stares at me with something approaching hatred and whispers, "I bloody hated going to the baths when I was at school, this looks as though it's going to be about ten times worse, I'll kill Sid if we ever survive this lot."

I was going to remind him that survival was what we were here for, but cowardice prevailed.

By now, however, our Instructor was in full flow and explaining the fun we were all going to have whilst in his tender care. After which, he favoured us with what he erroneously thought was a reassuring smile and, as an afterthought, asked a fairly important question, "By the way lads, is there anyone here who can't swim?"

We all looked at one another and then a short tubby guy with a crew-cut and acne scars, whose name, we learned later, was Ernie, stuck up his hand.

Seeing this, our host beamed at him and said, "No problem squire, we've not drowned anyone recently, don't worry, me and the lads'll keep an eye on you.

Bert said, "I think it's a case of Ernie being totally out of his depth."

For obvious reasons, Liam and I pretended not to hear.

"Right then, let's get started, first of all what I want you to do is practise getting into a liferaft. So put on one of the life-jackets, climb up to the top diving board, then on my signal, tuck your arms and legs into your body and jump in. Once in the water you need to swim to the raft and clamber in as quickly as you can, bearing in mind there will be six of you to each raft. Okay, off you go."

I won't bore you with the details regarding the next hour, suffice it to say we learned one fundamental lesson—clambering into a life-raft with rubber sides whilst wearing a lifejacket is not easy. The first guy to try, reached the raft, grabbed the rope fixed around the sides and gave an almighty heave to pull himself up. At which point, the raft turned over and landed on top of him. This little setback seemed to cause great amusement among the Jacques Cousteau brigade, as one of them swam over, flipped the raft upright, rescued our missing victim and then made matters ten times worse by slipping expertly aboard in one fluid motion. This, we felt, was to illustrate just how useless we were and just how good he was, but that could simply have been jealousy on our part. In the meantime, five other bodies have landed in the water and as they forgot to shut their eyes, can't see what the problem is. All they have in mind is to avoid drowning, get out of the water and kill the instructor.

After about an hour or two of this madness we were allowed to sit on the edge of the pool whilst our friend reminded us that in reality we would also be wearing a survival suit and how important it was to remove false teeth, spectacles and sharp objects, before jumping.

At the mention of false teeth, Liam, who remembered that Bert had earlier lost a brand-new set in an incident on our mooring buoy, said, "If we ever have to jump in, you'd better tie yours around your neck, because there's no way I'm going to try to explain to your wife once again that you've lost another bloody set."

"Sod off, Liam," said Bert.

At this point our Instructor decided we were now ready for the next phase.

"Right lads, it's time for some fun with the Escape Trainer. That's the thing you've all been staring at hanging above your heads. What we do is in four separate exercises, Surface Evacuation, where the helicopter lands on water and remains upright; Partial Submersion, where the chopper lands on the water, but starts to sink slowly; a Slow Capsize, where the chopper, having made a controlled landing, makes contact with the water, sinks to about chin height and then capsizes; and finally, the real fun part, a Rapid Capsize. This represents a descent onto the water at short notice, resulting in an immediate capsize. Is that clear to everybody?"

"Oh, it's bloody clear alright," said Liam, "We're about to be soaked to the skin, totally disorientated, completely knackered and scared to death. All because some prat discovered oil in the middle of the sea instead of on the sand dunes."

We nodded; sometimes you just don't want to be confronted with logic, especially when you're soaking wet.

I've noticed there are people who consider a fun day out is to take the train to Blackpool and once there, waste their money riding on big dippers, water slides, free-fall capsules, giant swings and eating a type of glass-fibre known as candy-floss. Then, having staggered off and been sick several times, they return home to regale their friends with tales of adventure holidays, derring-do, bravery in the face of untold danger and how they wouldn't have missed it for the world.

Well let me tell you, if you are ever seeking a real adrenalin rush, let some sadist strap you in a helicopter seat, drop it from a height, rapidly submerge it in water and just as you think it can't get any worse—have them turn the thing upside down.

You're now in the situation where, despite all the previous instructions, you have absolutely no idea what is happening. All you do know is that you're hanging upside down, you're under water and it's a hell of a long time since you last took a breath. The idea is for you to quickly undo your seat belt, grab the open window, pull yourself through and rise gracefully to the surface there to take an almighty gulp of fresh air.

Blackpool—a childish waste of time and money if you ask me.

The following day, having dried off, thanked the instructor (part cowardice, part upbringing) and received our Survival Certificates, we assembled at the aptly named "Fire Pad" near Portlethen. So having spent the previous day being alternately terrified and half-drowned, we were about to be placed in the tender care of a bunch of lads known as the Grampian Fire Brigade. Having run out of cats up trees to rescue, they'd seen a gap in the market for an official means of terrorising innocent offshore workers and had devised a training course loosely translated as 'ordeal by fire.'

This time, in anticipation of another type of excitement to come, we were issued with what was laughingly called 'protective clothing.' This consisted of trousers and a jacket made out of some fire-resistant material, but which was so stiff and heavy that just putting the gear on and remaining upright brought on severe exhaustion. The ensemble was completed by a pair of stout boots and a fireman's helmet. This latter garment weighed about a ton, wobbled about alarmingly and had an unnerving tendency to obliterate your vision if you were careless enough to nod your head. It's no wonder that Steve McQueen kept taking his helmet off whenever he spoke to Paul Newman in the 'Towering Inferno.' If he hadn't, there's no doubt in my mind, we would never have seen his face.

Once again we were subjected to what the senior officer considered to be a light-hearted briefing of the fun time they had in store for us. "Obviously, as we were merely amateurs, there was no way in which they could subject us to the true rigours of a proper fireman's lot." Liam said he thought this latter statement was said with some degree of regret.

"However," continued our new instructor, "They would do their best to provide us with as realistic conditions as possible."

Bert said, "There's really no need for them to bother," as he already had some experience of realistic conditions the time he set the barbecue on fire.

"Call that realistic?" sniffed Liam, "Wait until this lot get going."

As if on cue, the instructor said, "Right lads, what we'll do first is get you to run out some hoses and then douse a small fire with the water. Afterwards we'll get some breathing apparatus on and let you see what it's like to rescue someone from a smoke-filled building in the dark." And with that the sod beamed at us, as though we were being given a rare treat.

Liam said, "I like the 'we' part, what he really means is 'us' and it's not going to be pleasant I can tell you."

Having digested the instructions, we were then instructed to run to a container, grab a roll of hose, lay it out along the concrete, couple it up to a hydrant and, on his signal, grab the nozzle firmly, while one of our team turned on the water. This seemed easy until we realised that a stiff suit, strange boots and a wobbly helmet caused severe mobility problems. This minor setback paled into insignificance, however, when the bloke at the valve end turned on the water. In a mille-second the flat hose leaped off the floor, became as rigid as a steel pipe and weighed about a ton. And then things began to go seriously wrong as, working to instructions, the guy at the business end opened the nozzle. Water —at about the speed of a low-flying jet plane—shot out of the end, at which the nozzle leaped into the air with the guy frantically hanging on to the mechanism, but with all thoughts of aiming the jet in the desired direction long since forgotten. There was water everywhere, except largely where our instructor had said to we were to aim for. As is usual with experts, the firemen bystanders had somehow taken up positions of safety and were finding the whole fiasco amusing.

Finally, the screams of the nozzle man reached the ears of the valve man and the water was turned off. Our instructor reappeared from behind a nearby container and said, "Right lads, it's not as easy as you think is it? But never mind, now you've got the hang of it, we'll make it a bit more realistic and put out a real fire."

He then led us to a pile of old pallets and assorted solid rubbish, to which his men were just setting fire, and before we could back away, the whole lot became a sort of raging inferno. As one man —we backed away.

Our instructor beamed again and issued further suicidal instructions. "Right lads, same routine again with the hose, only this time you need to get really close to the fire and direct the water onto the flames, where it will have maximum effect —are we ready?"

Bert said, "If the bastard says 'right lads' once more I'm going to turn the sodding hose on him." You could tell by now that feelings were beginning to run dangerously high. Anyway, as instructed, we grabbed the hose and set off again, this time we felt pleased to find that most of the water was hitting the flames, until we realised that the instructor was screaming at us to get really close to the flames. "It's no bloody use lads," he yelled, "Standing so far back, you won't get burned, that's what the suits and helmets are for, get close in and put the sodding fire out."

So very reluctantly and neglecting the fact that our eyebrows were being singed, we crept closer until finally the flames went out.

"Great stuff lads, we'll make firemen of you yet, now we need to see how to handle a really hot fire, only this time we'll be using fire extinguishers. Follow me."

So, with increasing reluctance, we followed him until we came to what looked like a shallow steel tray about eight feet long and a foot deep, mounted on legs about three feet off the ground. His men had just finished filling the tray with what smelled like a mixture of diesel, kerosene, old sump oil and thinners, but it could have been anything equally appalling as far as we were concerned.

"Right lads, gather round and we'll run through the types of extinguisher to use in the event of a particular fire." After some (heated!) discussion, we agreed that powder or foam would be the thing to use on the hobgoblins sloshing about on the tray. This theory bit didn't seem too bad and we became quite blasé, which was a mistake, as at that moment, one of his men nipped out from behind the container and threw a match into the tray.

In an instant, there was a whoosh accompanied by an unbelievable surge of heat, followed by the blackest, thickest smoke we had ever seen.

As one man, we backed away again.

"Now come on lads, you know what to do, grab an extinguisher, get close in and douse the flames. You'll need to work as a team on this one; never mind the heat, it won't harm you, let's spray the bastard and get the job done."

So, with helmets falling over our eyes, sweat running off and into every orifice, whilst at the same time being convinced that at any minute our suits, boots and gloves would spontaneously combust —we put the damned thing out.

At this point in our fun-packed day we were now lying in a disgusting heap in pools of filthy water on the concrete, and such are the unworthy thoughts of a group of people in extremis, we hoped our host would be called away to a real fire or preferably, be sacked for extreme cruelty. Sadly, our immediate and heartfelt wish was not to be granted.

"Right lads...... "

"That's it" said Bert to no one in particular If I can just get up out of this puddle, I'll strangle the sod."

"Right lads, there's just time for a brew and a sandwich before we do the rescue operation." And with that, our instructor beamed again and led us off to the canteen.

"Have you noticed something," I said, "His bloody helmet doesn't wobble when he walks."

They both looked at me with something approaching pity and Liam said, "Is that the best you can do? If I know these masochists, it's probably glued to his bloody head."

Having, for the moment exhausted the desire to converse any further, we were enjoying the well-earned brew when Ernie, our non-swimmer friend, sat down and asked whether we knew what was next.

Apparently he was employed as a Steward on one of the many Drilling Rigs dotted around the North Sea and had recently joined the offshore game. He told us he'd previously been employed as a labourer in the Council's graveyard department and a mate told him there was untold wealth to be had on the Rigs. This was his second month on the job and he confessed to being baffled by the things you had to learn just in order to make beds and scrub floors.

Liam asked, "How come you're on one of these courses? Generally it's for blokes who are involved in safety matters."

"Ah well," said Ernie, "I've been wondering about that myself. It seems the man in charge, I think he's called the toolpusher, said they needed someone to keep an eye on things and as I'd had experience of fire hazards, he sort of volunteered me."

"How do you mean, fire hazard experience? I thought you said you were working for the Council."

"Well, I suppose it's because I mentioned I'd been seconded to the Crematorium for a while and the bastard said, well that's just what we need, someone who understands heat."

'"Bloody hell," said Bert, "You might find this afternoon a bit different from setting fire to coffins." And with that he gave a sort of shudder and said, "Sod that for a job."

"Right lads, time to move on, let's get you rigged out ready for the rescue in a smoke filled building exercise, the BA sets are over here."

"What's a BA set?" said Ernie to Liam.

"It's a portable Breathing Apparatus and you're just about to find out how useful they are because where we're going there won't be any air to breathe."

"Oh great, I've been half drowned now they're going to asphyxiate me," muttered Ernie.

So once again we gathered round while the instructor put us through our paces regarding the BA set, which was a bit of a doddle for us as, fortunately, we were all members of our platform rescue team. This was in no small measure thanks to Sid who decided that in his opinion, Maintenance guys had bugger all to do, and so were best placed to rescue anyone should the need arise. Sometimes we found it really hard to love Sid.

Anyway, the exercise was designed (if that's the word) for us to enter a sealed building which, while we were innocently eating our buns, the caring firemen had filled with black, acrid smoke. Obviously the place had no windows and in order to "Make it as realistic as possible," said the man, "There are two storeys with a set of stairs at one end. We've placed a dummy somewhere so that, when you locate it, you can carry out a proper rescue. Okay, it's time to get your sets on and we'll go in teams of four."

Ernie, having listened to all this, was in a state of terminal shock and quickly attached himself to us three in the manner of a lost child on a crowded beach. Feeling sorry for the poor guy, Liam helped him on with the heavy BA set, checked his air demand valve and showed him how to operate the unit. Finally he was ready, and all we could see through the window in his facemask was a pair of wildly staring eyes and a number of enlarged acne scares, due to the magnifying effect of the glass.

As we slowly approached the building, a smiling fireman opened the door, which allowed a large quantity of black smoke to come billowing out. At this point Ernie made a gallant but futile attempt to make a break for freedom but as he was firmly wedged between Bert and me, we managed to drag him into the building.

I won't bother you with the awful details, but suffice it to say we kept low, remained in contact with one another and negotiated our way through the ground floor with no sign of the blasted dummy. As we reluctantly felt our way up the stairs, there was a crash and a series of muffled but perfectly audible curses from Liam, who was leading the way. He had discovered, by the simple expedient of falling over, that the sadistic bastards had put the dummy at the top of the stairs. So, grabbing both the body and Ernie, together with a good deal of pushing, shoving, cursing, sweating, struggling and bumping into rails, the walls and each other, we finally staggered out into the fresh air.

"Right lads, well done," said Attila. "I hope you found that useful. Now, if you'll get out of your kit, there's a nice brew and a certificate waiting for you in the office."

"There you go Ernie," said Liam, "Two certificates to show the toolpusher when you get back on the rig, he'll be right proud of you."

Ernie stared at Liam, "Aye, and if he doesn't pay me some more money for having put meself through these two days of sodding torture, he can stuff his job and I'll go back to the Crematorium. At least it's nice and dry and they play some lovely music."

8. Glorious Boating Weather

For some unaccountable reason, lifeboats held a morbid fascination for Liam and Bert. This was probably based on the premise that as they had to maintain the boats' engines, davits, release mechanisms and winches, they felt very proprietorial when it came to their use. This determination by the intrepid duo to claim custodianship overlooked one salient fact —nobody else on the platform wanted anything to do with the ghastly things. Lifeboats were seen as inventions of the devil and represented pain and discomfort on an epic scale. No more so than when we were in the middle of our weekly safety exercise and, having ensured we were all present at the muster stations, Sid, in a fit of excess zeal, would sound the 'go to your lifeboats' alarm. This meant we had to try desperately to get those assembled to tie lifejackets in place without strangling themselves and then hand them over to Bert. His task, on the face of it, was also simple; all he had to do was usher them inside the boat, sit down and fasten themselves in. Sadly, the concept of occupancy, as defined by the manufacturer, turned out to have little relevance, especially when applied to hairy offshore workers, ensconced in polar jackets, overalls, boots, hard hats and huge ill-fitting lifejackets made up of solid lumps of foam—tied in random fashion around and under various parts of the body. This meant that after the first ten blokes had clambered aboard, the boat was comfortably full. Bert's dilemma was he still had about twenty guys outside the boat convinced that as there was no room for them, they should start to remove their lifejackets in readiness for a quick getaway. This mutinous behaviour meant that Bert had to take on a role somewhere between that of a Centurion, whipping reluctant gladiators into the Coliseum and that of an Indian train guard ensuring that all available space on the roof was taken up.

So, with a combination of pushing, cajoling, cursing, sweating and shoving, he finally got everyone aboard. Until, that is, Liam tried to take on his second role as official engine starter. As he was still outside it meant he had to clamber over about six tightly packed guys sitting in maximum discomfort across the entrance hatch. The upshot of which was a near riot as he fell into, and clambered over, the unfortunate group until he reached the relative safety of the engine bay.

And then a whole new process of epic proportions came into play as

Liam made preparations to start the engine. This simple task involved a three foot steel bar being inserted into a hole in the pneumatic starter and pulled back and forth for fifty strokes in order to prime the system. Unfortunately, as Liam pushed and pulled, the occupants felt able to relieve their discomfort by exhorting him to greater efforts, accompanied by ribald comments and overt criticism. Now, as he approached the thirty stroke mark, the pressure increased and so, of course, did the effort required to keep pumping, a situation which invariably brought out the worst in Liam. He sweated, stared with hatred at the passengers, and cursed Sid, Bert and me in random order. Finally the required strokes were completed and he sagged back against the side of the engine. This was a signal for Bert to spring into action and with a delicately poised finger, he pressed the starter button. Here again, this task was not without risk and Bert knew full well the cost of failure. Sure enough, on a number of occasions, there would be a resounding clunk as the starter engaged with the engine, only to find it failed to start. When this happened, Bert would groan, the passengers would stop chatting and Liam would become apoplectic. If, however, Bert's finger worked a miracle and immediately after the clunk, the engine roared into life, Bert would smile, Liam would wipe his forehead and the more emotional passengers would raise a cheer. This euphoric state was short-lived as the incredible noise of a badly insulated diesel engine in the confined space of a lifeboat precluded any form of conversation, ribald or otherwise. It was at this juncture that I was required to leap out of the boat and contact Sid with the good news that all was well and could we please shut the damned thing down and get the hell out of there.

There's no doubt that what took the shine off being in charge of the lifeboats as far as Liam and Bert were concerned, was the need to share them once a week with a bunch of unenthusiastic, ungrateful, unfeeling, recalcitrants. What they really enjoyed was playing with them during the week when things could be checked, monitored, examined, oiled, greased, tightened, replaced, repaired and tested. All carried out in peace and quiet and without having to make allowances for ungrateful sods getting in the way.

Of all the aforementioned activities their favourite was—without doubt—testing. This involved the use of electrical power, compressed air, hydraulics and fuel. The boat station would be cordoned-off, danger signs hung on handrails, the davit winches could be energised and oats could be lowered and raised. Then, on fine Sunday mornings, they achieved the ultimate in just reward for their efforts—a chosen lifeboat was lowered into the sea and a wee trip around the platform could be taken. The crew on these occasions generally consisted of the three of us (being maintenance men, this was serious business—or so we argued.) We would, however, often invite one or two lucky individuals to accompany us on the trip (sorry—integrity test run.) Generally, we chose guys from the catering department who otherwise saw little of the platform, being confined mainly to mopping floors, making beds and the production of custard.

And then one day, just such trip went horribly wrong. Sid informed the lads that a Board of Trade Inspector was to come aboard and carry out a check on our ability to communicate by radio with Stonehaven. This was a mandatory examination and we had to demonstrate our ship to shore capability in order that he might provide us with the appropriate Radio Communication Licence. As I recall, Bert became quite enthusiastic when he learned that an integral part of the test was to launch a lifeboat and sail some distance away in order to establish the maximum range of the radios. Liam wasn't so sure, having expressed the opinion that there may be a marked resistance on the part of the inspector to be lowered some forty feet on the end of two thin steel ropes, be cast adrift and transported away from the relative safety of the platform.

His fears were laid to rest when the inspector declared himself more than ready to conduct the test in a lifeboat. As he said, "It's a great way to measure the signal output in peace and quiet."

Liam said, "I don't know where he gets the quiet bit from, he obviously hasn't heard our lifeboat engines at full throttle. Still, if that's what he wants, who are we to stand in his way?"

Bert said he thought Liam was secretly pleased, but didn't want to show it.

And so the great day dawned, briefings were held, the radio operator was informed and Liam and Bert geared the Inspector up in a lifejacket and launched the boat.

At first all went well, the sea was relatively calm, the boat responded to the rudder and they headed out to begin testing. It was just after the Inspector had powered up his radio in readiness for the first test that things began to go wrong. The cabin started to fill up with blue smoke of the eye-watering, choking variety and the inspector virtually disappeared from view. Acting with remarkable speed, based mainly on the need to breathe, Liam and Bert dove for one of the access hatches and pushed it open. This cleared some of the smoke, but a glance back into the cabin revealed a considerable amount still pouring from the engine.

"We'll need to shut the bloody engine off," said Liam between choking coughs. "It's obvious the exhaust has broken or is at least leaking like a sieve."

Bert, with a remarkable distain for life, took a deep breath, dove back inside and shut off the engine. As the smoke cleared, he noticed the inspector still sitting at the side with tears streaming down his face and a handkerchief stuffed across his nose and mouth. Bert then tried to alleviate the situation by saying, "It looks as though we've got a small problem, won't take long to fix." As he said later, it was probably the most inaccurate description of the actual situation it was possible to imagine, but he didn't realise it at the time.

In the meantime, Liam had reappeared and together they tried to assess the situation. Using maintenance skills for which they were justly famous, they came to the conclusion there was a serious leak in the exhaust. Their diagnosis was based primarily in the fact that they could see a bloody great split running along the pipe as it emerged from the side of the engine.

In the meantime, what started off as a fairly minor issue was now growing in importance by the minute. This was due, in no small measure, to the fact that stability, as far as a lifeboat is concerned, is determined solely by its ability to travel forward through the water and obviously, in order to comply with this requirement, you need an engine. The other significant drawback in lifeboat design is the increasing tendency for a stationary boat to wallow. For those who are fortunate enough to have missed the experience—a word of explanation. The shape of the lifeboat resembles a fat lozenge and when placed in the water it bobs about like a cork, completely at the mercy of the waves. This is particularly marked when, as inevitably happens, the boat is pushed side-on to the swell. Not only does the boat rise and fall in time to the waves, it also rolls along its length. This motion is known as wallowing and lifeboats provide a prime example of the process.

To recap—the lads daren't try to start the engine for fear of being asphyxiated, the Inspector is taking no further part in the proceedings and Liam and Bert are staring at one another in horror. At this point, Bert begins to feel the detrimental effects of the up and down, side to side and rolling motion of the boat and is sick. For some unaccountable reason, this causes him to lose interest in the proceedings, preferring to hang out of the open hatch. Liam, no doubt influenced by the sight of Bert heaving and straining, starts to feel very queasy and is also sick. We now have what might be called an interesting situation—one chap is inside lying across the seats in the foetal position with a handkerchief stuffed in his mouth, two chaps are hanging out over the gunwales with their faces alternately in and above the waves; whilst the boat—carried by the wind and waves—is drifting away from the platform in the general direction of Iceland.

Fortunately for our brave sailors, the radio operator, puzzled by the complete absence of radio traffic, calls Sid to find out what's going on. Putting aside his half finished Telegraph crossword, Sid locates his binoculars and nips outside. Sure enough, having focussed the things, he spots the boat drifting away from the platform and sees a figure waving frantically from the open hatch. Moving with commendable speed, Sid orders another boat to be launched and in a scene reminiscent of those black and white wartime films of heroism at sea, the lads are towed back to the platform and winched up to safety.

We are now in the realm of what is known as 'mixed feelings.' Liam and Bert are soon feeling better and have started to blame one another for the debacle, the inspector has retired to his cabin for a lie-down and people are whistling sea-shanties whenever they come across our heroes. Sid has returned to his crossword and Bert, in a futile effort to explain the onset of sickness says, "I read somewhere that the best way to prevent being sick is to keep low in the boat and get plenty of fresh air."

Liam stared at his mate and replied, "You're a bloody idiot, if we'd tried to get any nearer the water, we'd have been in it—and as for fresh air—give me strength."

Bert said, "You're just pissed off because you were sick as well, and anyway, I'm just telling you what I read in a yachting magazine."

Fortunately, a strong brew and a sticky bun restored their equilibrium and Liam said, "I guess we'd better fix the sodding exhaust system before it makes you sick again."

"Agreed, but it wasn't the exhaust that caused the trouble and anyway, next time I go out in a lifeboat with you, I'm going to eat a pile of ginger first."

Liam said, "I wish you'd stop reading magazines that you don't understand and anyway, what's with the ginger?"

Bert said, "The article also said that eating ginger before you go on a boat can help to prevent seasickness."

Liam said, "We don't need any of that crap, all we need to do is keep the bloody engine running."

And so, full of buns and with a measure of agreement restored, they nipped out to take rightful ownership of the lifeboats once again.

The next two trips passed uneventfully, whistling had died away, drills were successfully held, maintenance routines were in full swing and Sid put away his binoculars. Until, that is, the episode of the 'killer shark.'

Up until then, as part of a lease-lend agreement, we had two American production supervisors, one from California and the other from Louisiana. For some unaccountable reason, Bill had come to the conclusion that California was preferable to Aberdeen and decided to return to the land of the free and hippy headquarters. Our replacement supervisor's name was Jim; he hailed from somewhere in the North East and spoke like Jimmy Nail. Having familiarised himself with the workings of the platform and found out when the sticky buns arrived, he became a regular member at Sid's daily meetings. Then one day, in what was obviously a moment of mental blackout, he said he would like to take a trip in a lifeboat the next time we launched one.

This request startled Sid, who until then had believed the guy to be reasonably sensible. "Are you sure about this?" asked Sid, who had often expressed the opinion that getting into a lifeboat would be, for him, tantamount to being launched into space.

Jim confirmed Sid's worst fears and agreed that indeed this was so.

Sid, looking at Jim with something approaching pity, said, "Well as long as you're sure, we'll get Liam and Bert to take you out on Sunday if the weather's good. But if I were you, I'd give it some careful thought between now and then."

This last guarded statement seemed to baffle Jim, but he still said he was keen to go.

Unfortunately, as it turned out, the weather on Sunday was perfect, there was not a cloud in the sky, the sea was playing at being a millpond, Bert and Liam were in charge of everything and Jim was resplendent in a bright red life-jacket.

So, with the engine running sweetly, a complete absence of exhaust fumes and the lads in their element, the boat was launched and away they sailed. Jim was enjoying the experience and commenting just how big the platform seemed when viewed from sea-level, when he spotted a sinister looking triangular shape in the water just off the starboard bow (for land-lubbers, this is the right-hand side.) Letting out an almighty scream, he pointed, gasped and shouted, "There's a bloody shark, oh my god, let's get out of here, we'll all be attacked and eaten if we don't move fast."

Liam and Bert peered in the direction of Jim's still rigid finger and sure enough, there, gliding through the water, was a massive triangular fin.

Now, you have to remember this was the 1970's and in 1975 Peter Benchley's best selling book 'Jaws' was turned into the scariest sea-saga ever filmed. With director Steven Spielberg creating maximum suspense in the first moments of the film enhanced by John Williams' music, it was the tale of a great white shark invading a peaceful New England resort and eating people. In fact, we were all very familiar with the film as our Company, convinced we needed reassurance, used to send it out at regular intervals.

Now as far as Jim was concerned, being too scared to eat your orange while watching in the safety of the recreation room, was one thing. Seeing, in close-up, a monstrous fin circling round just yards away from you was something else. He let out another yell and tried to climb on top of the boat, an action which Liam, as Captain, couldn't tolerate.

"Get back down you daft bugger and sit inside where you'll be safe."

"Safe, safe," shouted Jim, "What the bloody hell are you on about? —Safe? We're all about to be eaten by a bloody great shark and all you can do is tell me to sit down."

"It's a Basking Shark," said Bert.

"What?"

"It's a Basking Shark; they're harmless."

"How the hell do you know what kind of sodding shark it is, it looks horribly dangerous to me," said Jim, still staring at the fin.

Liam said, "You can tell it's a Basking Shark because its snout is visible above the water. It's a filter feeder and swims with its mouth wide open. Some of them are over thirty feet long."

Bert, trying gamely to lighten the situation, added, "You can tell it's a Basking Shark because it's floating on its back taking in the sunshine."

Jim stared at Liam and Bert with something approaching hatred and said, "Never mind all the funnies and zoological crap, I still don't like that bloody great fin circling round, so just get me back to the platform and off this sodding boat."

Bert said, "It's a pity really, you don't often see them this far out;

they're generally much closer inshore."

"Inshore—that's just where I wish I was. I must have been mad to come out with you two."

Some time later Sid bumped into the lads and not having heard about the saga, asked them how Jim had enjoyed his wee sail around the platform.

Liam said, "I don't think it went too well. We had a close encounter with a Basking Shark which seemed to put the fear of God into Jim."

Sid chuckled, "That'll teach him to mess about in boats. Oh, and while I think about it, perhaps you'd better warn him about the film tonight. Andy tells me it's about a giant octopus which slithers out of the sea at night and terrorises a small seaside town."

9. Welcome Aboard

There are few things more unsettling than arriving for the first time on a new Installation. It's even more disconcerting when not only are you a stranger on the platform, it's also the very first time you've ever been offshore. The feeling of uncertainty started some time previously when you arrived at the Heliport to check-in for your flight. The place is heaving with blokes, luggage, queues and incomprehensible tannoy instructions. It all seemed so straightforward when you were in the office and an administration lady said, "You're to go offshore this afternoon to visit your new platform. It's all arranged; I've sent a telex to the Installation Manager so they'll be expecting you and a bed has been allocated. Now, a taxi will take you to the Heliport where you'll check in for the flight. Any questions?"

Of course you can't think of anything that won't make you look like a prat, so you confirm that everything is okay, no problem.

So, you're now in the Heliport and you're beginning to feel the same as you did on holiday last year when, for some unaccountable reason, you decided it would be a good idea to drive through Paris on your way to the camp site in the Dordogne.

The journey starts off all right, just keep to the right, take it slowly, look for the direction signs and don't forget to signal. This strategy holds good until you find yourself driving down the Avenue des Champs-Elysees towards the Arc de Triomphe. It's then you find yourself locked in lane five of a seven lane mass of French motorists, all of whom know exactly where they are going and will commit every motoring offence in the book to get there.

Funnily enough, this nightmare scenario is treated as the norm, despite being accompanied by an almost continuous cacophony of horns. The problem for you is that as you approach the monument, you find you're in entirely the wrong lane for the required turn off to the south. Glancing nervously to the left all you can see is a line of wall-to-wall motorists, none of who are taking the least bit of notice of your flashing indicators. A vague attempt on your part to move into the next lane is met with a fresh blast of horns and a shaking of fists. There's only one course of action now open to you—carry on going round and round until you realise if you're ever going to reach the camp site—you'll have to adopt the same suicidal driving technique as the locals.

Finally, by ignoring all the noise, gestures and a distinct risk of both personal and bodywork damage, you manage to get into the correct lane and freedom. The only trouble now is the experience has left you in a state of nervous exhaustion and an abiding hatred of all things French.

Whilst I can't pretend that entering the Heliport for the first time is directly comparable to motoring in the French Capital, the feeling of uncertainty is similar. Everyone except you knows what queue to join, the tannoy announcements produce a concerted movement though a series of doors and slowly you begin to find the crowd thinning to such an extent that if you don't make a move soon, you'll be the only one left in the building. On perusal of a number of signs donating destinations, you approach the check-in desk. Documents are produced, torn out, stamped and returned to you with instructions to go thought door 'F' where your luggage will be examined before proceeding onwards to the survival suit and safety briefing area. With a sigh of relief, you're just about to move off when the check-in lady issues a throw-away line.

"Don't forget, your platform is the third drop-off."

"Sorry, what did you say?"

"I said remember, this isn't a regular crew-change flight, so the chopper is doing what we call the 'milk-run.' Yours is the third stop-off, so make sure you don't get off on the wrong platform."

"Oh right," you say, with as much confidence as you can muster.

Time for the next phase, as you stagger through the third door on the left. I won't bore you with the trauma of donning the safety suit, this was dealt with in some detail in book one, suffice it to say that by the time you've been searched, dressed, briefed, questioned and re-checked, you're exhausted and you've not yet left Aberdeen.

At last, it's time to clamber aboard the chopper, having been careful to place your luggage in the correct heap so the ground crew can load it in the hold in order of disembarkation—or so you hope. The Co-Pilot gives a further safety briefing, with what you consider to be an undue emphasis on something called 'ditching' and what to do in the event of it happening. Then finally you're airborne and as you gaze out of the window at the coast below, you notice that other than the crew, you're the only one awake. Now we're over the sea and suddenly it dawns on you that this is not like crossing the River Mersey to New Brighton. The North Sea looks bigger, colder, deeper and you can't see the edges. And then, after what seems like a lifetime of engine noise, the Pilot says,

"Ten minutes gentlemen before we land on the first installation."

At this some of the lads wake up, you sit bolt upright in your seat and remember that yours is the third stop. We then circle around the first platform and you can see the helideck out of the window. The thing that now occurs to you is that it's far too small and there's no way a huge helicopter like this one can fit onto such a small circle. You sit even further upright in your seat as we descend towards this tiny speck in the sea and then, by some trick of the light, the deck looks as though it will just about fit and within a couple of minutes we land with a bump. One down—two to go.

Finally, it's your turn and you step out onto the helideck, where a member of the Deck Crew escorts you to the stairs. It's then that you find something else to worry about. As the helideck is cantilevered out over the end of the modules beneath, stepping onto the stairs for the first time means that the only thing between you and the sea some eighty feet below, is a thin piece of steel lattice-work. This means that on looking down you have an uninterrupted view of the water, which, for some reason is disconcerting. Still, as there are half a dozen blokes behind you, there's nothing for it but to keep your eyes on the horizon and stumble on downwards, clutching your luggage and a coat, which you now realise was a mistake, due to the fact that a howling gale keeps trying to wrap it around your head.

However, you're now safe inside and a kindly man is issuing you with a room number and so, being anxious to meet up with your contact, you find the room, change into work clothes and venture down several flights of stairs only to meet a steward at the bottom who, without any preamble says, "What the bloody hell are you doing wearing safety boots in the accommodation?"

The realisation that you have unwittingly broken some unwritten code is somewhat embarrassing and so you nip back to the room, put your shoes back on and go down the stairs again. On meeting the boot critic once more, you ask where your contact's office is located and having been nodded in the general direction, knock on the door.

A voice tells you to come in and you find yourself face to face with a guy who is scrabbling about with a huge drawing, while at the same time trying to carry out a telephone conversation with someone who is obviously desperate for information. As you stand there trying to look inconspicuous, the door opens and another guy enters, ignores you and proceeds to search frantically for some documents in a nearby filing cabinet.

You realise, as your contact drops the drawing on the floor and begins to yell profanities down the phone—that he's going to be really glad to see you.

This same scenario was played out all over the North Sea and none of us were immune from the feeling of total hopelessness it engendered.

For instance, I recall one occasion when a new chap, dressed in a brand-new stiff pair of overalls, arrived in my office clutching his boots, a pair of artificial leather gloves, a shiny helmet, ear defenders and safety goggles. It wasn't that I hadn't expected him, it was just that as usual, I was up to my eyes in something or other. In these circumstances, there is a pressing need to buy some time so the first thing you do is to send the newcomer off for a cup of coffee, then, once he's done so, you contact the Safety Representative and arrange for him to have an immediate and preferably lengthy, safety briefing.

Finally, having run out of delaying tactics, I suggested he might like to have a look around, but as he couldn't go on his own, I arranged for him to meet Bert at the entrance to one of the lower modules. I remember making some vague arrangements with Bert regarding the newcomer's need to have a taste of what we did during an average shift and I also recall Bert making some equally vague statement like, "Okay, leave it to me."

The day wore on and it was some time after our evening meal that Liam and Bert popped into the office for a brew and a chat. Seeing Bert, I remembered our visitor and asked where he was. Bert said, "Well, I took him to the galley for dinner and suggested that afterwards he might like to meet you. He said he was absolutely knackered and thought he would have an early night. He said I was to apologise to you and that he'd see you in the morning."

"That's fine," I said. "By the way, what did you do to entertain him during the shift?"

"Well, when we met, he asked me what was I doing and I said I was tidying up the Mechanical Stores. He asked if he could come with me and after he'd been watching for a while, I thought, sod this; he might as well be earning his living as just watching me."

At this revelation, a sort of cold feeling began to take hold and I said, "What did you get him to do?"

Bert said, "I gave him a brush and told him he might as well sweep up the floor which was full of rubbish from all the packing cases.

He didn't seem to mind, but I couldn't help noticing he looked a bit puzzled."

"Puzzled, puzzled, I'll say he must have looked puzzled, don't you remember me telling you who he was?" I said.

"You never said anything to me, I just thought he was a new technician come out to join the team."

"Why, who is he?" said Liam, who'd been listening to our conversation with growing interest.

"I'll tell you who he is," I muttered, "He's only the new Platform Engineer who's been appointed to take charge of the opposite shift; he's been sent out for a couple of days to see how we manage the business. Give me strength—god knows what he'll think—he's been shunted around all afternoon and finally been issued with a brush by some idiot."

"It's not me that's the idiot," said Bert, with some feeling, "I didn't know who the hell he was, he didn't tell me, you didn't tell me and all I did was to keep the sod out of your way."

Liam said, "He can't have been that bright—if anyone had given me a brush, I'd have told him what to do with it."

I had to agree he had a point. It was time to change the subject, so I said, "What's the film tonight?"

Liam said, "It's something called The Fuller Brush Man."

"Are you trying to be funny?" asked Bert suspiciously.

"No, I'm just telling you what it's called; it's got someone called Red Skelton in it."

I said, "I don't think we'll bother, it's another of those bloody films where everyone who was in it died before we were born—I reckon it's time for another brew and some sticky cakes."

10. Oh Buoy

Faithful readers may remember the role played by the remote Buoy in the rapid ageing process of Liam, Bert and me. Well your faith is about to be rewarded because lurking in the memory are yet more adventures which, for the sake of posterity need to be told—or so I've been telling myself. But first it might be as well to set the scene, so to speak.

As there were no storage facilities on our platform, oil had to be transported by ship to a refinery in Teesport. This meant we could only produce oil when a tanker was available and in order to make loading possible, we had installed a special Buoy about a mile away which was connected to us by a pipeline on the seabed.

The buoy was really a 'fishing float' of gigantic proportions; with a draught about as deep as three cricket pitches. The submerged portion consisted of a central shaft with the surrounding area filled with water ballast and buoyancy compartments. Massive four tonne counterweights hung down the shaft, which were used to counteract the pull of the Tanker on the oil hose and mooring rope. The entire unit was held in place by eight anchors on chains, which extended outwards from the structure for about two hundred yards and served to minimise roll and heave in bad sea conditions.

The superstructure of the Buoy could rotate around 360 degrees which enabled the moored tanker to 'weathervane' through a complete circle and adopt a position of least resistance to the combined forces of wind, waves and current. It was also capable of landing a helicopter on its ninety-foot deck, (a not insignificant facility as we will see.)

The structure under the helideck housed the fifteen foot diameter reels for coiling the hose and mooring line, a long mooring extension arm, an emergency generator and very basic accommodation capable of housing up to three unfortunates in great discomfort.

The structure above and just below the waterline was protected by a circle of huge wooden fenders, designed to collapse progressively in the event of a ship drifting into the buoy.

Sorry about the technicalities, but the main thing to remember is that it was remote, it had very little protection from the elements and was generally very cold, even in the summer. Oh, I nearly forgot, it was painted in a tasteful bright yellow, so from a distance it looked like a one-eyed man with a big nose, wearing a wooden skirt and a flat red hat, floating in the water.

The most civilised way of getting on and off the buoy was by helicopter and fortunately, we had the use of one all to ourselves. This was a 'Bolkow,' a fantastic machine, made in Germany with a big perspex bubble forming the cab. There were two seats in front and room for three behind the pilot. Our pilot was Andy, an ex-army flier who could do wonderful things with the machine. Sadly, for us anyway, there were times when the Bolkow was out of action and consequently other, more hairy, modes of transport had to be used. These generally required an innovative use of water borne transport, none of which were looked on with gleeful anticipation by the lads. In fact, any such requests on my part were met with a blank refusal, invoking my dubious parentage, lack of feeling, failure to understand, deliberate lying, gross exaggeration, victimisation and sundry other moans and groans. This, at times, led me to adopt a number of managerial tactics of which Edmond Blackadder would have been proud. In essence, I was required to lie a good deal whilst adopting a hurt look on my face.

About once a week we had what the deskbound chaps in the meteorological office called 'the hundred year storm.' In our naivety, we thought the title explained everything and that the chance of our being involved would be fairly remote, say, once in a hundred years, for example. Apparently not, as I'd just received word from the tanker that he'd beaten a hasty retreat due to the bad weather and had left the hose and mooring rope in a state of what he referred to as 'jammed.' This highly technical explanation, whilst having the benefit of brevity, didn't really give us much in the way of detail. There was only one thing for it —we needed volunteers.

Another small difficulty was the time; it was about five thirty in the morning and the lads were in bed, however, sacrifices had to be made, so I knocked on Bert's door and went in. I often find it best, in these cases, to attack straightaway before the sleeper has quite woken up.

"There's been a bit of a problem on the buoy and I need you to pop over and take a look."

"What," mumbled Bert? "Fly across at this time of the morning? Get lost." And with that he sagged back, pulled the blanket over his chin and shut his eyes.

"Well," I said, speaking quickly and realising that the operative word 'pop' hadn't evinced the desired effect. "It's not quite as easy as that, the weather's too bad for the Bolkow to take off, so you'll have to go over by supply boat."

At this revelation, Bet heaved himself upright and said, "You must be bloody mad if you think I'm getting involved in that lunacy! No fear, forget it." And with that, he sagged back once more.

I could see this was going to be more difficult than I had thought; it was time to play the 'appeal to the better nature' card. So, leaving the cabin, I stood outside for a couple of minutes and went back in.

"Bert, I've just spoken to Liam and he's volunteered to go across; surely you're not going to let your mate down and leave him to manage on his own? Besides I've more or less promised him that you're happy to go as well."

"You bastard," said Bert, "You know full well I can't let Liam think I'm feared, I'll never hear the end of it. Pass me those bloody trousers."

Phase one complete, I thought, now for Liam's cabin.

So, about twenty minutes later the lads were full of tea and a bacon bap, the insulated overalls were on, radios were slung over shoulders, tools were bagged and no one was speaking to me. Which, in view of what was about to happen, was perhaps prescient. It was only later, on their return that Liam, in a moment of weakness, revealed the awful tale, which went roughly as follows:

The first hurdle they had to overcome was to get off the platform and onto a supply boat moored underneath. This involved the lads waiting on the open deck for a crane to lift them off in a basket and lower them onto the back of the boat. This, in itself, was something you didn't look forward to, as a good deal depended on the skill of the crane driver. The basket was reminiscent of a giant inner-tube with a rubber floor and was fixed to the crane hook by a rope net, which stretched from the outside of the inner-tube up to a loop about eight feet above. The best way to manage this mode of transport was to stand on the outer rim, grasp the net with both hands and pray. Lifting off wasn't too much of a problem, the fun started as the basket was lowered onto the heaving deck of a boat.

If the driver timed it just right, he touched the deck just as the boat was about to rise, you stepped smartly off, were caught by the deck crew and the crane lifted the empty basket out of the way. If, however, the driver was half asleep, he would still be lowering you as the boat started to rise rapidly on the swell. This meant that, as you were being lowered, the deck gave you an almighty upward kick, the crane rope went slack and you fell off the basket onto a soaking wet deck. Then, as the deck went down, the crane rope tightened and the basket swung around in a mad arc, intent on using you as a human skittle. Liam, who was a natural genius at crane driving, used to hate the thought of placing life and limb in the hands of someone who, having failed at being a deckhand, had been given a crane to drive.

Liam took up the story, "We landed okay, got clear of the platform and set off towards the Buoy; the wind was quite strong and the boat was ploughing through the waves with spray everywhere. The idea was that, on nearing the buoy, the boat would reverse towards the iron ladder which was fixed between the wooden fenders. This would enable Bert and me to step off the back of the boat and onto the ladder. We were just fighting about who would go first when the skipper shouted that it was too rough to come in close and he proposed to lower the inflatable Zodiac and a couple of his lads would take us in to the ladder."

I said, "Bloody hell, I've got terrible memories of travelling by Zodiac before; remember the day we had to leave the buoy and climb up the rope ladder at the side of a diving vessel?"

"It's something I'll never forget," said Liam, "And when the skipper mentioned we would have to get into one of those awful rubber dinghies, Bert started to curse you all over again. As he said—if the sea's too rough for a bloody big supply boat—what chance do we stand on a silly bit of inflatable rubber?"

"So what happened next?"

"Well, the skipper hove-to about two hundred feet away and tried to keep us in the lee of the waves. The Zodiac was lowered and two of the deck crew clambered aboard. Holding on to the side, they shouted for us to get aboard. All the time we're trying to clamber aboard, the blasted thing is leaping up and down so as usual, we fell into a heap in the bottom and away we shot towards the fenders. As we got closer, it was obvious we were in for a hairy time, as the damned Zodiac was going up and down in the swell, so one minute we could see almost the entire ladder, the next minute it disappeared and the dinghy was almost at the top of the fenders."

Adopting my 'caring for the troops' persona, but conscious of not having had to be there, I said, "But it all went okay, I mean you made it onto the buoy alright?"

Liam stared into space for a minute and said, "Well, as we got closer to the fenders we could see that the ladder was badly damaged; there were sharp bits of rusty metal sticking out at the sides and the Mate said, 'You're going to have to be quick or I'll catch the Zodiac on a sharp piece. So when we get close, I'll shout jump and you leap onto the ladder as quick as you can.'"

At this point, Liam stopped and said to Bert, "You tell him what happened next."

"It was bloody terrifying. As the mate brought the dinghy in close to the ladder, there was a huge swell and as soon as we reached the top, he shouted 'jump' at which Liam took off and hung onto the ladder. The boat then went down some ten to fifteen feet and, as it rose up again, I looked at the mate and he shouted, 'jump you bastard, jump.' So I did.

Unfortunately, just as I leaped into the air, I realised that Liam hadn't moved, so instead of grabbing a rung, I found myself hanging on to Liam's waist. As we both hung there, Liam on a rung and me on Liam, the bloody swell came up again and I was soaked from the waist down.

"I'm now yelling at Liam to get a move on, he's doing his best to climb upward with me hanging onto his overalls until finally, we made it to the top of the fenders. I thought for some time I was a goner, but once we made it onto the walkway, we collapsed into a shivering heap and began to laugh —I think its called hysterics."

"Wow," I said.

"You might well go 'Wow," said Liam, "The only thing that kept us going for the rest of the day, was the thought of getting back and throwing you overboard."

Thinking quickly and trying desperately to avoid harm to the person, I said the only thing I could think of to diffuse the situation, "I've a nice brew and some sticky cakes in the office."

Works every time.

It was during another one of our restorative brews that Liam said, "That bloody Buoy has been trouble from day one. I did think that once we got the thing up and running we could sit back and leave it alone."

"Fat chance," said Bert, "I remember all sorts going wrong from the day it was floated out."

I said, "Are you sure we want to resurrect old wounds? After all, reminiscing isn't all it's cracked up to be."

"Aye well," said Bert, "It'll help pass the time while we get another brew and some of those pink icing cakes."

"If I remember rightly Bert, you were out before us," said Liam.

"That's right; I'd just joined the Company and had no idea what I was letting myself in for. In fact, the platform was still being piled into the seabed and the buoy had already been anchored in place. We were living on a giant crane barge and in December we had a spell of really bad weather so she sailed off into a sheltered location.

"It was during this stormy spell that we received some bad news from a boat that was fishing in the area. He'd reported that the Navigation Lights on the buoy had gone out and consequently, he felt we were a danger to shipping. A helicopter was sent out just before Christmas to check on the lights and on arrival found they were on, but unfortunately, the sodding Buoy had sunk to the level of the generator room, just under the helideck."

"What you might call a minor setback," said Liam.

Bert stared at Liam, and was just about to say something, when he decided to take another bite of cake instead. Feeling suitably refreshed, he continued.

"Obviously we couldn't just leave it there and I flew out to the crane barge, ready to sail when the weather abated. The good thing was that I was able to see in the New Year twice, as the boat's time was an hour ahead of UK time. So, we had drinks with the Captain and then drinks with our team, as much as you wanted—and all free."

At this snippet of news, Liam and I looked at each other and pretended we didn't care. "Never mind all that rubbish," said Liam, "What about the buoy?"

"Well, the weather finally calmed down and off we sailed. The idea was that the crane would lift the buoy out of the water to about the right height. We would then attach four massive 'yokohama' fenders to the sides to keep it afloat while we sorted out the problem."

(Now, what on earth, I hear you ask, is a 'yokohama fender'? Well, contrary to popular belief it's nothing to do with that strange looking woman who persuaded John Lennon to live in a bed, at least for a short time, while he was in the USA.

Think, instead, of a giant lozenge some ten feet in diameter and twenty feet long. This lozenge is made of rubber and inflated. Wound around the body of the thing are a number of chains running both along and around the perimeter. Attached to every junction, where the chains cross over one another, are what look like giant lorry inner-tubes and the whole ensemble is completed by having lifting hooks attached to the chains at each end.

All in all, they're not something you would want to trip over in the dark, or even worse, have one roll over on you, as they weighed about six tons. They're generally placed between a harbour wall and the side of a ship to avoid damage when docking.)

Bert said, "We manoeuvred the crane barge into position and the crew fixed lifting hooks to the helideck. When all was ready, the crane took the weight and slowly the Buoy was lifted out of the water. As soon as the wooden fenders were showing above the water line, we attached four yokohamas to the buoy. The idea was they would provide buoyancy while we carried out repairs. I know this sounds easy, but the bloody things had to be floated into position and held in place while we fastened them to the sides with wire ropes. All this time, the crane is holding the buoy out of the water, the sea, although calm, is still moving with about a three foot swell. Anyway, after a time, the teams had fixed them in place and we all retired to the deck of the barge.

"Having checked and re-checked everything, word was given for the crane to slack off and let the yokohamas take over. For the first few minutes all seemed well, the crane was released, and the buoy settled in the water with the yokohamas holding it in place just like a wee child in the swimming pool, floating happily, with a big rubber ring around its waist. And then all hell broke loose."

Consumed with a sort of morbid curiosity, I asked, "What happened?"

Bert said, "I need another brew."

Liam, who had also been uncharacteristically silent while his mate recounted the awful events, said, "Stay there, I'll get them and I'll see if there's any more of those sticky cakes."

On his return, we all took a well-earned sup of Yorkshire's finest and asked Bert to continue.

"Well, just as we were planning the next move, there was an almighty bang as one of the wire ropes holding a yokohama snapped and the sodding thing floated away. The problem then was that the weight of the buoy was now being taken by three instead of four buoyancy aids, and within a couple more minutes the other wire ropes snapped. The buoy, realising it was no longer being held out of the water, began to sink again.

We couldn't believe our eyes, the buoy is rapidly disappearing and the sea is full of bloody useless yokohamas floating about in the water. We held our breaths as it continued to sink and for a time we thought we'd lost it forever. Then, just as we were about to close our eyes, it slowed down and came to rest with the helideck about three feet above the waves."

"What you might call—back to square one," said Liam.

Bert gave him one of his stares and, between mouthfuls of cake, said, "Do you want to hear the rest of the story or not?"

"Of course we do," I said, "After all you must have been successful because we're never off the blasted thing."

Liam plopped down three more cups; after all, when you're busy solving complex problems; a regular brew is an essential aid to the thought processes.

Bert took a sip and continued, "After a great deal of consultation and recriminations, the next idea was to get the divers to burn a hole in the main ballast tank and pump millions of polystyrene pellets into the space. The central section of the helideck was then removed and once the pellets had raised the buoy to the first deck level, we lowered pumps into the counterweight and ventilation shafts and pumped out the water. At last the buoy was secure, but there was now a mammoth amount of work to do to get it ready for production."

Having digested this tale of sorrow and woe, we all felt a bit tired and decided to call it a day, have dinner and watch a film. As Liam remarked, "We're in luck, we've a new film on board, its got someone called Margaret Lockwood in it and it's about spying or something."

I said, "What's it called?"

"The Lady Vanishes."

"Bloody hell," said Bert, "It's an old black and white film; I remember my granny used to watch these films on Sunday afternoons."

"Well," said Liam, somewhat defensively, "I haven't seen it."

"No you won't have, you're too bloody young," said Bert. "Still it's got to be better than work; I'll go and get the toffees."

The following day saw us back in our usual position on the buoy. We'd just moored up a fresh tanker and were having a well earned brew when Liam said, "So what happened next?"

Well," said Bert, staring once more into space, "We had to carry out a good deal of minor work prior to a full scale refurbishment and as there was nowhere to live, we'd no option but to make day trips out and back from Aberdeen. That's two rotten trips a day in a helicopter and every now and then the blasted buoy was moving about too much for it to land, which meant we had to jump in or out of the cargo door while it hovered above the deck."

"Still," said Liam, "You joined for the adventure."

"No I bloody didn't, I joined because I thought it would be better than working in a paper mill. Anyway, the next thing that happened was I transferred to a converted Yugoslav trawler crewed by great hairy Germans, who'd been hired to assist with removal of the polystyrene pellets. The good bit was the price of whisky, which was a £1 a bottle and lager was £5 for twenty four cans—marvellous. The bad bit was the weather blew up again and we were forced to sail round and round for a week, which meant I was unable to drink anything due to being violently sick.

"Then later on, work started again and we resumed our daily shifts on the buoy. When the nights became lighter, we used to do a night shift as well. The only problem was, we were stuck there without any food, so some genius came up with the bright idea of microwave meals. A microwave oven was brought out and coupled up to an emergency generator. Then, before we set off from Dyce, we picked up our microwave meals ready to cook during the night."

Liam said, "That all sounds like a bit of fun, not only did you have to work on a remote location, but you had to cook your own food as well —that's a caring company for you."

Bert said, "Well, it was a novelty at first as I'd never seen a microwave before and in a moment of madness, I bought one for the house—which turned out to be the most expensive kitchen clock I've ever bought.

"And then things started to go wrong because, for some reason, the blasted ovens kept blowing up just as we were cooking our supper. The company sent out a unit every other week before we found out what was causing the explosions. What we hadn't realised, and nobody had told us, was that you can't cook your food on a metal plate, so every time we put the plate in the oven and switched on, there would be a flash followed by a loud bang, food would be spread all over the inside, the generator would trip out on overload and we had nothing to sodding well eat."

Liam said, "We need another brew, all this suffering has made me thirsty. I often think this bloody buoy will be the death of me, what with the ways in which we have to get on and off the blasted thing, the lack of accommodation, the freezing weather and the times we've missed a film —it's a wonder we're not certifiable."

I said, "Working with you two makes it hard to tell, besides the films are rubbish."

"That's not the point," said Liam, "Even watching that woman with the spot on her face is better than being over here."

"I take it you're referring to Margaret Lockwood who, may I remind you, was a big star during the Second World War. Although I have to agree, she was no Sophia Loren."

"You're right there," said Bert in a rare show of solidarity. "Mind you I'd have settled for any of them to keep me warm, when we were over here at night, trying to manually operate the turntable every time a tanker was moored. I used to wear a couple of boiler suits, one of which was padded, big gloves, a helmet with an inner bonnet with lugs that came down over your ears and a black plastic bag over my head, with holes cut out for the eyes. I've never been so cold, in fact I was convinced I'd got hypothermia by the time came for a shift change."

Liam said, "Seeing you in a black plastic bag wouldn't have done a great deal for your macho image as far as Sophia was concerned, in fact she'd have run a mile at the awful sight. Mind you, I think it might be worth trying the bag routine when you get home, you never know your luck."

Thinking I ought to change the subject before fighting broke out, I said, "Oh, look here comes the chopper." So, off we went for a hot shower, a big feed and another film with a star-studded cast—all of whom had one thing in common—they were all dead.

The Buoy, one desirable residence with sea views

Do you think the skipper's seen us?

Bert looking lost in the legs.

11. Revenge Is What We Need

Those of you lucky enough to have read the first of these offshore saga's, may remember my agreeing, in all innocence, to Liam's contention that the west crane engine had to be removed. And, in a stroke of what we thought of, at the time, as genius, he and Bert lifted it out with the east crane. This meant that for a while, we had no cranes available for use. Unbeknown to me at the time, this sudden lack of availability caused the drilling fraternity some inconvenience. The upshot of which was that I found myself being pursued by a homicidal toolpusher wielding a large spanner. (I think it was a two inch Whitworth, but in missing me, it partially destroyed Sid's desk, so I didn't stay to get a proper look.)

An understanding of his murderous intent was later explained to me by Sid. Apparently, he had been too long in the tropics, where he held ultimate power over life and death of everyone on the drilling rig. Sadly, on being posted to UK waters, he found that having to share the platform with a bunch of people who were surplus to (his) requirements was a step too far.

Fortunately, soon after, he was sent to some sort of retirement home for demented toolpushers and a replacement was sent out to join our happy band. Again, he was a native of the land that gave us cheese full of holes with a distinct lack of flavour. He too, had been drilling in the more remote areas of the world, but was younger and sported a goatee beard, in the manner of a Dutch painter. We were introduced to him by Sid and for a time we harboured a hope that he was au fait with the concept of sharing. (His opposite number, a guy named Guus, was a joy to work with, despite the fact that he displayed an unhealthy appetite for ice-cream.)

Sadly, it was not to be. Although our bearded friend appeared to be civilised, we pretty soon found it to be just another a shallow veneer. Once again, all was well as long as we didn't, as he succinctly expressed it, 'get in his goddam way.' This translated to our being confined to the maintenance office, not touching any of the plant or machinery, keeping well away from the cranes, not speaking to his staff, never using the Telex machine or contacting Wick Radio.

His reaction to our having to isolate equipment in order to carry out maintenance duties could best be described as caustic. He would lose no time in openly criticising our timing, intellect, capability and technical competence. This irritated the hell out of Bert who said, "There's no pleasing the sod, I've a good mind to let the whole plant just break down and then see what he's got to say for himself." This was Bert displaying some kind of inner turmoil, as he liked things to be orderly, "If we can't stick to the maintenance schedule, how the hell are we ever going to see the start of the evening film?"

However, this deep and emotional concern displayed by Bert, paled into insignificance when Liam realised our goatee friend wanted to deny him free access to his beloved cranes. This, as far as Liam was concerned, was akin to having your car repossessed when you were up to date on your repayments. In Liam's mind, cranes were there to be cosseted; nursed, oiled, cleaned, tested and carefully driven. It was a well-known fact that in bad weather, supply boat skippers would actually ask for him to lift containers off a heaving deck rather than the regular drivers.

One of the best illustrations of Liam's prowess with cranes occurred one afternoon when Ken in the radio room received a call from one of our supply boat skippers asking for Liam. Apparently, he'd been contacted by a fishing vessel in the vicinity asking for assistance with one of their crew. The chap had been taken ill with severe abdominal pain which had now localised on the lower right hand side. The skipper had consulted his bumper book of fishing diseases and come to the conclusion that his lad was suffering from Appendicitis. He'd contacted the supply boat to see whether they could take the patient back to Aberdeen, since it would be far quicker than his trawler. The supply boat skipper readily agreed, but wondered how they were going to be able to transfer the guy from one boat to the other. It was then he remembered Liam and the upshot of the call was to ask him whether he could lower the crane basket onto the trawler and transfer him across to the deck of the supply boat.

Liam, being Liam, readily agreed and the trawler was summoned alongside the waiting supply boat and in the lee of the platform.

It was then, on looking down, we noticed a slight snag. The trawler was considerably smaller than the supply boat, it also had very little clear deck space and to cap it all was bristling with radio antenna, winches, nets and had a wheel house amidships. Even the supply boat skipper was concerned and said as much to Liam on the radio.

It was as though our hero hadn't heard a word, the basket was hooked up to the crane and the trawler skipper was told to be ready to grab the thing as soon as it touched the small clearing on his deck. Liam gently lowered the line and with considerable skill, gently placed the basket exactly where he said he would. Willing hands held on to it while the patient was placed inside the rope mesh, at which point Liam said he was ready to raise the line. This was accomplished by him having a very delicate touch on the controls, as slowly the basket was raised clear of the boat's superstructure and in one smooth motion, swung the crane across until he was immediately above the deck of the supply boat. He then contacted the skipper and informed him he was ready to lower the patient onto his deck. This next operation took just a couple of minutes and on landing, the patient was lifted out of the basket into the safe hands of the crew.

Unbelievably, we found that throughout the whole operation, nobody had breathed and on realising that all was well, the crew on both boats gave Liam a wave and a cheer. Then, as Liam sagged back in his seat, the skipper of the supply boat came back on the radio and said that as far as he was concerned, he'd never seen a crane handled so capably and that Liam should be in line for a commendation. Despite his determination to remain unimpressed, Bert was very proud of his mate's efforts and clearly, on this occasion, the tea and cakes were on him.

Sadly, episodes such as this didn't endear Liam to some of the regular drivers, but he didn't care —wellbeing of the cranes took priority.

So with ownership of the cranes clearly established, (at least as far as we were concerned) the scene was set for that well-loved management strategy known as confrontation. This adversarial way of working had been honed to perfection in the 1960's by British Leyland when confronting (without success) the Unions, led with considerable zeal by a guy called 'Red Robbo.' The process consisted primarily of the manufacturer making what was known as a derisory offer, the unions flatly refusing, a walk-out being initiated, pickets being placed at the gates, braziers being lit and no Austin Metro cars being produced. Although in hindsight, this was perhaps no bad thing.

Fortunately, in our case we had Sid, who was called upon to mediate between the opposing factions and, having been associated with the drilling fraternity in the past, was able to negotiate an uneasy truce. The upshot was that we could maintain things as long as Beardy was given lots of advance notice and we promised not to interfere with his drilling rig. As it happened, there was very little chance of that, as the unit was an old refurbished thing belonging to Santé Fe. It was painted a tasteful shade of battleship grey and known affectionately as Rig 87 (but not by us.)

And so, as the weeks went by, we kept out of one another's way, he dining alone and the three of us laughing a good deal whilst consuming steak and chips, something which also seemed to upset him (the laughing, that is—not the chips.)

Then one day, after another near confrontation, Beardy hit on what he considered to be a cunning ploy—he started broadcasting over the tannoy.

You have to remember these were early days offshore and although we had already been victims of a spurious alarm when some idiot put out a 'man overboard' call; the danger of misuse obviously hadn't percolated down to our friend. Anyway, witness our amazement during yet another futile attempt to start a turbine, when the tannoy blared out the following message, "Maintenance are assholes." We looked at one another, "Did you hear what I think I heard?" said Bert.

"Definitely," said Liam, "It sounds like our idiot toolpusher - what a prat." We agreed and tried once more to solve the mystery of the broken fuel pump springs, but realised the solution could only be found after a strong brew. We re-convened in my office—well, when I say office, I'm really referring to a table, purloined from the mess and re-located to my bedroom.

The following day, same again, this time with a variation to the script —"All maintenance are useless." Followed by—"Maintenance people should be sacked." This was now causing sniggers from bystanders wherever we went, especially each time he reverted to his obvious favourite—"All maintenance are assholes." By now Liam, Bert and I were becoming distinctly tense and in order to try and diffuse the situation, I suggested we get Sid to 'have a word.' Bert said, "No, I'm not having that sod think we can't manage our own affairs; besides it'll just play into his hands if he thinks he's having the desired effect on us."

"I agree," said Liam, "We need to sort this out for ourselves."

Bert said, "We need to dream up some sort of revenge on the sod, that's what."

"Revenge is a dish best served cold, according to someone or other," I said.

"Never mind all that crap," said Liam, "I want revenge served now and if possible—often."

We all nodded; once again Liam had put his finger on the key requirement, but having thought for a moment, we couldn't come up with anything suitable, other than throwing the enemy overboard. "The only trouble with that," said Bert "Is no one would miss the bastard."

Proving that revenge needs careful thought and having exhausted our immediate repertoire on possible methods, there was only one course of action left to open us—we needed another brew and a sticky bun.

Then, as things sometimes do, the answer came to us two days later from a most unlikely source. We had, in our tender care, a number of submersible pumps and there was one in particular which used to cause us more grief than the others. This was a Sumo pump and the name was strikingly appropriate as we continually wrestled with the damned thing, due primarily to the fact that its electrics were rubbish.

The pump was located on the main deck and was lowered into the water through a large open ended pipe known as a caisson. As it was a long way down from the deck to the water, the pump was made up of a number of eight foot pipe sections bolted together. An electric cable ran down the outside and was connected to the pump motor by a waterproof coupling. Each time we had a problem, the entire unit had to be pulled out of the caisson and unbolted section by section until the pump unit itself appeared at deck level. Then, in order to lower the replacement pump back into the water, the whole sequence had to be repeated. It has to be said, that tending the Sumo pump wasn't very high on our list of exciting maintenance jobs and pulling up an extremely heavy unit eight feet at a time using a block and tackle fixed to a girder, soon lost its romantic appeal. Until, that is, Liam had one of his better ideas.

This required me to order a three-ton winch (no questions asked) which, on arrival, was firmly bolted to the floor adjacent to the pump caisson. A pulley was fixed to the girder, a wire rope was threaded through and down to the top of the pump and 'hey presto,' all we had to do was start the winch and up came the pump, as if by magic. Bert and I both agreed that at times, Liam was a genius, but that might have been due to a surfeit of sticky buns.

A couple of trips later we had just removed the pump once more when Bert began to speculate on how wonderful it would be if we could pull the blasted thing out in one complete length. Such was our hatred of the thing that far from calling him an idiot, we started to develop the possibilities of just such an action. As usual, it was Liam who came up with the answer.

"This could easily be done," he said, "If we could utilise the west crane. It would easily pick up the whole assembly and lay it down nicely on the helideck, where we could simply uncouple the pump, fit a new one and then lower the whole thing back down again."

Bert said, "We'd need to cut hatches in each deck so we could feed the crane rope through, then, when we weren't pulling a pump, we could fit a lid over the hatch to prevent anyone falling through."

This was awesome—talk about innovative thinking—it was a privilege just to be nominally in charge of such brain-power. Then just as we were about to do a little dance, Beardy spoiled the moment with one of his broadcasts, 'All maintenances are assholes.'

"I'll swing for the bastard," said Bert.

"Hang on a minute," said Liam, "I've got an idea, we know the access hatches have to come through the Accommodation to get to the helideck, but what if two of the hatches just happened to go through Beardy's office?"

Bert and I stared at Liam—brilliant!—This could be it, revenge at last; time for a brew while we planned the campaign.

And so, in the best traditions of maintenance, we sacrificed a film, worked far into the night, sketching and measuring, checking and cross-checking and supping tea. As Bert commented, "This is far too important to worry about missing a shortened version of 'Some Like it Hot;' after all we've seen it at least four times before."

Liam said, "That's all very well, but I could watch Marilyn Monroe every day." We knew how he felt, but were safe in the knowledge that the film would no doubt be sent out yet again.

The following morning we put phase one of our plan into action. We decided to start gently and so, when Beardy was safely ensconced on the rig, probably making the driller's life a misery, we nipped into his office, moved his desk back towards the window, removed four of his carpet tiles and drew an eighteen inch circle on the floor. We heard nothing until I had popped into Sid's office about something and he said, "Hey, I've had a query from the toolpusher, he wanted to know who'd moved his desk and chalked a circle on the floor."

I had long ago realised there was no point in trying to hide things from Sid, especially as I was his reluctant Secretary when he held his staff committee meetings. So, embroidering things a little, I told him how Beardy's broadcasts were getting on our collective nerves and how we'd hit on a wheeze to seek some revenge. I have to confess that during my explanation, I was less than sure what Sid's reaction would be, even though I'd stressed the fact that it was just a harmless prank.

Sid listened in silence, heaved a great sigh and said, "You're all bloody mad! This is supposed to be a sensible, highly efficient production platform and you lot a larking about with a senior member of staff. Mind you, it'd be good to see the arrogant bastard taken down a peg or two."

"So you approve of what we're doing then?"

"Like hell I do, and if anyone asks me what's going on, I'll deny all knowledge."

The next morning, we nipped in to Beardy's office again, removed the carpet tiles he'd put back and this time we removed four ceiling tiles immediately above. While Liam and Bert were so engaged, I inadvertently left a detailed drawing on his desk showing a cross-section of the platform with dotted lines coming from the Sumo pump, travelling up through the turbine hall, into the accommodation and up onto the helideck. It was nicely detailed with scale measurements, annotated sections, route identification, material requirements and a proposed completion date.

Keeping well out of Beardy's way, we waited for the explosion. In our excitement however, we'd forgotten one crucial point, it was crew-change day and so without any further contact, he went off on the afternoon chopper. Realising that Guus would be coming on board and not wishing to baffle him; we nipped back into his office and tidied everything up. I was just about to leave when I remembered the drawing; only to find it was no longer there. A quick search revealed nothing and I thought, oh well, he must have thrown it in the bin before he left. Then, just as we were about to leave, Guus appeared.

"Hi Guus, had a good leave."

"Hi lads, yes but it was too short, what are you doing in my office?"

"Er, nothing Guus, we were just looking for a drawing."

Over a restorative brew, we carried out an in-depth review of the situation. Bert said, "Well that was a bloody waste of time, he's gone off for two weeks and we can't start it all over again when the sod comes back, what a shambles."

Liam said, "The problem was we didn't realise he was crew-changing the day after we started; now we'll just have to think of something else."

"Never mind," I said, "It could have been fun and we tried our best." I think this puerile statement was a pathetic attempt to cheer up the team and obviously it didn't work, as Liam gave me one of his pitying looks and said, "Sod off Brian."

There were, however, two things we didn't yet know. One was that he'd left Guus a resume of our proposal in his handover notes and the other was that he hadn't thrown the drawing away.

The first unknown came to light when Guus, being puzzled by the note, popped into see Sid and asked what was going on with regard to maintenance carrying out radical alterations to his office.

Sid, like us, had a good deal of respect for Guus and immediately put him at his ease, saying it was just the daft maintenance crew having some sort of a joke on his opposite number. Sid said to me later, "Guus looked a bit bewildered, but I think I convinced him there was nothing to worry about and to just forget the whole thing. You bloody clowns will be the death of me yet, but it's a bit of a shame you couldn't have thought of it earlier."

The second unknown revealed itself the following day when I received a telex from Karl, my Boss. Apparently he'd had a visit from the Area Drilling Superintendent who was waving some kind of drawing which identified radical changes to his toolpusher's office. Fortunately, my boss was the same guy who'd hired me and we got on well together, but in view of the potential embarrassment, I thought a phone call might be a better way to try and explain the unexplainable.

Now, telling your boss, who until that moment, thought you were fairly level headed, that what he was hearing from the Superintendent was a joke, needed some careful thought. The other uncertainty I felt was that he was from the same country as our intended victim. Finally, Wick Radio connected me and I did my best to explain. I used words and phrases such as light-hearted, bit of fun, just a joke, meant no harm, good for morale, harmless and other assorted rubbish.

He listened in silence and even when I said 'over,' for a minute there was no reply. Liam and Bert, who were crowded in the radio room to hear my attempts to avoid us all being sacked, looked fearful. And then, just when I thought we'd been cut-off, Karl said, "Brian, between you and me, I've worked abroad with that miserable devil. It's a pity you miss-timed his off-duty, it would have been interesting to see what his reaction had been if you'd carried on with your little escapade. By the way, if you quote me on this I'll sack the three of you. But, just to satisfy my curiosity, what did you intend to do next?"

Bert said, "We were going to bring in the portable oxy-acetylene set to convince him we were ready to burn a hole in his floor.

Liam, cleared his throat and said, "We'd cut a seven foot piece of twelve inch pipe and we were then going to place it in his office with one end sticking through the ceiling and the other on the floor where the chalk mark was."

Karl chuckled, "Bloody hell, it's probably a good job you lot weren't able to carry out the mad scheme, he'd have thrown a fit—still, it would have been good to see it. By the way, did the Installation Manager have any idea what you were up to?"

"Partly," I said, trying desperately to sound confidently vague and not wishing to involve Sid.

"Alright, I'll ask no more questions, leave the superintendent to me."

When I returned onshore, it was my habit to call into the office and have a de-briefing meeting with Karl. On this occasion, I was a bit unsure what his reaction might be and I sure as hell didn't want to bump into the Drilling Superintendent. Fortunately, I needn't have worried, he explained that after our phone call, he'd popped into the Super's office and said, "Your man's going barmy. I've checked with the platform and they assure me the drawing he stole was simply a tentative proposal, but the lads had realised it was a non starter as soon as they'd finished taking measurements."

"Bloody hell," was all I could think of saying, "But it would have been nice to have scared the sod for a bit longer."

"Maybe it would, but don't you lot ever put me in that position again —now are we going out for a drink?"

Funnily enough, we never did hear any more abusive broadcasts during our next trip together, but the best news finally came from Sid, telling me the sod was being transferred to another drilling rig. Bert thought he'd asked for a move due to us, but Liam was convinced he hadn't the brains to engineer such a move by himself. Either way, it was nice to see the back of him. The funny thing was—pulling the Sumo pump in and out afterwards—didn't seem half as bad.

12. The Hippocratic Thingy

Our regular Medic was a tall guy named Andy, a hairy character about six feet two inches tall who hailed from Tyneside. This made consultation somewhat difficult, as most of the patients couldn't understand his questions or, possibly more importantly, his diagnosis. Although (when viewed in poor light) he resembled Klinger from MASH, his bedside manner more closely resembled that of Sir Alan Sugar on a bad day. Malcontents were swiftly dispatched; moaners were given a dose of some strange smelling liquid, which for some reason generally meant the recipient never returned for a follow-up dose.

His inner sanctum was the Sick Bay and the one area of the platform where cleanliness was next to wotsisname. It was clearly identified with a big green cross on the door and kept locked with the keys chained to Andy's belt. Obviously, as he was the chap designated by Sid to run our film shows, the need to safeguard the film projector was paramount. For some strange reason, the Company believed they had to justify the cost of providing us with medical care on board and they felt this was difficult to do if he just sat around all day waiting hopefully for someone to become ill or injured. So, in the early days, Andy also took on the role of Helideck Landing Officer. Fortunately, he had a relaxed attitude to work and was often seen helping out when the sick bay was closed. As he said, sitting there on his own and waiting for a chance to show off his medical skills, was somewhat boring.

We, on the contrary, felt that our continued good health was based on the premise that Andy's key role was never disrupted. I refer of course, to his custodianship of the projector, splicing gear and re-winding machine. All of which he lovingly maintained.

Such was his awareness of the importance of recreation to our wellbeing; he'd also created an unofficial lending library. Consisting mainly of dog-eared paperbacks it could, nevertheless, be a life-saver if you ran out of something to read. He started the collection by simply purloining any carelessly discarded books left in the recreation area. Should a forgetful reader return to find his book had disappeared into Andy's collection, pleas for it back were generally met with an admonition to 'sod off.' Interestingly, nobody ever pursued the matter of ownership; as Liam said, "Annoying the medic is a risky thing to do, particularly if you're not feeling well the next day."

In between the important work of looking after our cinematic needs and the discharge of library books, there was still time for Andy to offer medical consultation. He had a fund of stories regarding the average male's approach to issues of a medical nature and we had many interesting discussions late at night, while taking a mug of restorative tea in the sick-bay.

The four of us were chatting one evening and I asked Andy about his role in landing helicopters, what training he'd received and whether he'd volunteered for the job. At this he became rather vague on detail, preferring instead to illustrate his expertise by waving his arms about in a rather alarming manner. When tackled about the meaning behind the increasingly manic signals, he said, "It's not difficult, the movements are coordinated to let the pilot know where the centre of the helideck is, how far he is above the deck and when he's landed that he can slow the engine down and open the door."

Liam said, "If I were the pilot, all that arm waving would put the fear of god up me. You're supposed to be calm, what you do is reminiscent of someone with his foot caught in the tramlines."

Bert said, "I can vouch for that; we were just returning to the platform in the Bolkow when we noticed Andy at the side of the helideck waving his arms and jumping up and down like a madman. Allan, our pilot said, what the hell's Andy up to and are the signals supposed to be meant for me? I stared out of the side window and sure enough he was going frantic and making all sorts of incomprehensible signals. Allan said, 'The daft sod, I'm just going to land, and then perhaps we can figure out what he's on about.'

"So we landed as usual, only to find Andy still pointing at the top of the engine. We couldn't figure out why he was still gesticulating as we'd landed okay and Allan had shut the engine down. However, as we got out, we looked up to see what he was going on about and noticed that the exhaust cowl inside the engine compartment had come adrift and the fibreglass body had started to melt."

I said, "Crikey, what did Allan say?"

"Well he kind of apologised to Andy, but confessed he hadn't understood the signals; in any case, he had no option but to land anyway."

Andy, who'd been listening to all this, said, "I don't know why I bother. You're a bunch of ungrateful sods—nobody told me what signal

I was supposed to make when a helicopter is coming towards you and bits of the engine start falling off."

Liam said, "Are we having another brew?"

"I suppose you lot think that multi-tasking is not something you expect from a medic, but let me tell you I'm pretty adept at many things."

Andy's outburst in defence of his hidden capabilities was a bit of a surprise and we felt it was somewhat lacking in specifics. Lancing the odd boil, showing films and waving his arms about a lot, seemed to sum up his day as far as we were concerned. He did, however, display one dubious skill regarding dentistry, which Bert was to experience to his cost a couple of weeks later.

And then Liam, in what can only be described as a fit of pique said, "Multi-tasking, you call what you do multi-tasking, let me tell you, when I first joined this benighted Company on the Southern gas platforms, the mechanical staff were expected to do all sorts of bloody strange jobs."

Now both Bert and I were aware that Liam had a certain degree of prior knowledge when it came to offshore maintenance work and that he'd gained this experience somewhere in the south, near a strange place called Lowestoft. What we hadn't realised until now, was to what extent their regime differed from ours. And then Andy said the wrong thing.

"What kind of multi-tasking could you possibly be involved in on a small gas platform?"

"What kind, what kind? I'll tell you what sodding kind!In addition to my normal duties, I had to become competent in crane driving, lifeboat training, radio operating, production supervision, and medical assistance. And as if that wasn't enough," said Liam, warming to the theme, "I had to assist the electrical and instrument technicians whenever they got bloody stuck."

We stared at Liam with renewed interest; here was a man with hidden depths, just as Bert had been when gamely trying to keep the buoy afloat. Obviously I'd had the good fortune to link up with such a capable pair, but I did, however, vow silently never to let them know my feelings —you can go too far with admiration. Besides, if they did get to know, I'd find myself having to organise brews and sticky cakes for evermore.

And then Andy, obviously struggling with some inner concerns regarding his job, said, "What's all this about you being the medic?"

"Ah well," said Liam, "I'm talking about the days before each platform had a medic, so in order to make sure we could treat injuries, we had to have an advanced First-aider on board. As I said, the person chosen to occupy this post was the mechanic and I had to undertake special training so that I could perform critical operations on unsuspecting operators."

"I don't believe this," said Bert, "When I got hurt on the buoy the other week, all you did was laugh."

"True enough," said Liam, "But you have to remember I'm no longer the medic, you're now in the tender care of Andy instead."

Andy said, "Never mind all that, what I want to know is what kind of training you received."

"Well, we learned all sorts of useless things, one of which was, we had to practise using a hypodermic syringe by injecting it into an orange and I remember wondering at the time whether a human arm would be softer or harder than an orange."

"Is that bloody it?" said Andy, "You call that medical training."

"No, we also went on a visit to the Accident and Emergency department at the local hospital to see how the professionals did things. I remember looking forward with great anticipation as the first casualty was brought in, but unfortunately, it was a man who'd lost his thumb on one hand. The thought crossed my mind that this must be why they choose mechanics for this job, as I guess we're the most likely people to lose a limb or two. Then things got really busy and some of the casualties came in with much more serious injuries and two guys from the other platforms fainted. I remember then thinking I was glad I'd decided against being a surgeon."

I said, "There's still something bothering me about your training."

"What's that?" said Liam.

"Well, you said you practised carrying out injections on an orange."

"That's right, although I hoped and prayed I'd never have to use the thing in anger."

"Right—but what I want to know is—what was the syringe full of?"

"Water."

"No, I don't mean when you were practising, what would it be filled with if you had to do it for real?"

"I've no idea; we never got that far and anyway, the orange just about burst when we forced the water in. It was then I thought sod this, if anyone gets injured, I'll just bandage them up and wait for a helicopter to take them ashore."

As Liam then took a nice long swig of Yorkshire's finest, I realised we were at the end of his tale of advanced medical training. Even so, I'm pretty sure I heard a distinct sigh of relief from Andy—although I could have been wrong—it might just have been wind.

A couple of trips later, we'd just finished dinner and Liam suggested we nip into the Sickbay for a chat with Andy. We were just about to move off when Bert said, "Hang on; I'm off Andy at the moment."

I said, "Why's that, what's he done to upset you?"

"It's not so much upsetting as bloody embarrassing."

We leaned forward......

"Well?" said Liam, "What happened?"

"As you know, I had all my teeth out and a new set fitted....."

"Aye and then lost them overboard due to carelessness," interrupted Liam.

"Never mind that now," I said, "Just get on with the story."

"Well," said Bert, staring at Liam with something approaching hatred, "As I was saying, before they were removed I used to suffer something terrible with toothache and Andy professed to be well versed in the art of dentistry."

"And you believed him?" said Liam.

"If you had toothache like I did, you'd try anything. Anyway, Andy started poking about and after a while he decided I needed a few fillings. Now, as you know, Andy is very tall, and while I sat low down in the chair, he was on his knees in front of me, when the door opened and a steward came in. He took one look at what seemed to him to be some sort of illicit sexual act and beat a hasty retreat. I lived in mortal dread he'd tell everyone that he'd just disturbed a secret liaison between two consenting adults, but fortunately, he must have been too taken aback to say anything. The only thing was he kept avoiding me for the next couple of trips.

"But that wasn't the end of it, because it turned out that Andy wasn't as good at dentistry as he made out, and when I eventually went to get my teeth sorted, the Dentist, while making a final examination, remarked on something mysterious he'd not seen before."

"What was that?" said Liam.

"He said a number of my teeth appeared to have been cemented together."

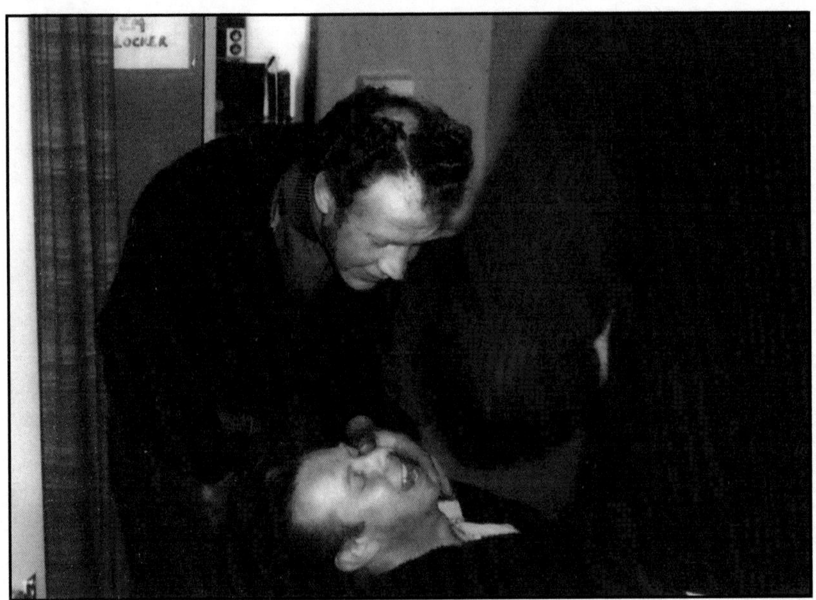

Liam doing a maintenance check on Bert’s teeth.

13. Ornithology Beats Snooker Any Day

You can't beat boredom for bringing out the very best in British lunacy. The search for innocent enjoyment knows no bounds and a sudden interest in bird life was no exception. In the first volume, I recounted the late lamented attempts to form fishing clubs on our platforms. Each angler claimed to have a unique insight with regard to 'the perfect spot' for casting their lines. At first these were closely guarded secrets. However, it wasn't long before the custodians had an irresistible urge to boast and it was amazing, listening to the unconvincing garbage they spouted to account for their success, or more generally—failure.

The fishing craze soon caught on and clubs were inaugurated. This meant that appropriate club names had to be thought of, a president, secretary and treasurer had to be appointed and regular meetings convened. It was astounding to see just how formal things were becoming, with club rules, fishing spots allocated on a rota basis and catches weighed, measured and recorded. Photographs of significant species began to appear on notice boards and one or two idiots even began to don fishing apparel prior to venturing forth. This landed gentry look was somewhat diminished by having to wear a bright yellow safety helmet in conjunction with Harris Tweed overalls.

And then, sadly, it all fell apart as they started to catch divers instead of fish.

So, in a game attempt to find a less dangerous pastime, somebody, having spotted a bird perched on a rail at the south end of the platform, decided to write it down in a book and tell everyone about his find. Within a short time, the majority of the crew had divided into two camps - the new bird enthusiasts and the cynics.

There is something mysterious which happens to the psyche of the average offshore worker when confronted with an opportunity to become an enthusiast. Especially if it concerns something which, in the normal course of events, he wouldn't be seen dead doing when on leave. And so I watched in amazement at the rapid onset of bird watching as a pastime. All it seemed to need was for some idiot to say, "I saw a Skua this morning," for some other idiot to reply, "That's nothing; I saw two lesser-spotted thingys near the flare boom." Within minutes, proof was demanded, records needed to be kept and a club was formed. By the next trip, copies of books with compulsive titles such as All the World's Sea Birds, Birding for Beginners, Eye Spy Sparrowhawks and You too Can Hand Feed Robins began to appear. The fact that there was little likelihood of seeing most of the birds listed in the books, appeared to make no difference; the objective was to show erudition in the new subject.

I recall being caught up in matters ornithological when one of our technicians said, "There's a bloody big bird perched on the helideck rail and it's not moving or anything." Now as his pronouncement fell someway short of a concise description, I plodded up onto the helideck for a look. On sighting the bird, I was forced to re-evaluate my criticism of his narrative capabilities. It was 'bloody big,' it wasn't moving and what's more, it was staring at me in a most disconcerting manner. Not wishing to be carried off to its lair, I summoned support from the cohorts. And after what seemed like a lifetime, Liam and Bert finally arrived and I pointed to the occupant of the railing.

Bert said, "That's a bloody big bird, what's it doing here?"

I said, "Give me strength—if I knew the answer to that, I wouldn't have needed to send for you two."

Liam said, "It's a Snowy Owl."

"What?"

"It's a Snowy Owl."

"How the hell do you know that?" said Bert, who considered himself to be something of a nature buff.

"Because," said Liam, "It's big, its head swivels and it's white."

Just then the creature, still staring at us, stretched its wings and we had to agree that Liam had a point. The creature's wingtips reached beyond the uprights of the railing and, as Bert observed, "Do you realise that the blasted bird's wing span must be at least five feet, because the uprights are set at four feet six inches apart? What's more, I don't like the way the flaming thing keeps staring at me, I'm off down for a brew."

Once again, Bert had summed up our feelings perfectly, a brew was definitely called for and Liam promised he would nip into the galley for some sticky cakes.

Later, as we were enjoying our well-earned repast, I asked Liam how he knew what kind of bird it was.

He said, "Ah well, I saw an article in the paper where a bloke had spotted one in the Cairngorms and managed to take a photo of the creature. Apparently they're very rare and you're lucky to see one in the

UK."

Bert said, "Remind me never to go into the Cairngorms. I don't fancy coming face to face with one of those monsters, especially if I'm sitting on a rock enjoying a butty."

Still curious, I ventured up to the helideck that evening and it was still in exactly the same place and still staring at me —so I left it there.

One thing we did enjoy was dropping our sighting into a casual conversation with a well-known 'twitcher'. He stared at us in a mixture of hatred and disbelief.

"You're a shower of bastards, why didn't you tell me it was there? Bloody hell, all I've seen so far is about forty bloody seagulls! I could have been the envy of all the other watchers."

"Well," said Liam, "We thought it best not to frighten the owl and besides, it's dangerous up on the helideck."

I don't think he believed Liam for a minute, but we did enjoy the sight of a grown man's face twitching uncontrollably.

And then there were the cynics, a breed of person generally found welded to the snooker table. In their dreams they believed themselves to be the offshore reincarnation of 'Fast' Eddie Felson, as played by the late, great, Paul Newman in 'The Hustler.' In reality, they more closely resembled Paul Gascoigne and were just about as sensible. They had no interest in reading, darts, quizzes, crosswords, films, idle chat, being outside, phoning home or doing overtime. As far as they were concerned, 'Pot Black' was the finest thing to come out of the BBC and they were convinced that 'The Crucible' by Arthur Miller was a documentary about a place in Sheffield where they held the World Snooker Championships.

An indication of their somewhat limited outlook was evidenced one day when a newcomer appeared on board and was spotted by one of the snooker fraternity, who pronounced in hushed tones that he, the newcomer, was something of a legend in the local pool hall. This adoration backfired somewhat when the 'worshipper' tried to tempt his idol onto the team —only to be informed that he, the newcomer, couldn't possibly join in, as we only had a half-sized table and to play in such reduced circumstances would, on his return onshore, spoil his potting capabilities. What was even more pathetic was the fact that the 'worshipper,' on hearing this load of old rubbish, nodded in agreement.

Any attempt, therefore, to interest the snooker fraternity in the delights to be had in standing on a wind-swept deck, waiting to spot a stray cormorant, was met with, at best, derision and at worst, total incomprehension. A notable exception to the derisory school of thought was Sid, our esteemed Installation Manager. Any, or all of the lads' attempts to relieve boredom by forming a club of some sort were met with his disdain, but never criticism. All he asked of life on board was to have a copy of the Times or Telegraph crossword, the odd film to see and some decent conversation over a brew. We realised very early on, during our time together, the futility of trying to interest him in any form of extra-curricular activity, and as the months passed, I began to see the sense in this approach. There really was nothing better than a late night brew and putting the world to rights in the company of Sid, Liam, Bert and Andy.

In spite of our lack of interest in birds there was, later on, an irresistible rise in twitching, culminating in the formation of a thing called the North Sea Bird Club. This was initiated by a guy in BP who should have known better. He invited the major oil companies to subscribe to a new club with the aim of improving the knowledge of North Sea bird life. Despite a degree of scepticism from other birding organisations, the club grew in strength and was seen as a useful way of charting the migration patterns of many rare visitors to the UK. It's perhaps fortunate for our sanity that, at the time of its inauguration, Bill Oddie was still a 'Goodie' and content to ride around on a three-seater bicycle.

14. The Company Expects........

Everything was carefully prepared; the lounge on our Accommodation Rig had been cleaned, polished, curtained and the seating arranged according to rank. A steward had delivered an extraordinary selection of cakes, tea and coffee was delivered hot and strong, copies of the latest progress reports were laid out on each chair (coloured and annotated in order to convince the reader that the project was currently ahead of schedule and considerably under budget.)

This then was the setting for the bi-monthly progress meeting with our major Partner. The VIP's would be arriving at two o'clock; we had been up most of the night trying desperately to anticipate thorny questions and more importantly, be able to provide answers. Our gang arrived early, as you do if you're wise, and were stood around trying to look relaxed. Then, bang on time, the door opened and in trouped our interrogators. That afternoon we were blessed with the presence of the Project Director, the Company Chief Engineer, the Production Manager (designate) and bringing up the rear our Partner representative. All we knew was that he was from Texas, had been in the oil industry longer than the rest of us put together and spoke like Charles Bronson. In fact, he looked a lot like him, dressed as he was in the usual attire of well washed jeans, a tooled leather belt, a muted check shirt (with pearl buttons) and nicely polished black shoes.

Without any preamble, he walked over, introduced himself and said we were to be sure to call him Chuck. After all, he said, this is the big oil and gas industry and we weren't to stand on ceremony —just tell it like it is.

Now, as telling it like it is, was just about the last thing we wanted to do, there were some nervous replies along vague lines of, "No problem, Chuck, that's why we're all here."

Thankfully, at this point, our director gave one of those senior type coughs and said, "Well gentlemen, if we're all ready, I suggest we make a start. Has everybody availed themselves of the excellent repast our hosts have kindly laid on? If you wouldn't mind then, Harry, why don't you provide us with a resume of progress to date."

Harry was our duty project manager who worked opposite Vince for two weeks on and two weeks off. As the Platform Engineer on this Project, I had the dubious pleasure of working a week at a time with each of them and their approaches to the job couldn't have been more dissimilar. Whereas Vince ran the project as a sort of personal fiefdom, Harry was organised, democratic and calm, believed in critical path analysis and smoked a big curved pipe. We felt it was, therefore, fortunate it was Harry presenting our case and not Vince.

Anyway the meeting proceeded as meetings do, with some key points made, some general waffle, the occasional laugh (not overdone and somewhat nervously.) Until that is, just about the time we thought, 'bloody hell, we've got away with it,' Chuck, who until then had made notes and smiled a lot (marvellous teeth,) said, "Hey you guys, just before we wrap up, I've a question I'd like to ask."

Lulled into what turned out to be a completely false sense of security, our director said, "Certainly Chuck, fire away, I'm sure we'll be only too pleased to hear what our partner thinks." (The patronising sod.)

Chuck said, "Well boys, I've heard a lot of good stuff here this afternoon, but what I seem to be missing is this —just when do you intend to start up those big Export pumps that we helped to pay for and when are we going to start getting some goddam payback?"

To say this brought about a stunned silence would be putting it mildly; it was as though a sex maniac had nipped into a convent and shouted 'right girls let's be having you.'

Trying gamely to recover, our director looked at Harry, who with remarkable speed, turned to George, the Piping Engineer and said, "I think the answer will be better coming from the chap who's been very closely involved with the export pumps."

We all leaned foreword to hear what George had to say. But then, with equally remarkable speed, George said, "I think Brian has more up to date information than me, after all his chaps have been commissioning the pumps for some time now."

And with that admittedly brilliant side-step, he smiled at me and sat down.

There are the odd occasions in life where I believe a phenomenon called 'mixed emotions' occurs in spades and this was one of them.

Again, there was a silence you could cut with a knife, all eyes swivelled around to stare in my direction and there were facial expressions an actor would die for. The director stared at me with something approaching hatred, Chuck looked slightly amused, Harry looked worried, the production manager looked curious, George looked the other way and I looked stricken (I guess.)

I don't really know what I said, only that it was mostly rubbish, but presented with what I hoped was sincerity and confidence. I rambled on about our difficulties in aligning the thirty six inch pipework to the pump intakes, how we had sent for a piping expert (who turned out to be a lady) and how we were working flat out to achieve success.

Realising I had actually nothing of interest to say, the director brought the meeting to a swift close and we all started to troop out. All I really wanted to do was kill George slowly and with malice. However, just as we reached the door, Chuck stopped, turned to me and said, "Say Brian, we've a bit of time before the flight back—why don't you show me the pumps for myself? I guess I'm just a curious son of a gun." And with that he flashed his teeth at me, gripped me by the arm and said, "Okay, let's move out."

Once again I realised my worst nightmare was far from over; the last thing I wanted was to have Chuck all to myself for the next hour and, interestingly, neither did our director. Moving swiftly back into the room he tried to disengage me from Chuck and said," I really don't think you've time Chuck, the chopper could be here early you know."

"Don't worry," said Chuck, "I'm sure I'm in good hands and I guess Brian here can see me back in time. Okay, Brian, ready to move when you are." Then with another flash of teeth, this time at our director, we sallied forth.

Even though I took the long way round, we finally arrived at the pumps and I launched into yet another pathetic spiel about capacity, delivery, power requirements, control mechanisms and pipework problems causing unplanned delays. Then, having listened in silence, he waved an arm and said, "Goddam it Brian, cut the crap. I know all about the pumps, what I'm trying to find out is just what your management are on about, because whenever I ask about start up dates, they give me some goddam rubbish about manpower problems, trade-mixes, manufacturer's delays and a load of baloney like that."

"Chuck, I'd like to help, but I'm just at the sharp end and we really are doing the best we can to get the things running." Even as I said it, I thought, this isn't going to convince a child of five, let alone someone like Chuck.

He then took the wind right out of my sails by saying, "Man, I know it's not your fault and your so-called mates have tried to put you on the spot. No—there's something else going on here and it's my guess there's goddam politics behind it. I think there's a problem on one or two of your feeder platforms, ones in which my company aren't involved and the bastards are playing a delaying game to give them time to sort it out. Well let me tell you Brian, I ain't standing for it, I've been in this game too long to be fed crap. I just wanted to see the pumps for myself and it looks to me as though you could fire them up pretty soon, so just give me a straight answer—am I right?"

There seemed to no point in further self-sacrifice on behalf of an unfeeling Company, so I said, "Yes, Chuck, my lads tell me we could run the pumps within the next week, just as soon as our alignment calculations are verified."

"Good man! I thought so—okay, let's head on out of here, I need a few well chosen words with your bosses." Then, seeing me looking even more stricken (pathetic really,) he said, "Brian, there's no need to worry, I ain't about to quote you. I can see for myself the goddam pumps are pretty well finished. Now, let's move it, I need to sort a few things out. My company ain't used to being asked for millions of dollars just to be fed a load of horse-shit."

And with that, Chuck smiled at me once more and we went back to the accommodation.

There comes a time when you realise you're completely out of your depth and are being used for political ends, about which you know nothing. However, having said that, I enjoyed meeting Chuck. Only afterwards it dawned on me that when he smiled he reminded me of an alligator.

15. Lights Out

Picture if you will, the scenes of unrestrained joy when Ant and Decking reveal on prime-time television that you're the lucky winner of some useless contest. You dance about, the feeling is one of euphoria, the family are cheering, Reporters are queuing for interviews, flash-photos are being taken, and the audience are going spontaneously bananas, as instructed by the Producer. Ant (or is it Decking) is opening a bottle of champagne, Lulu is waiting in the wings to present the cheque, people you only vaguely know are slapping you on the back and the unlucky contestants are trying to look pleased for you.

Well, sadly, going into production for the first time thirty years ago was nothing like that. For a start, the two cheeky chappies from the arctic wastes of the north east were far to young to be celebrities and Lulu was still going around 'shouting' at anyone who'd listen. For the last three hectic years we'd been assembling, banging, hammering, arguing, modifying, cleaning, repairing, breaking, mending, recruiting, sacking, bonding, lying, exaggerating, promising, reporting, cajoling and energising. We were bloody well exhausted but, at last, everything was in place, tests had been carried out, machinery was working, wells had been drilled, pipes had been connected and we were ready to produce oil.

The great day finally dawned and several of us gathered expectantly around the Christmas Tree. In addition to yours truly, there was Phil, the Production Supervisor, a couple of production technicians, the Installation Manager and Pete, our Mechanical Commissioning Engineer. Significant by his absence from our little gathering was Vince, our Project Manager. He'd decided the place for him to be was in his office, ostensibly to keep things 'running smoothly' (which for Vince was an oxymoron.) We, on the other hand, knew the reason he'd stayed put was so that his would be the first telex ashore conveying the momentous news.

"Thereby," said Pete, "Ensuring that any congratulations would be delivered directly back to the crafty sod." Some felt this to be a somewhat cynical viewpoint but—on the other hand—it was probably accurate.

Now for those readers who are still baffled by jargon, remember, the christmas tree is simply a great big block of steel weighing about seven tonnes and is so called because in the olden days in America it had a number of valves sticking out from its body, which, to some backwoods oil man (probably high on funny tobacco) made it look just like a christmas tree. You can see how easy it is to get stuck with a wholly inappropriate name—a bit like calling someone Marion Morrison, when all the time he wanted to be known as John Wayne. Anyway, here we were staring at our christmas tree and in particular at a valve known as a 'Choke' (don't ask.) All you need to know is that on opening said 'Choke,' oil will begin to flow from the well into the production facilities. Witness then my utter amazement when Phil said, "I think Brian should be given the honour of opening the choke, as he's been here battling with the elements since the platform was in bits in Norway."

Now, it's easy to be cynical, but I have to say on this occasion that I was both touched and delighted at the gesture. So I graciously accepted and gingerly opened the choke valve for the first time. There was a momentary silence and then the oil, under extremely high reservoir pressure, began to blast its way through the valve, along the connecting pipes and into the pressure vessels. There were handshakes all round and big grins—happy in the knowledge that, at last,we were a 'live' platform.

Phil contacted the control room to see that all the necessary flashing lights were indeed flashing and then passed the good news to Vince.

Pete then turned to me and said, "Nice one, but I can't wait to see Vince's face when he hears it was you that opened the choke. I reckon if he'd known that Phil wasn't going to do the honours himself, he'd have been down here like a shot."

But, as I still had a sort of silly smile on my face, I just nodded. As far as I was concerned, all was right with the world, together we'd overcome some amazing problems and had succeeded. I was well pleased, a feeling which, as it turned out, was somewhat premature.

Slowly the vessels were filled, the pressure of the oil was dropped to atmospheric and started to pour into the huge storage tanks at the base of the platform. Obviously, as we dropped the pressure, gas started to be released (just like it does when you open a bottle of champagne—or coca-cola if you're poor.) This meant we needed to ignite the flare to dispose of the gas. I did have a momentary feeling of panic and wondered whether there might be another idiot in a transfixed state at the top of the flare, but I thought, oh well, when we light this lot, he'll come down soon enough—I think it's called paranoia.

Now, if I might just wax lyrical for a minute, it's a late afternoon in December, we're closer to Norway than Aberdeen, the light is beginning to fade and the flare has been lit. Slowly, word gets around the platform and people begin to meander outside the production areas and accommodation blocks for a glimpse at a gigantic flame leaping out of the end of the flare boom. This awesome sight summed up just what our efforts were all about, we're on a three hundred and twenty seven thousand tonne monster in four hundred and ninety two feet of water and there in front of our eyes was the evidence of our efforts for all to see. Even Vince was affected and was heard to remark— "Bloody marvellous."

Please don't ask me for a rational explanation for the lunacy that followed. I blamed Pete and, contrary to all that was logical—he blamed me. As the flare was now well and truly into its stride and Vince was composing ever more grandiose telexes to everyone in the known universe; one of us (and it wasn't me) suggested we nip down to the base of the flare to see that the system was working as designed. Then, having arrived, we carried out a few fairly meaningless checks, whilst all the time keeping a reasonable distance from the intense heat given off by the inferno above our heads.

It was at about this time that one of us had a complete brainstorm (it wasn't me) and suggested this would be good to turn on the flare cooling system.

Experience on earlier platforms had confirmed the fact that the tips of our flares weren't lasting very long due to the blowlamp effect on the outermost tip. In fact, on a previous platform, the maintenance lads changed a flare tip by having a helicopter hover above the end with a new tip slung underneath. The idea (which was a good one) was to save us having to build complex scaffolding at the end of the boom so that we could winch up a new flare tip off the deck of a supply boat. A slight drawback to the helicopter plan was the downdraft from the blades, which meant we had to tie ourselves on with safety harnesses to avoid being blown into the sea.

Anyway, in order to increase the life of the flare, we had installed a water pipe up the side of the boom, ending in a ring around the base of the flare tip. This ring was perforated with a series of holes and the pressure of the water formed a cooling circle around the flare.

So, having finished our checks, one of us (it definitely wasn't me) decided it would be a good idea to switch on the cooling water and one of us pressed the pump starter button (not me.) Then, as we peered through the brightness, we noticed a complete curtain of water had formed around the bottom of the flame, as it emerged from the tip. We were ecstatic, another triumph for commissioning and a lengthier life for the flare.

A few minutes later, we noticed the flame appeared to become smaller. Pete said, "I guess the production boys are reducing the flow from the well." And, for a second or two, this seemed to be a reasonable conclusion. But sadly, it was becoming increasingly obvious that Pete's pronouncement was bloody rubbish as—in front of our eyes—the water took a greater hold, the flame became smaller and then, in the manner of someone snuffing out a candle, the sodding flame went out.

In a futile gesture, before running away, I said, "Quick, shut the bloody water off."

Pete did so, and we were now faced with the sight and sound of millions of cubic feet of raw gas filling the evening sky.

Just as we were preparing to leg it, there was a clatter of feet behind us and a production technician arrived panting, to see what had happened.

"What the bloody hell's going on—what have you two daft sods done to me bloody flare?"

Notice, if you will, a certain lack of restraint and awareness of rank during this outburst, it did, however, deserve a reply; the only problem was we couldn't think of one.

"You've been playing with the cooling system! Why can't you mind your own business? It's our sodding plant now, so just go away while I sort things out. The problem is, we'll have to shut the well down while we de-pressurise the gas header vessel."

It then dawned on me that Vince who was, at this moment, still ensconced in his office and no doubt sending telexes proudly letting the world know we were in production — was oblivious to the fact that we had suffered a serious setback as far as boasting was concerned.

So, in the space of about thirty minutes I had gone from hero (ceremoniously opening the well) to bloody idiot (putting out the flare.) My worst fears were borne out when, having had to rescind a number of congratulatory replies, Vince sent one more telex to base. For some masochistic reason; I still have a copy to this day. It is succinct and whilst not overtly accusing me of ineptitude, the message is perfectly clear. It says:

From: The Project Manager
To: Base Management
Daily Report for Tuesday 11th December 1979.
Flare lit successfully at 1745 hrs this day.
Flare put out by Page at 1750 hrs—yes the flare spray does work.
Flare re-lit at 1755 hrs.
What do we do when it rains?

Even today—as I look back—I still think it was Pete's fault.

Section 2

Onshore Adventures

1. A New Job

It may surprise you to know there were a good many people in our company who occupied what were known as 'Senior Positions'. This meant that as well as telling everyone else what to do, they met at intervals to decide what the proletariat should do after they'd done what they'd been doing quite happily for some time. This was also euphemistically known as 'Career Planning' and occupied a good deal of time in the Personnel, sorry — Human Resources — Department. Such important decision making was based on advanced psychological methods consisting of impenetrable information based loosely on chats with supervisors, 'what if' scenarios, annual appraisals, not knowing what to do with someone, sidelining before they destroy a platform, foreign postings and other subtle means by which your future prospects (if any) were assessed and determined.

And so, inevitably, one day it was my turn. Summoned to see a senior person whom I'd never met, I found his office and was ushered into the presence. In addition to him and me there was also a lady named Marjorie from Human Resources, who appeared to be leafing through a huge file with my name on it.

"We understand you've been offshore now for some eight years and in that time have been involved in several large projects." He looked up as if asking for confirmation but then, without waiting for a reply, continued, "Well we think that's quite long enough and it's time for you to take on some fresh challenges, as I'm sure you'll agree."

As I had no idea what he meant by 'fresh challenges' it was difficult to make an informed comment, so I asked what he had in mind.

"Well now, we'd like you to take up the post of Head of Commissioning across the company. As you know we have several major projects underway at present and your role will be to ensure that company standards are consistently applied throughout." And with that he beamed at me, assumed I'd already agreed and said to Marjorie "Well, that's that then, see to the changes, will you."

It sounded alright, but then I remembered two fairly important things, on the one hand it would mean moving the family from Cheshire to Aberdeen, selling our house, finding a new one, choosing schools for three children and not least of all, having my wife lose her post as a Lecturer. On the other hand was the fact that I had just spent over four years in harness with Vince, my current Project Manager, whose managerial style was somewhere to the right of Kemal Ataturk. The thought that I was now about to take on the combined might of several other project managers made me somewhat cautious, so the idea, therefore, of leaping up and shaking my new benefactor by the hand was not exactly uppermost in my mind. However, it was promotion and I would have my own group of dedicated Commissioning Engineers, a desk, secretarial assistance, a pint after work, a dress code that didn't include safety boots and freedom to travel to exotic locations like, Leeds and Hull. (It's not that I have anything against Leeds you understand, it's just that for some unaccountable reason, it was typical of the locations where we built offshore equipment.) I've waxed lyrical about Vince on a number of occasions, but, as I've tried to hint already, new readers shouldn't confuse my erstwhile project manager with some quietly spoken sophisticate. Don't get me wrong, I learned a great deal from him and he was very good at his job. Once, that is, you'd learned to ignore the fact that anyone foolish enough to disagree with his pronouncements was summarily sacked. This was somewhat unnerving for newcomers, until they realised it was simply his method of stifling what he considered to be a rebellious attitude.

Interestingly, in the whole time I worked for him, he only got rid of one chap. This unfortunate bloke was seconded to us from a partner company and was appointed to be my opposite number. To compound the problem, Daniel had a sort of unworldly air about him and it soon became obvious that he wasn't cut-out for the hurly-burly of project work. He was a gangly sort of chap with blond hair which had a tendency to fall over his eyes as he spoke. Being tall, he reminded me of Jacques Tati in his most famous role as Monsieur Hulot. (The French film entitled 'Monsieur Hulot's Holiday' is a comedy classic and the character Tati created predated Mr Bean by about thirty years.)

Anyway, as time went on Vince became less and less enamoured with Daniel, whom he complained was vague about progress, had a tendency to miss meetings, retired early to bed and exercised insufficient control over the lads.

Vince collared me one day and said, "You're his oppo, what do you make of the idle bastard? I need to sack him and get someone else in his place. I know what you're thinking, but he's bloody rubbish and we've a long way to go yet."

Trying once again to tread that fine line between sycophancy and cowardice, I said, "I agree he's not the best oppo I've ever had, but we need to be careful. As you know, he's the eyes and ears of our partner, and sacking him isn't going to be easy."

"I know what you mean," said Vince in a rarely seen air of wistfulness. "But we've got to find a way."

As I left his office, I couldn't help pondering with some misgiving about Vince's use of the collective word 'we.'

On my arrival the following week there was pandemonium, telex's were flying about, Vince was, as usual, yelling down the phone and a senior human resources person was expected out on the next flight. On entering his office, he looked up, beamed at me (a frightening experience,) gave a thumbs up sign, put his hand over the mouthpiece and said, "Got the bastard."

He put the phone down and said, "I knew I'd find a way—it's a safety matter, not something we can ignore, rules are rules. Walter, the Installation Manager agrees—well he will when I've finished with him. I've just got to make it official with Charlie from human resources, when he arrives."

"How the hell have you managed it Vince?" I said. "The last time we spoke it seemed impossible."

"Ah it's the safety angle you see, no company can ignore that aspect. As you know I'm red-hot on safety and that prat Daniel has been acting in an unsafe manner, so I had no option but to fire him."

This red-hot on safety bit was news to me; although Vince was as safety conscious as the rest of us, it was not unusual to see him arguing with the safety representative over the timing of a lifeboat drill interfering with his afternoon nap. However, I was curious to find out what had tipped the balance, so I said, "What did the poor sod do to deserve the sack?"

"I'll tell you what he did, he only went down the leg on his own without telling anybody, that's what. We can't have that, it sends the wrong sort of signal to the workers seeing a senior person setting such a bad example, and furthermore it's bad for morale, I can't have that, no matter who it is."

A word here about the 'leg'—our platform was, at the time, the biggest we'd built. It was a concrete structure with space in the base to store a million barrels of oil. Four giant legs arose from the base to a height above the water of some sixty feet, on top of which was the deck, the accommodation and all the equipment modules. It was possible to go down the legs to a point just above the storage dome, remembering that at this depth you were a long way below the water-line. Escape meant you had to climb a series of vertical ladders, followed by numerous flights of stairs. To go into the depths on your own was at the least foolish and in Vince's considered opinion, "The act of a bloody madman."

As Vince and morale were not two words I was used to hearing in the same breath, I began to get the feeling that his uncharacteristically emotional explanation was some sort of rehearsal for the meeting with Charlie. Privately, I wasn't too surprised that Daniel had wandered off on his own and for a moment I felt quite sorry for him until, that is, I remembered his hand-over notes were based solely on the unquestioned, and at times highly imaginative, rubbish fed to him by the lads.

I remember asking Charlie whether we had abused the standard protocol regarding dismissal, such as verbal and then written warnings, interviews, tribunals and so on.

"Ah well," he said, "In theory we haven't actually sacked him, as he isn't our employee to start with, and all we're really asking is for him to be transferred back to his parent company. Mind you, I will say this insistence on our part is causing them some embarrassment and I'm sure they won't forget it in a hurry."

Before I left the tender care of Vince and the Platform I had learned to love, Vince and I had one more adventure together which, in view of the Daniel episode, was somewhat ironic. It came about because we'd encountered a serious problem to do with some pipework down one of the legs, the source of which was to be found just above the point where the pipe entered the top of one of the storage domes. Now in normal circumstances, there would be no access to this pipe, as some way above was what was known as the 'gas-tight floor.' This was located part way down the leg and was reached by a series of metal stairs. As its name suggests, the floor was meant to be sealed during operations and was only open to us while we were still in the construction phase. Entry through the floor was via a manhole and further downward progress could only be made via a vertical ladder fixed to the concrete wall of the leg.

It's hard to describe the awfulness of the journey from the top of the leg to the bottom, it was hot and became hotter and just as you had arrived at the base of the stairs you realised there was a manhole to negotiate followed by a climb down a nasty metal ladder. And that was just to get down—coming back up was a nightmare.

Anyway, as the pipe problem refused to go away, there was no option but to see the thing for ourselves. In my case, wandering about the platform was part of the job; in Vince's case this meant a rare and unenthusiastic journey into the depths.

Obviously safety precautions were taken, access to the leg was limited, there was a chap stationed at the top that took your name, time of entry and exit and was responsible for seeing that breathing apparatus was in place and functioning in case anything went wrong. The other interesting thing was that, in order to ensure an ample supply of fresh air reached the top of the dome, a temporary fan was installed and a flexible tube about two feet in diameter carried the air down through the manhole.

This meant that not only had you to negotiate the hole then feel for the rungs of the ladder, but you were also forced into intimate contact with the damned tube. As Vince remarked with some asperity, "It was like being crushed against a very large buxom woman, while you did your best to slide gently past."

I said, "We should be so lucky."

Anyway, on this particular morning there were four of us at the scene of the problem, Vince, me and two young pipe fitters, whom we'd brought down with us in case we needed to arrange for modifications to be made. So, here we were debating what to do, when suddenly we heard the Platform alarms go off and the safety guy called us on our Motorola radio to come out immediately and go to our Muster Stations.

Off we set, back up the ladders, squeezed past the fat lady, climbed up the stairs, landed at the top, gasped a good deal, sweated considerably and made our way up four more flights of stairs to our muster stations. At this point the alarms stopped and Walter came on the tannoy to say it was a false alarm and that it was okay to return to work.

Vince said, "Sod that, I need a cup of tea and a bun before we go back." Being aware of Vince's view that what he wanted, we all wanted, there was general agreement. Then, having been fed and watered and facing the inevitable, we proceeded downwards, past the fat lady, until we landed on top of the dome once more.

And then—and this is true—the alarms went off again. We looked at one another and Vince let out a stream of invective the like of which brought exclamations of admiration from the two lads, but which, fortunately, I can't do justice to, as this is a family book. So, off we set again, back up the ladders, squeezed past the fat lady, climbed up the stairs, landed at the top, gasped a good deal more, sweated uncontrollably and staggered up four more flights of stairs to our muster stations. The only bright part of the climb in my view was the fact that as Vince and I were hauling ourselves up the ladders, we became dimly aware that our two lads were climbing whilst carrying on an animated conversation regarding the relative merits of Marilyn Monroe as an actress or as an object of desire (from what I could make out, the 'object of desire' aspect was winning hands down.)

However, just as we emerged from the clutches of the fat lady, Vince let out a sort of strangled cry which brought everyone to a stop. Then, in between gasps and ragged intakes of air, he addressed the two lads, "Listen you two bastards, when you're climbing the ladders, just keep sodding quiet, I'm sick and tired of listening to you rabbiting on as though you're on a bloody stroll, just keep shtum, because if I hear another word, I'll sack the pair of you—now have I made myself clear—keep bloody quiet." This last outburst took all of Vince's remaining air and he sagged back against the bottom stair.

The lads, who obviously thought they were in the presence of a madman, muttered their apologies and off we went on the next leg up the stairs. On finally reaching deck level, the alarm stopped and Walter's dulcet tones were heard once more informing us that, "Another false alarm I'm afraid, back to work everyone while we try to sort out the source of the problem." For a moment I wasn't too sure whether the 'I'm afraid' part indicated a degree of regret that the alarm wasn't for real—but it could just have been Walter in broadcasting mode. By now Vince's face had returned from puce to a healthier bright red colour and in a futile effort at levity, I said, "Well at least we don't have to climb up to the muster station."

Vince stared at me and said, "Never mind all that crap, if I had my way I'd sack you, Walter, the safety officer and I'd keel-haul the Fire and Gas Detection Engineer, because the sod's obviously bloody incompetent."

There was a lengthy pause, then, recognising the inevitable, the demands of management, the need to resolve the problem and the fact that Vince, in a rare moment of weakness promised the Designers that he would personally report back—we went back down again.

And the alarm went off.…….

The two lads started to make a (silent) ascent up the ladder; I was plunged into a sort of exhausted despondency and once again staggered to my feet and was just about to heave myself onto the bottom rung when I realised that Vince wasn't behind me. I turned around to see where he was, only to find him sitting on a horizontal section of pipe.

"Are you coming?" I said. This was, to my mind, a rhetorical question; you didn't give Vince orders if you wanted to remain in employment.

"No, I'm bloody not coming, I'm staying right here, I'm sick and bloody tired of this farce, so let's just do what we have to do and get the hell out of here once and for all. So get down off the bloody ladder and let's finish the survey."

I was just about to mention the fact that we both occupied managerial positions and, as such, it could be argued that we were expected to set some sort of good example, when the man at the top contacted me by radio. I listened carefully and relayed the message.

"Vince, he wants to know where we are, the two lads have arrived and he says he can't see us coming up the stairs."

"That's because were not coming up the sodding stairs, just tell him what I've told you, we're staying put."

"But Vince, it might be for real this time."

"I don't care if the QE2 has hit the platform, we're going nowhere, tell the sod to mind his own business. No, wait a minute, ask him to call Walter and find out whether this is just another bloody false alarm."

I did as I was told and asked for clarification and a couple of nerve-wracking minutes later he came back on to confirm it was a false alarm. He then rather spoiled things by saying he was duty bound to report Vince for disobeying a Station Bill and even more unfortunately, Vince heard him. The radio was snatched out of my hand and Vince yelled into the mouthpiece, "Report me, bloody report me, I'll give you report me you miserable sod, you can consider yourself sacked with immediate effect."

I managed to retrieve the radio before Vince decided to clear the platform, when I heard the rather plaintive voice say, "He can't talk to me like that, I'm just doing my job, I'll see the Installation Manager about this."

I said, "Aye, that's the best thing to do."

I was remembering a previous episode concerning Vince, Walter and the Camp Boss, when a steward rather foolishly told Vince he couldn't have a sheet and two blankets on his bed instead of a duvet. The upshot of which was that Vince issued one of his most famous ultimatums— "Either I get my sheets by tonight or you get the sack."

This then, is what made me somewhat nervous at the prospect of meeting and dealing with several more assorted project managers, none of whom I had ever met. Would they be in the Vince mode, or would they be quietly organised like Harry? The answer, as I was to find out, was yes on both counts.

Now, I'm not about to overly criticise project managers, they had an unenviable task and were daily trying to balance the needs of the project with the demands of the company's Senior Executives, the Government, Partner's, Certifying Authorities and a myriad of Contractors. What was interesting (if that's the word) was the difference in approach to the task ahead. For instance, we had one American manager who, it was rumoured, had been the choice of our partner and, as such, we never knew to what extent we could trust him. We also had another project running in parallel with that of our American friend and it was well known that he'd each bet the other guy a crate of malt whisky on who would finish first.

On the face of it, the bet could be seen as a great morale booster; unfortunately, the determination to win at all costs meant they would brook no interference from any source, however well merited. To that extent, the American had a notice nailed above his door which read — 'Plan the Work, Work the Plan.' Now, whilst this might be considered a laudable philosophy in itself, it was translated in its most literal sense and any attempt to suggest an improvement or modification was met with a stream of invective and a blank refusal to even consider. A bit like asking your best mate for a loan of his vintage Porsche in order to go rallying on Anglesey.

His rival in this race for project supremacy and scotch, whilst not quite as bloody single-minded, was still difficult to influence. In fact, between the two of them, I found myself to be fighting a constant rearguard action, as they blithely shortened or cancelled a number of key commissioning activities. If I remember rightly, our American manager finished first and was delighted to receive the crate of scotch. It was only sometime later, when we were checking the 'Handover' documents that my guys noticed the Gas Export System hadn't been commissioned at all. Obviously, by then, our friend had long since returned to the good old US of A and was incommunicado. I did manage, however, to track down one of his engineers who rather sheepishly confirmed that, as there was a distinct danger they would lose the bet, he had decided to cancel some of the outstanding work.

I said, "How the hell can you just make arbitrary decisions like that?"

He said, "There were times when, if you wanted to stay employed, you didn't argue, and this was one of them."

"But it means that we've now got to mobilise a complete crew, flush out all the pipework, pressure test the system, monitor the control facilities and delay production. It'll cost a fortune."

"You're probably right, but he did say he would set aside a sum of money for Operations to finish off; his argument at the time was that you were the best people to do the job."

He stared at me for a minute and with an air of wistfulness, said, "I've decided that instead of listing this job on my resume, I'm going to put down that I was in prison for stealing from orphans."

Conned yet again by a mad project manager, this time a smooth-talking American bastard—will I never learn?

2. Trust me — I'm an Auditor

As time went by, the Company found it had enough platforms for the time being and as our existing projects were reaching completion, the need for a Commissioning department diminished accordingly. In other words, I was beginning to work myself out of a job.

This state of affairs had also dawned on others in the organisation and once more I was summoned into the presence of another senior person whom I had also never met. Again, on entering his office (desk with matching bookcase, hat stand, view of the main road, fawn carpet tiles and venetian blinds) I found the second seat to be occupied, as before, by Marjorie, still clutching what appeared to be a secret file with my name on it.

My new boss re-stated the position vis-à-vis the reduced need for commissioning and said he was sure I would be pleased to know they had a new challenging job for me and what did I think?

As I had no idea what he had in mind, I muttered in agreement, while privately becoming increasingly concerned about the word 'challenge.' In my experience people who have been on McKinsey type courses are trained to use the word challenge when they actually mean 'problem.' I gather the substitution is meant to cover you in a positive aura and make you feel empowered (whatever that means.) I've sometimes tried to imagine what would have happened if we'd had the benefit of these Guru's during the Second World War and one of them had tried to convince Winston Churchill that having thousands of men trapped on the beaches at Dunkerque was actually a challenge rather than a problem.

Anyway, whilst I was still daydreaming, he smiled, turned to Marjorie and said, "Are we agreed then, Brian is the 'best fit' for this new job?" She nodded, somewhat guardedly I thought.

"Okay Brian, down to business, we want you to set up a company-wide audit programme, specifically so that we can assess the capabilities of suppliers before deciding whether to grant them a contract. You'll need to recruit a small team and develop a system for putting the idea into practise. How does that sound?"

Being, as I now was, an old hand, I had long since realised the futility of asking for details about a new job. It's my contention (based on experience) that the person giving you the job was generally the last person who was able to explain in detail what it was all about, and so, working on the premise that a refusal would offend, I said, "Fine."

You can't fault that for a concise, yet erudite, answer.

Therefore, having been trained to obey the last order, I duly set up, developed, recruited and started auditing a considerable number of largely unsuspecting, somewhat cynical, sometimes devious, occasionally obstructive—but generally helpful—suppliers and contractors.

A word about auditing: At the risk of being accused of sexism, but recognising that it is still, for the most part the ladies who have to contend with the thorny problem of weekly shopping—I want you to imagine for a moment a perfect world where every lady was able to turn the tables on the supermarkets. So, instead of them making cynical and mostly meaningless promises that shopping with them will make your life easier, cheaper and a joyful experience—you reverse the process.

Now, in my perfect world, the power rests entirely with you. They can supply you with goods only if you agree they are fit do so. This means that Sainsbury's, Asda, Safeway, etc. have to be audited by you before they can sell you anything. To do this, you draw up a list of questions (of your choice) make an appointment to interview them all (remember in our world, they can't refuse to see you.) You can challenge any contention, for example "Call that a cabbage I've seen better on my dad's allotment!" Then having asked all your questions, and verified that your every requirement has been fulfilled, you decide which one offers the best service and after a lengthy wait, you notify them that they've been accepted. You also remind them that the arrangement can be terminated instantly should they fail to comply with your requirements and that you may re-audit them at any time.

The other powerful part of this audit business is your ability to make them treat their sub-contractors fairly. Image for a moment being able to say, "I notice that you're only paying the dairy farmer a pittance for milk —this practise must cease forthwith. From now on, you will negotiate a price which is acceptable to them, which I will then approve. Oh, and by the way, you will do so within your current profit margin—or else."

This then, is exactly what happens in the oil industry during an audit. We short-list a number of companies who are anxious to do business with us; we draw up a list of questions, carry out an audit and, based on the findings, provide them with a contract.

This is why—in general—auditors are universally hated, feared, bribed, threatened, cajoled, pleaded with and (very) occasionally thanked.

Mind you, having said all that, there are some auditors who should never be allowed out. These are the ones with a totally deluded sense of power and believe the way forward is to uncover fault at any price, nit-pick to the n'th degree, disbelieve everything that's said and when unsure, are unable to give the benefit of the doubt. You can always tell such idiots, as they will never look you in the eye, rely entirely in pre-prepared, often irrelevant questions and were probably bullied at school.

I wonder if there's any chance that the government might take up my proposal for the right of the public to audit supermarkets, instead of the other way round. What do you think? Perhaps it might be worthwhile my making contact with Hugh Dicky-Whittington. I digress, the scene is now set for a foray into the peculiar world of the auditor; let battle commence, as they say.

3. There Are Some Things You Just Don't Want to Know

I almost ran up the wooden stairs thinking, for God's sake Les don't ask question fifteen, I think I know the answer and if you start probing, we'll probably be thrown out on our respective ears.

But hang on, I hear you say, who's this guy Les? Well, he was an engineer whom I'd had the great good fortune to tempt out of semi-retirement. He brought with him a wealth of knowledge, a good track record in auditing and was, importantly as it turned out, totally unflappable.

So, on this particular morning, I reached the dingy office at the top of the stairs in time to hear the owner of the haulage company telling Les how easy it was to falsify a Tachometer reading. On entering, I found that Les had his back to the door while the owner was staring at me in some confusion from across his desk. I say desk, but it was hard to tell really, as the entire top was covered with what looked like a mammoth collection of charts, invoices, bills of lading, time sheets, spares catalogues, spanners, old air filters and the remnants of several sandwiches. How the hell was I to get Les to abort the audit without arousing suspicion? All I could think of on the spur of the moment was to say, "Oh Les, sorry to butt in; I've just remembered we need to be at the docks within the next ten minutes, I've just had word the boat is arriving early and we have to witness the unloading." You can see that an ability to lie convincingly is an important attribute of a successful auditor.

Les, even though he knew I was talking rubbish, but not why, turned to me and said, "Well I've nearly finished here, can't we just hold on for a couple of minutes? There's only question fifteen to go."

On the one hand, I had to admire Les's ability to keep calm, when he'd no idea what I was talking about with regard to boats. On the other hand, his laudable attempt to finish the job had to be stopped at all costs.

I tried again, "Les, we've run out of time and we need to go pronto." I turned to the owner and said, "Sorry to cut the interview short, but we'll be in touch. Now come on Les, let's get out of here."

Half grabbing and half pushing my mystified mate, we shot back down the stairs and out into the sunshine. At which point, Les could contain himself no longer. "What's the hell's going on? What's all this rubbish about a boat? If you'd given me five more minutes we could have wrapped this one up, all I needed to ask was question fifteen—How and where do you safely dispose of your waste sump oil?"

"Because, Les," I said, "I'm pretty sure I know the answer. As far as I can tell, it all goes into a horrible looking grid in the middle of their workshop floor and my guess is, it's then flushed away into the river."

"Bloody hell," said Les.

I told you he was unflappable.

This saga started one day when Frank, our Transport Manager asked me to nip in and see him. Having nipped, he waved a newspaper at me (purveyor of local news since 1747) and said, "Have you seen this?"

I confessed that I had and what's more their ace reporters were having a field day at our expense. "Aye, and it's not just the paper, I've already had several 'ho-ho' calls from my colleagues in rival organisations who, for some reason, seem to think it's funny."

The article to which he was referring was prominently displayed on the front page and what made it worse, it was accompanied by a colour picture —splashed (as we say in the media) across several columns.

There, displayed in all its glory was one of our precious christmas trees lying at an acute angle half way round one of the busiest roundabouts in Aberdeen. Apparently, the haulage company contracted to carry this precious cargo to the docks had engaged a driver who momentarily forgot he was driving a thirty tonne lorry and had decided the best way to negotiate a roundabout was to power slide the unit through the bend, in the manner of Tommi Makinen.

(For younger readers, Tommi Makinen is a recently retired Finn and was one of the most successful World Rally Championship drivers of all time. He is a four-time World Rally Champion, a series he first won, and then successfully defended, continuously throughout 1996, 1997, 1998 and 1999, on all occasions driving a Mitsubishi Lancer Evolution. He also aided Mitsubishi to the 1998 World Constructor's Title as well as winning the 2000 Race of Champions.)

As far as we could tell, the lorry driver's attempt to emulate Makinen must have started off all right, but part way through this daring manoeuvre, the tree, which incidentally was made from a solid block of steel weighting some seven tonnes, decided to obey another one of Newton's Laws. This is the one which states that a body in motion will, if given half a chance, continue in the direction in which it started. In this case, the opposing forces caused the tie-ropes to snap and the tree parted company with the lorry, which was now on a highly curved trajectory of its own.

So, we now had the interesting situation where seven tonnes of steel were in mid-air and travelling at about thirty miles per hour until, that is, gravity took over and the thing tried to dig itself into the road. As it was early morning, there were a number of other road users also intent on using the same roundabout, only to find a large piece of platform descending from the sky immediately in front of the leading car. For some reason, the sudden appearance of a giant lump of shiny metal had a disconcerting effect on the first driver who, until then, had been happily listening to the latest chart-topper on NorthSound.

Fortunately, no one was hurt if, that is; you discount mental trauma, anguish, anger and the overwhelming need to blame someone.

But the real purpose behind Frank's request to see me was the caption to the article. This stated that our company (printed in bold capital letters with accompanying coloured logo) had been careless with their equipment, had attempted to destroy a perfectly good road, disrupted rush-hour traffic, caused general mayhem with bus schedules and had frightened half a dozen drivers to death.

Interestingly, in all of this criticism, there was no mention at all of the haulage company.

Frank said, "I don't know how the hell we're going to live this down. I'm already getting calls from our Public Affairs people, the local radio station want to do an interview and the paper wants a follow-up article based, I understand, on their considered opinion that we're a bunch of dangerous incompetents. I'm going to have to do something to demonstrate that we take these things seriously and I want to say, that as part of an immediate response, we've engaged a specialist group to examine every detail, make recommendations and report back."

"Where do I fit in?" (A foolish question.)

"You're the bloody specialist group and I want you to carry out audits on all of our haulage contractors. They need to be thorough, not just how they keep the bloody stuff on a lorry, but what kind of organisation they run, how they demonstrate compliance with rules and environmental regulations, you know the kind of thing. Oh, and if I'm to survive this lot, I need the results as soon as possible—preferably by next week"

"How many contractors do we use?

"Nineteen."

"What?"

"Nineteen."

"Bloody hell, this is going to take some organising and I assume the 'next week' deadline is wishful thinking."

"Aye well, just be as quick as you can then."

Working selflessly in the cause of mutual survival, Les and I set up a programme, developed a questionnaire and started auditing. I won't bore you with the details but—as you might have guessed from the overly dramatic start to this section—one of the key questions was to find out how they managed waste oil products in an environmentally friendly manner.

(Please note that in caring for the climate, Les and I were streets ahead of the year 2000 Presidential Candidate in the United States who, having failed to master the voting system in Florida, decided instead, to worry about polar bears.)

Anyway, all was going well, the people were co-operative and we began to enjoy the task, until, that is, when having interviewed about half the companies, we both began to pick up on veiled comments from a number of individual managers. This was particularly apparent in the case of the smaller companies; at first we were unsure of what was being hinted at, but even more puzzling was a general reluctance to elaborate. What we did observe was a sort of veiled hint, where people would say cryptic things such as:

"I hope you're going to treat all the companies the same way."

"Will you being asking the same questions of all the hauliers?" This last query always emphasised the word 'all.'

"We've invested a lot of money in setting up our systems; it wouldn't be fair to have one rule for one and not for the others."

"We can't figure out how some people got a contract from you in the first place."

Despite our requests for folk to elaborate, all we got was a pursing of lips or head shaking. Only one manager was slightly more forthcoming, but even then his comment lacked a certain amount of specificity, as he said, "Have any of the other companies mentioned anything?" We agreed they had, but the only thing we'd gleaned was the need for us to treat everyone consistently. "Aye well, that's good, you'll know what we're on about when you get to them." And with that, he offered us a cup of tea and some shortbread.

In between our next batch of audits and having compared notes, Les and I agreed there was definitely some underlying grievance, but that no one was prepared to speak openly. "I'm fed up with this," said Les. "I play golf with one of the haulage managers, I'll ask him for a direct answer or at least get a proper clue, something's upsetting them and we need to know what it is." Good old Detective Inspector Les, I thought. (I'm prone to such idiot thoughts at times.)

The following day, after having lost a number of balls, the game and several drinks afterward, Les said, "I think I've wheedled the information out of my mate. What they're all bothered about is a company we've yet to do called Norbert's; apparently they're on the same call-off contract as the others, but the word is they haven't invested in anything like the facilities we've insisted on across the board. There's no doubt that if we don't treat them the same as everyone else, we'll lose all credibility."

"Bloody hell," I said, "Aren't we seeing them next?"

"I'm afraid so," replied Les.

So, the following morning we're both stood outside Norbert's premises and I have to say it didn't look too good. Up until now we'd been very impressed by the layout, cleanliness, facilities, attitude, organisation, systems and procedures of the other companies. Vehicles were shiny, workshops resembled a Formula 1 layout, overalls had logos, but most of all there was pride in their being able to demonstrate considerable investment in state of the art equipment for gathering waste oil, including in many cases, a facility for separating the contents into re-usable elements.

These feelings came to the fore as we stood staring at the outside of a rather dingy building with obvious signs of past and recent spillage on their hard standing. There were broken pallets in a heap at the side, the double doors looked as though they'd been retrieved from HMS Victory then distressed to look old and the only window was in an advanced state of spider occupancy. All in all—we felt a distinct lack of confidence.

"Still," said Les, "We need to be fair, maybe it's a lot better inside." Sometimes Les's optimism is a right pain. He plunged on, "I'll do the usual and meet with the owner to go over his procedures and controls, while you look at the technical aspects with his mechanics."

So saying, we left the sunshine, opened a small door located in one corner of the big wooden doors and stepped inside.

It was like stepping onto the set of Dootheboys Hall, just as Dickens must have imagined it in Nickolas Nickelby. At first we thought the place was in darkness, then as our eyes became accustomed to the gloom, we realised there was light. This was provided by two bare bulbs of about fifty watts hanging from the ceiling some way above. This gallant attempt at illumination was immediately counteracted by the fact that the ceiling and walls were rendered a tasteful dark oak colour by what we took to be many years of welding fumes together with a liberal coating of dust and sooty deposits. There was not a window to be seen (no pun intended) as the one we'd spotted from the outside had been boarded over with some old packing case planks and in the distance we could just see a lorry with the chassis supported on some old railway sleepers and its wheels missing.

Then, just as we were gazing around in awe, accompanied by a growing feeling of despondency, a chap appeared out of the gloom and introduced himself as the owner. He was a large man wearing a pair of what appeared to be shiny overalls and looked, as far as I could tell in the gloom, like an unwashed version of Ray Winstone—only taller. He said we were to call him Norb and assured us that nobody messed about with him. Not having understood a word of what he was on about, but determined not to mess with him, we said something pithy like, "Okay Norb," and proceeded to tell him what we wanted to do. He nodded and suggested that Les accompany him up to his office, which I could see cheered Les up no end, while I cast around on the shop floor —so to speak.

Peering into the darkness, I spotted a couple of lads clad in matching shiny overalls and having persuaded them to stop trying to remove a huge dent in the offside wing of the lorry with a couple of five pound hammers, I started chatting. Sadly, within a short time, it became obvious that we were on something of a different wavelength as far as technical issues such as oil separation centrifuges or computerised checks were concerned.

Whenever I raised the subject of waste oil disposal in accordance with environmental best practise, there was a considerable amount of feet shuffling, nervous glances and pathetic attempts to change the subject. Recognising the futility of carrying on with this line of questioning, I was just about to brave a look in another black hole which one of the lads had referred to as 'the stores,' when I noticed a very dirty oil streaked drain in the middle of the floor. They also noticed me looking at it and tried to usher me into the corridor leading to the store. It was then that I remembered question fifteen, panicked and ran for the stairs……..

The upshot of all this dedicated auditing was that every one of the companies were re-engaged except of course, Norb's. This bad news didn't sit too well with him and he rang our company several times trying to arrange a meeting. Fortunately, remembering his adage that "nobody messes with me," we'd left town—or at least our secretary pretended we had.

A couple of months later, Les bumped into his golf-playing friend who gave us some very good news from the consortium.

"You know, we never thought you'd have the bottle to do it. You guys have certainly gone up in our estimation and if you ever want anything shifting with a lorry—just give one of us a ring." Praise indeed, but for some time afterwards, we were both careful never to drive anywhere near Norb's premises—just in case, you understand.

4. It's Easy to Love Lerwick

This was Les at his very best; every now and then he would pop his head around my office door and utter the immortal words— "I've arranged a nice wee trip for us."

What this somewhat cryptic message meant was that we were bound, once again, for the Shetland Isles.

The routine was always the same, Les would go into full travel agent mode; an audit programme would be prepared, companies would be informed, our hotel and hire car would be booked and we would set off on a crew-change flight to Sumburgh. Once there we would pick up a car and drive to Lerwick, but before checking in at our hotel, we would divert to the only Chinese restaurant on the island and book a table for that evening.

You see, work is okay and obviously has a certain priority, but there are some things in life that take precedence and a Chinese meal is one of them. We learned this the hard way, as the first time we went north, we thought—incorrectly as it turned out—we could just turn up, as you do in London, and a table would be made available. Not so in Lerwick. We were ignominiously turned away by a smiling Chinese person and what was worse, without ever having sampled the delights of a curried prawns and fried rice —Shetland style. Our discovery of this excellent establishment provided me with further proof that Chinese people are the great silent integrators. They make no fuss and have an uncanny ability to provide a service that you didn't know you needed. I asked one of the lads at the base one day when it was they'd arrived in Lerwick, and he confirmed my contention, by saying the locals just woke up one morning to find a Chinese restaurant had appeared as if by magic and was open for business. Not only that, he said, "But at the end of the meal, we were issued with something mysterious called a 'fortune cookie.'" This apparently went down a storm with the locals, even though no one had any idea what they were for and many diners, on being given one for the first time, simply popped it into their mouths—only to find the filling was made of paper.

So, having ensured our evening meal was safe; the next priority was to book in at our hotel. This was an establishment near the harbour and about two minutes drive from our Operations base, on whose behalf we were carrying out the audits. Les, being in sole charge of administration arrangements, checked us in and then moved swiftly onto priority number two—lunch. This was taken in the hotel and invariably consisted of a bowl of very thick soup, a brown crusty roll and a pot of tea. You may be somewhat surprised to read about what might be termed an unhealthy emphasis on the consumption of food. Not so, this was all part of Les's oft repeated philosophy: 'a person should eat when they can—not when they need to.' Who was I to overrule such deeply held, almost religious, beliefs? Besides, Les was two years older than me and knew lots of things that I didn't. The one thing I did find mildly upsetting was the fact that although Les was as tall as me (six feet two inches,) he was built like a whippet and consumed food with scant regard for silly things like calories.

Everything was in now order, sleeping arrangements had been made, potential starvation had been averted and so we were now free to deal with the other reason for our being here—work.

The office at the base was staffed by a small, friendly group of Shetlanders. They were cheerfully non-political, healthily cynical of us lot on the mainland and firmly believed there was more to life than work —fishing and keeping sheep for instance. It was they who had asked us to see whether we could bring some of their local contractors, kicking and screaming, into the twentieth century. As the last thing we all needed was to alienate people who lived, worked and played together for the rest of the week, we had to develop a rather more gentle approach to auditing and, fortunately, Les excelled at this. He had adopted a fatherly persona towards our victims and often came up on his own to assist various companies with this new-fangled way of working.

Don't get me wrong, these people were no fools, a contention borne out by their success in single-handedly holding the world's major oil companies to ransom over access to Sullom Voe. No, it was just that they had been working (successfully) within their own bailiwick for a long time before we arrived on the scene and they realised there was an opportunity to work for us. Unfortunately, in a number of cases, this brought about two problems; on the one hand, we were appalled at their informality regarding a lack of systems and procedures; whilst on the other hand, they couldn't for the life of them figure out why they needed to produce all this new-fangled rubbish.

Enter Les. Armed only with a pencil and some reference documents he cajoled, persuaded, mildly threatened, pleaded with, and finally convinced the majority to change the way in which they worked or at least, pretend to do so, while they worked for us.

A suspicion that one or two reverted back to the good old ways of fishing boat repair, was borne out on one visit to a small boatyard who were contracted to refurbish chain for us. This came in various sizes and, having been subjected to wear and tear offshore, was shipped to them for cleaning, testing and re-certifying. Les had paid particular attention to the manager of this company and having been persuaded by a master tactician, he'd engaged the services of a consultant to develop the necessary documents on their behalf.

When Les heard the good news, he was delighted and a visit to their premises to inspect the newly acquired documents, was high on the agenda.

Having lunched and checked in at the base, we drove to the boatyard, climbed the narrow wooden stairs and, on entering the office, were struck once more by the wonderful array of pictures portraying the scope of work undertaken by the company over many years. There were photos of numerous fishing boats, some in dry-dock, some newly cleaned and painted, while others were shown setting out to sea. This historical success story, was something we had to remind ourselves of, when enforcing a multi-national company's onerous requirements on such a firm.

Les introducing me to the general manager and opened the proceedings, saying, "Now George, I hear that you've made excellent progress towards the introduction of your new documented systems."

This opening gambit achieved two things; George looked at the far wall, then swivelled around in his chair and stared wistfully at the scene below. The view was of a fishing boat up on stilts,being lovingly restored by his workers to its former glory.

Les persisted. "George, I understand that your consultant has completed the package for you and that it's now in operation."

This evoked even more silent gazing, accompanied by another swivel to stare at what could only be seen as freedom, as far as George was concerned.

"Aye, well, we do have a fine set of books to be sure."

"Where are they? Can we see them?

Another swivel, this time accompanied by a huge sigh as he turned back towards us. "I'm not just too sure we were wise to go down this route; it's all very strange working for you people, after all, it's only a bit of chain we're looking after for you."

Les went into kindly uncle mode. "Now look George, we've been over this a number of times, the work is good, you have a decent contract, all we need is some sort documented proof that your procedures are being worked to and we have evidence to back it up."

This provoked yet another sigh and a lengthy stare once again at the far wall. I did notice he seemed to be looking at the portrait of a Victorian looking chap in a dark suit, complete with a watch chain looped across an ample stomach and complete with a fine set of mutton-chop whiskers. I guessed this was some deceased Chairman and as George gazed at the portrait, he was probably worried that he might return from the grave to see what the hell he was up to—but I could have been wrong.

Les again, "George, this is getting us nowhere, do you have the documents that the consultant has developed for you?"

"Oh yes," said George.

"Well where are they? Can we see them?"

"Oh yes, I keep them in that cupboard over there; they cost us an awful lot of money, I'm not sure it was worth it."

Then with one more wistful look out of the window, George opened his desk drawer, took out a bunch of keys and slowly walked across to a big old fashioned cupboard to retrieve the documents. Bringing them over, he gingerly placed them down in front of Les.

"Great stuff," said Les. "These look to be just the job. Now all we need to know is—are you all working to them?

This last question evoked a stricken look in George; it was as though he'd suddenly been informed his house had burned down. There was now what can only be described as a complete gamut of emotions, as George sighed, swivelled, stared and randomly flicked open the pages of one of the documents. We waited.

Finally, he looked first at Les, then at me and said, "Well, not exactly. I've shown them to the lads downstairs, but they didn't seem too keen, so I thought I'd give them a bit longer to—you know—get used to them, so I put them back in the cupboard for safe keeping; after all they weren't cheap."

Les said, "Okay George, but they're not much use in a cupboard and you won't get value for money unless you use them. We'll leave it at that for now."

This time, George's sigh of relief could be heard in the street outside, and then with one more swivel and a glance below, he said, "Is that it then?"

"Yes, that's it for now George, thanks for your time."

As we went back down the stairs, I said, "Bloody hell Les, what are we going to do with guys like that?"

Les said, "We'll just report back to the lads at the base, They all know one another and are probably the only ones who can persuade George to bite the bullet. I honestly haven't the heart to lean on him any more."

So, we did what we always did in such cases—we made up a nice report, handed it in and went off for a well-deserved sweet and sour pork with fried rice and a decent bottle of wine.

The following morning, refreshed and ready for almost anything, we decided to split up. Les was off to see a pipe fabricator and I was to see a firm specialising in the re-calibration of the safe load indicators on our dockside cranes. This piece of kit was a mandatory safety feature fitted to all our cranes. In order to comply with the regulations, they were removed at regular intervals and sent to a qualified company for re-calibration. But before venturing into Liam's world of cranes, I had to pop into the base to pick up some papers.

As I may have mentioned, the base was literally about two minutes away from the hotel, so nipping into our hire car, I drove out of the car-park and along the front of the hotel en route to the base just across the road. Witness my surprise, therefore, when a constable, who was standing at the kerb, moved forward and waved me down. "There's been an accident," I thought, so I dutifully stopped, wound down the window and said something fatuous like,

"Good morning Officer, how can I help?"

"Well sir," He said, in the musically lilting tones of a true Shetlander. "It's not so much how you can help me; it's rather that I see you're not wearing your seat belt. Now as you are aware sir, it's against the law to be driving with your seat belt unfastened and I'm afraid I'm going to have to report the fact and unfortunately, there will be a fine to accompany the infringement."

I then said something even more fatuous. "But Officer, I always fasten my seat belt, it's just that I am in a bit of a hurry to get to the base across the road and forgot to do it up on this occasion."

He then said something unexpected. "I do understand sir; it's just that my Sergeant has sent us out this morning to have what he calls a purge on people driving without their seat belts fastened. Unfortunately, you're the first person I spotted and so I waved you down. I didn't know at the time you were a visitor, we're really after the locals you see."

I thought, "Great, I'm on a winner here."

"Does that mean I'm free to go with a caution then?"

"Oh no sir, I've already entered the details I'm afraid."

The bastard.

Still fuming, I forgot all about the base, looked at the map and found that the premises I was looking for were located in a road not far away and so I set off with my seat belt fastened, my interior mirror in its correct orientation, my indicators flashing and my brake lights working. The only thing was, that having set off in something approaching a general hatred of the law, I couldn't find the place. I drove up and down, counting the numbers, cross-checking with my instructions and still there was no sign of a factory unit. In desperation, I stopped outside a shop selling what I took to be garden tools and equipment and nipped in to ask for help. The lady behind the counter said, "Oh yes, this is the right address; you need to see Michael, he'll be downstairs in the workshop."

Somewhat reassured, but still mystified, I went down some stairs in the corner and found myself in a small workshop consisting largely of a bench along one wall and a number of assorted lawnmowers in various stages of dismemberment.

Michael introduced himself and I again tried to confirm an association of this workshop with the re-certification of critical safety devices. Michael explained that he'd sent for the relevant crane handbooks, invested in the requisite test gear and, as far as he was concerned, was in business. Besides, he said, "I don't get enough lawnmowers to service in the winter and this job is a fine standby."

So, I asked my questions, he answered them and I was up the stairs and out of the door in about fifteen minutes. Twenty-five years later, it still ranks as the quickest audit I've ever undertaken.

It's now about a quarter past nine, I'm standing in a side road and Les, unaware of my rapid progress vis-à-vis lawnmowers, would be just settling in to his pipe fabricator audit. I thought, sod it, I can't stand here for another three hours, I'll go down and see what he's up to.

When I arrived on the scene, Les looked somewhat bemused and said, "I thought we were going to meet at lunch-time; what happened to your audit?"

"It's a long story," I said—which I thought was kind of funny.

Having recovered enough to introduce me, the pipe man looked slightly bemused until Les, thinking on his feet, suggested that I take care of the technical details while he spent some time going through the necessary documentation. At this, our man looked a bit sheepish and confessed he wouldn't be much use as it was his wife who looked after the books and paperwork.

"No problem," said Les "Is she in your office?" pointing to a small area at the rear of the workshop.

"Er, no, that's where we brew up. She'll be at home, that's where the books are kept. I could phone her and you could pop up and go through them there, if you like."

"Perfect," said Les, who could sense an escape route from five miles. "Where do you live?"

"Just across the way, it's the bungalow facing the sea; you can walk up if you like."

"Right," said Les, "You ring her and tell her I'm on my way and I'll see you later." And with that the swine sauntered off.

Realising that my bad hair day wasn't yet over, the pipe man and I got down to the enchanting subject of welding qualifications, care of welding rods, pre-heating and other assorted rubbish. After about two hours of checking and verifying in accordance with best practise, there was no doubt the guy had everything under control and so I thanked him, saying, "I'll get out of your way and pop up to the house to catch up with Les." At this release from lunacy, the guy breathed an audible sigh of relief, a reaction that generally occurred when we announced our departure from our victims and so I popped off — as they say.

Strolling up the path to the front door, I couldn't help noticing a large picture window in what I took to be the lounge. What took me aback, however, was the sight of Les sitting on a settee in very close proximity to a rather good looking lady. Their heads were bent close together and they appeared to be chuckling about something. I stopped for a moment and adopting a voyeuristic mode, continued to peer in (as you do,) just as the lady leaned across Les once more and it was apparent they were having a good laugh together.

At this point my imagination began to run away with me. Had Les struck lucky? Should I slope off? What about her husband just down the road? We'd all heard stories of bribes and favours' being offered to ensure a contract was offered. Was this what was happening to Les?

And then I thought, "Don't talk bloody rubbish," And knocked on the door.

I mentioned my imaginings to Les over Szechwan king prawns in black bean sauce that evening and he said, "The trouble with you is you watch too many bloody films." And then he paused, took a nice mouthful and said, "Aye, but she were a comely lass and no mistake."

Thinking back, I'm not sure there wasn't a note of wistfulness in Les's voice for a moment. On the other hand it could just have been due to the hot black bean sauce.

My wife also had an interesting experience whilst on the Shetlands. She'd been corresponding for some time with a lady named Vera, regarding their common interest in hand-spinning. Vera was incredibly bright and had, at the time, one of the highest Mensa scores in the country, I reckoned she was one of the first 'drop-outs,' as she explained that one day about thirty years ago, she came to the Shetland Isles for a week's holiday, liked what she saw, bought a tiny cottage right by the water and never went back to her job as an industrial chemist.

The upshot of their correspondence was that Bobbie was invited to call in any time she happened to be in the vicinity. So one day, being what was laughingly known as 'in charge,' I modified Les's arrangements to include her on our itinerary (the trip, not the audits.)

I recall it being one of those lovely summer days which make the Islands look magical, and as we were once again driving to Lerwick, we diverted to drop Bobbie off at Vera's cottage. The arrangement was that she would spend the day with Vera, taking in all things artistic and woollen, Vera would then drive her to meet Les and me in Lerwick, where we'd booked a table for three at the Chinese emporium.

Our day went well, Les and I audited our little socks off and at about seven o'clock that evening, we were waiting outside the Town hall for Bobbie to be delivered. Vera had informed us earlier that she wasn't a Chinese food person, which just goes to show that having a high IQ isn't all it's cracked up to be. We were whiling away the time discussing the relative merits of Sophia Loren and Janet Leigh (no contest as far as I was concerned,) when a battered Reliant Robin, made up of what looked to be random parts, accompanied by an engine note similar to that of a banshee in terminal agony, veered around the corner, crossed over the central white line, corrected itself by veering back towards the kerb and screeched to a stop, assisted—to a great extent—by the front wheel being jammed at right angles into the kerb.

The perpetrator of this exercise in terminal driving turned out to be Vera and sitting very still beside her, with a sort of glazed expression on her face, was my wife. At first she seemed reluctant to disembark, but we later learned that she was simply trying to reduce her pulse rate and start breathing normally again.

Finally she clambered out, waved goodbye to Vera and with Les and I supporting her, started walking towards the restaurant. As we moved slowly along the road, we heard the same banshee wail coming closer and Vera reappeared heading in our direction. As she came level with us, she glanced over and letting go of the steering wheel with one hand, gave us a goodbye wave. This kindly act had the most alarming effect on the Reliant's equilibrium as the car turned sharply in the direction of the wave. This, in turn, had an equally alarming effect on the three of us, a couple walking their dog and two cyclists, who, with commendable foresight, mounted the pavement. Then, wave completed, Vera re-engaged with the steering wheel, there was an overcorrecting lurch back onto the centre of the road and she was away out of sight—but not for a long time—out of hearing.

Bobbie stared into the distance and said, "It's been like that all day; I really do need a drink."

Les said, "Bloody hell Bob, you mean to tell me she drives like that all the time? And where on earth is that terrible noise coming from."

"It's coming from the engine. I found out during the day that she doesn't ever change out of second gear, even when we're on the main road; and if you think its noisy outside, you want to spend the day on the inside. I feel as though my ears have been ripped out. There's also another interesting aspect to Vera's driving—she's got cataracts in both eyes, so road signs or crossings mean nothing to her—she just ploughs straight on. In sheer desperation, part way through the day, I said I'd always wanted to drive a three-wheeler and suggested I might have a go.

"Unfortunately, Vera said she wouldn't hear of it; I was her guest and anyway she didn't think she was insured for anyone else. Then, as if that wasn't enough, I also found out that she can't reverse. This became clear as we approached a cake shop and she said it would be nice to get something for our lunch. Unfortunately, just as we arrived, she found the only parking space would need to be reversed into. "Can't do that," she said, accelerating away, "I'll pull in on the way back."

"How come she hasn't been killed?" said Les.

"I wondered about that and I learned the reason from a sheep farmer we went to visit; he asked me how I found Vera's driving and I said it was unnerving to say the least. He said, 'Aye, fortunately, all the locals know both the sound and sight of Vera's vehicle and they instinctively know to take avoiding action.'

"Incidentally, while we were there, he opened his barn door to show us a number of lamb carcases hanging from the rafters and he offered me one for thirty-five pence."

"You mean pounds," said Les.

"No it was pence, apparently he can't sell them. I would have loved one, but couldn't see how we could get it back on the company flight."

Les said, "Well, having witnessed a brief example of her unique driving skills, it's a good job for Vera that Mensa didn't carry out a driving test as part of their assessment."

Bob nodded in agreement, but I did notice that it wasn't until we were three parts through a fine chicken with green peppers and cashew n uts that she finally started to relax.

5. They all Speak English — I Hope

It's all very exciting auditing in the UK, but if you want a real thrill, try auditing abroad. For instance, I've been shouted at in Germany, arrested in Holland, violently sick in Spain, enchanted in France, baffled in Italy, very nervous in Kazakhstan and frustrated in Africa.

Requests to carry out what we seasoned travellers call 'sods law' audits, generally came from the working side of the business and, as is the way with customers, my instructions were often quite vague. For instance, one afternoon I received an urgent call from our Maintenance Department, asking if I would go to Holland and do a quick audit on a turbine repair company. The best way to get there, they said, was to fly to Dusseldorf, hire a car, drive down the autobahn and cross the border into Holland. A hotel would be booked for me close to the factory and a report was needed soonest. Risking an in-depth question in my never ending search for clarity, I said, "What is it you're specifically looking for?"

I should have known better, as I received the stock reply from those who reckon an audit will solve all their problems — but don't know why. "Ah well, just sound them out, have a good look around, see what you think, but let's have your conclusions as quick as you can."

So, armed with my client's idea of a detailed work scope, I duly flew to Dusseldorf and that's where the nightmare began. For a start, the plane was late arriving (hard to believe, I know) which meant that I reported to the car hire desk at eight o'clock at night instead of seven. The fraulein at the desk was what I believe is known in certain pretentious magazines as 'statuesque.' She had long blonde hair done up in a sort of coil on the top of her head, a figure-hugging dark blue suit and all and all, was extremely easy on the eye (not that I noticed, you understand.) Unfortunately, even though I'd been staring at her for about half an hour, she completely ignored my presence until, in desperation, I gave a sort of nervous cough, at the sound of which she stopped studying her nails and looked up.

"Ja, what is it you want?"

"Hello, I've a hire car booked with you for this evening."

Then, fixing me with an icy stare, she said, "Your name?"

"Brian Page."

This information evoked a long sigh, followed by a reluctant perusal of her computer screen.

"Ja, but here it states that you will pick up the car at seven o'clock, you are now one hour late."

Then, having imparted this nugget of information, she went back into nail staring mode.

"Look, I realise I'm late but the plane has just landed. Now can I have my car please, I've a long way to go."

Another audible sigh, followed by a further bout of screen staring, then some work on the keys and finally, the rattle of a printer. A length of paper was then torn bodily from the machine and flashed in front of me.

"You will sign here, these are the keys. Your car is a Ford Taunus and you will find it in bay number thirty-two." Back to the nails again.

"Thank you."

I headed off to the reservation bays and at last came to thirty-two, only to find it was occupied by a Volkswagen. Thinking there'd been some mistake; I tried the key and checked the registration number, but to no avail. It was clearly the wrong car. Back to the nail fetishist.

More ignoring.

Another cough.

"Ja, what is it you want?"

"I'm afraid you've given me the wrong bay number; the car isn't a Ford, it's a Volkswagen."

"Impossible, you have gone to the wrong bay; you will need to check again." I also noticed that the sighs were now being forced through clenched teeth.

Back to the nails.

Now I still don't know why, I don't think it was anything to do with the war, but I actually went back a second time to check on something to which I already knew the answer. I can only think that when I returned I would find, by some miracle, she had gone back to her day job in Spandau and a human being had taken her place. The trouble was, the time was now nearly nine pm and I still hadn't any idea if, or when, I might be permitted to leave the blasted airport.

Another cough.

Another "Ja?"

"Look, this is ridiculous; I've checked the same bay twice, the car definitely isn't there."

On hearing this latest news, she stared at me with a look similar to that favoured by Judge Jeffries on realising he'd just been stopped from hanging an innocent criminal and said, "You will wait one moment."

This brought about another session on the computer, lots of lip pursing, fearsome glances in my direction and finally, a call to someone on the phone.

"What's happening?"

"You will wait please."

The phone rang. After some minutes of what seemed to be a one-sided conversation, she put the phone down and said, "You will go immediately to the front of the Terminal building, a man will bring the car to you."

"Right." I said.

I was going to ask her where the sodding car had been parked, but she was once again deeply engrossed in her nails. I also felt that a thank you didn't seem to be warranted and anyway by now, my nerves were in shreds, wondering whether I would ever reach my destination. It also occurred to me later, that if there was an idiot anywhere who thought that marriage to a woman who exercised total domination would be the thing to have —he should get in touch with me — I've got just the right person in mind.

So, following my orders from the blonde horror, I found my way to the exit and was met with a scene from the film 'Speed.' You know the one where there's a bomb on board a school bus and they daren't go less than fifty mph or it will explode until, that is, our hero in the shape of Keanu Reeves has managed to leap on board and disarm the thing.

Except that this wasn't the USA, it was Germany, it was dark, it was raining and there were buses, coaches and cars zooming past, stopping for about ten seconds, flinging passengers and luggage onto the pavement and accelerating away again.

Standing in the middle of all this mayhem, I'm now looking for a Ford with a licence plate I can't read, in a colour unknown to me and driven by a man I've never seen. Just as I was beginning to panic for the fifth time, a car whizzed in beside me and with one smooth movement a chap in car hire livery leaped out, left the drivers door open, the engine running and waved at me to get in.

Now this was just about the last thing I wanted to do. My plan had been to sit quietly in Bay 32, familiarise myself gently with the layout, controls, lights, indicators and, most of all, study the map giving me directions. Now I'm sitting in a car with a left hand drive, the gear lever on the wrong side, light and wiper switches god knows where, and a man in uniform with a gun, obviously a relative of the nail fetishist, was gesticulating for me to get out of the way.

So, in order to avoid being shot at, I set off into the darkness, engulfed in three lanes of traffic consisting mostly of Mercedes taxis, all of whom knew exactly where they were going. Desperately looking up, down, sideways and in front, I navigated my way out and found myself on an autobahn. At that point I didn't really care if I was going to Poland, as long as the signs didn't say Dusseldorf Airport.

After what seemed like the drive from hell, where travelling at 120 kph meant that you were being overtaken by everything else on the road, I crossed the border into Holland and finally arrived at the hotel at about eleven-thirty. As I was now in an advanced state of nervous and physical exhaustion, the thought of a good meal with a restorative bottle of wine became something of a priority, to be shattered when I discovered that the restaurant had been closed for about two hours. This devastating news wasn't really alleviated by my having to manage on two shortbread biscuits thoughtfully accompanied by a sachet of caffeine-free coffee, with one sliver of sugar, but no milk.

Although the biscuits were wrapped in some kind of unbreakable tartan plastic, the taste, when the wrapping was finally removed, wouldn't be recognised by any self respecting Scottish person. This of course, could be due to the fact that in my increasingly violent attempts to undo the damn things, the biscuits had disintegrated. Considering for a moment that my normal working day was supposed to finish at five pm, you can perhaps see just how glamorous auditing on foreign soil really is.

The following afternoon, having recovered to some degree, I was chatting with the manager of the factory and he asked about my journey. Not wishing to break down in front of him, I simply mentioned that I had driven from Dusseldorf.

He said, "Who on earth told you to take that route? It's just about the worst way to get out of the country. No, what you should have done is come via Schiphol Airport in the normal way and simply driven north; you'd have been here by seven o'clock."

I must have looked even more stricken, because he said, "If you like I'll get your flight changed and you can have a leisurely drive down to Schiphol when we've finished."

He did and then I did, but what made the return journey special was the sight of a steel girder bridge which, for some reason, I thought I recognised. So slowing down as I approached, I noticed the name; it was the bridge over the Rhine at Arnhem.

I don't know why, but I suddenly felt a little bit emotional, remembering the epic struggle our troops had trying to gain control of this bridge some forty years earlier.

Then I thought, as I trundled across —auditing does have its rewards —occasionally.

(For younger readers —The Rank Organisation made a film in 1976 called 'A Bridge Too Far' which portrayed both the strategy and the epic battle. Even by today's standards it's worth watching, despite the fact that nobody swore.)

While we're in the Low Countries, so to speak, I had a rather alien experience once in Schiphol and it was all the fault of a misplaced ego. I'd received an urgent call from the manager of our International Training Establishment in Holland. Could I come over and give a lecture on their Project Management course, he said they'd be particularly interested hearing my views on external auditing. Wow, I thought, fame at last.

An expectation which, as it turned out, was rubbish.

Anyway, I grabbed my bits and pieces and caught the next flight to Schiphol. Joining the queue for the Customs inspection, I fished in my briefcase for my passport, only to discover it wasn't there. I think the immediate emotion is called panic.

Picture the scene, the queue is moving steadily forward, I'm in the middle of it and everyone else is brandishing their passports except me. Should I move out of the queue? If I do, where do I move to? Looking up I notice a uniformed chap is staring at me and he's got a gun. Unable to think of a counter-move, I get to the front and another uniformed chap holds out his hand and says, "Passport please."

I'm now in a sort of mental lock-down, so I say, "I don't have it with me." This, although accurate, seems just a little bit inadequate. At this point, the chap signals to the first man with a gun and motions me to one side. The gunman approaches and says, "Sir, what is the problem?"

"I appear to have forgotten my passport." Note the futile attempt to minimise the problem by using the word 'appear.'

"You will come with me please."

The one unique thing about Holland is that everyone in business or public office speaks English to a degree which would be the envy of most schools in the UK. For some reason, I found this to be somewhat reassuring, after all, how can people who are so polite throw you in jail without the option? Or so I told myself.

I dutifully followed and after losing sight of the other law-abiding passengers, our man said, "Wait there please."

There, turned out to be a short queue of people standing outside an office. So, not wishing to give him an opportunity to use his gun I joined the end. This part was no problem and I thought might impress my captors, after all I reasoned, it was the Brit's who invented queuing. As I settled down to wait, I managed to risk a glance at my fellow captors. One thing was immediately clear; I was the only one wearing a suit and clutching a briefcase. They, in turn, started to check me out and it became clear we had very little in common. I don't want to sound judgemental, but to me, my companions all looked kind of shifty. This was borne out by the fact that they were poorly dressed, shuffled their feet a lot, and jumped every time the office door opened or closed. This reaction was heightened whenever a Firearms Officer went past, especially the ones clutching semi-automatics across their chests.

After what seemed like an age, my fellow malcontents were led away and I never saw them again. So I'm now standing all alone and getting even more nervous when I'm escorted into a nearby office. Now I'm confronted by another Customs Officer standing behind a desk. There is, however, a subtle difference—she's about five foot two, blonde, gorgeous (possibly enhanced by the uniform) and has a smile that would melt steel.

"Please sit down."

I sat, ever mindful of the Heckler and wotsisname hanging at her side.

"Why are you here?"

I spilled the beans (early reading of Mickey Spillane) this was no time for vagaries.

"Can anyone vouch for you?"

"Yes, the Training Director can." Hoping and praying that this was true.

"You have his number?"

"Yes." Thank God. (Remember—the mobile phone hadn't been invented.)

She telephoned and for the first time, lapsed into Dutch.

She put the phone down and smiled again (I wished she wouldn't keep doing that.) "I will give you a clearance paper, keep it with you and show it to one of my officers on your return. You are free to go."

I thought, "Good heavens—she just said 'One of MY officers.'"

Later on, when I'd recovered with the help of several Heineken beers, I got to thinking about the differences between our nearby European countries. In a short space of time I'd met two women whose approach couldn't have been more dissimilar. Although both were very attractive, one had all of the customer—client relations of Idi Amin and the other carried a gun. Still, if I had to choose, give me the Dutch lady every time, I think it's got something to do with the uniform. This is probably because I was struck dumb with desire the first time I saw my wife-to-be in her nurse's uniform. Enough already.

Some countries attempt to lure the unsuspecting auditor with food. For instance, I was carrying out an audit on a company in northern Spain and at the end of the day was invited to join the manager for a meal. Having gratefully accepted, he picked me up and we drove to his favourite sea-food restaurant. I have to say the meal was quite something and contained a considerable variety of fish, molluscs, prawns, langoustines, crab and lobster claws. In addition, there were a number of subsea specimens of indeterminate origin and I was encouraged by my host to try everything. As he was tucking in with evident relish, I did the same. He was an excellent host, the Rioja flowed freely and we spent a good three hours dining on god knows what, most of which was probably fished out of the estuary at the mouth of the River Ebro.

At about three am, I awoke in a sweat, dove for the bathroom and spent the next four hours wanting to die. In fact, at one point I thought I had. In between times I ran the whole gamut of nausea, vomiting, fatigue, weakness, headache, cramps, dizziness, rapid pulse, agitation, confusion, disorientation and self-pity. All in all, I wasn't very well.

Occasionally, it occurred to me that a) I would somehow have to get showered and dressed and b) I was due to make a presentation of the audit findings to their Senior Management Team at nine am. By about seven o'clock and still in the throes of self-pity, I managed to lie semi-comatose in the shower, get partly dried and dressed, then stagger out of the hotel, desperate to find a chemist (or, as we linguists say - a 'farmathya.') After some time I did and the chap behind the counter gave me two things, a pitying smile and some incredible stuff to drink. Fortunately for me and, I suppose, everyone else in the vicinity, it worked and although I felt as though I'd been run over by a Sherman tank, I got through the day.

Probably the worst part was having to pretend to my host that the meal had been most enjoyable. However, their kindness was again manifested when they drove me to the airport and presented me with two bottles of Rioja. One if which was a 1974 vintage and I still have it at home —just to prove I can't be bribed.

And then I went to France or, more accurately, Paris. I was asked to go over by a French company to make a presentation to their management about something or other on the following day. I was ensconced in a lovely hotel (big white towels, dressing gown, after-shave lotion, drinks cabinet, coffee machine, view of the Eiffel Tower, and instructions to "Just ask the concierge if there's anything you want.") I did want, and asked him to get me a taxi to Notre Dame.

If you haven't seen it, make an effort the next time you're in Paris, the beauty of the light shining through the magnificent stained glass window at end of the south transept is beyond description. Anyway, having failed to spot either Esmeralda or Quasimodo, I mistakenly decided to stroll back to the hotel. Off I set and, having strolled through the Paris suburbs for about an hour, I turned a corner and found myself in front of Notre Dame. So I took a taxi back.

The following afternoon, I made my presentation and it couldn't have been too dismal as my host said he would pick me up at seven o'clock and we would all go for a nice meal. Now, what you have to remember is that a visiting dignitary (I know, in this case it was only me) gives the guys who invited you an excuse to dine out and is often referred to as 'legitimate expenses' (a bit like those claimed by MP's, I understand.) I was duly picked up and we arrived outside a place I had seen in magazines but never thought I'd visit. It was the famous Lido de Paris Nightclub and a table for six had been booked on the front row of the elevated section, directly facing the stage. We settled into our seats and with military precision, a sumptuous meal was served. Just as we were part way through this gastronomic feast, the orchestra struck up and a chap in evening dress bounded onto the stage. He gave an incomprehensible introduction, accompanied by a number of rather feminine hand flourishes and out of the wings came a group of the most gorgeous high-kicking girls with all of their chestal areas on full display.

The incredible sight of all this feminine pulchritude meant I forgot to eat for a while. Then, as the entire ensemble arrived at the front of the stage, they parted in the centre and another girl appeared with all of her accoutrements on show—as they say. She was obviously the star performer and very tasty she looked—and look we all did. Now don't get me wrong, I've been to clubs before, mainly miners' clubs I must admit, but entertainment, mining style, was generally restricted to some middle aged woman trying desperately to fool us into thinking she was Ruby Murray. No, the Lido was a bit different and as well as the gorgeous girls, there were numerous other attractions, perhaps the most interesting of which involved two skaters whirling round on a circular stage. Their grand finale consisted of the chap holding the girl by her feet and whirling her round horizontally, so on every complete revolution we had a wonderful, but fleeting, view of her womanly bits in mid-air and clearly under the influence of centripetal acceleration. Trying gamely to forget the incredible sight and failing, I found the following acts to be reminiscent of those we used to see at the Liverpool Empire in support of the star of the show — generally someone like Frankie Vaughan or Eddie Calvert (the man with the golden trumpet.) You don't get acts like that on 'Who wants to be a Millionaire Pop Star up the Jungle.'

Another grand night out and what I suppose you might call an 'eye-opener.' Incidentally, I've still got both the programme and a giant poster showing our star performer in all her glory; I discovered them again the other week when I was looking for my medical records (don't ask) and I have absolutely no intention of throwing them away. They beat stamp collecting every time.

Although there's one thing that continues to puzzle me about the evening—I've absolutely no recollection of what it was we had to eat —isn't that strange?

And then of course, there's Italy, but hey, someone's got to do it. This time I was casting an eye over two of their national power generation outfits. We visited several power stations and talked at length about exciting things like megawatts, grids (not the ones in the middle of the road,) power sharing, load shedding, uptime, downtime, distribution networks, demand surges, Sophia Loren and food.

In the evening we were invited to a family run trattoria and again, you have to remember this was not a bribe —honestly. One thing I learned about the Italians is that they are unfailingly polite, devious when necessary and lovers of good food. Sadly, in some ways, bribery never reared its ugly head and sometimes you felt it would be good to have an opportunity to resist—or not—as the case may be.

A table was reserved at the trattoria and each course was delivered with a flourish by the owner or a member of his family. Dish after dish was presented, each one more tempting than the last. Wine - of course there was wine - local to the region obviously and jolly good it was too. As I recall, each meal took us about three to four hours to consume, what with good conversation and superb coffee to follow.

For instance, during the course of one evening, I learned something from a power engineer which comes under the heading of 'useless information' but which has stuck in my mind ever since. It concerns the layout of the square in St Peter's in Rome.

"Brian, did you know," he said, "That the double rows of columns around the perimeter are in the exact shape of an ellipse, and if you stand in front of a column on one side and look across to a column on the other side, you cannot see the second row?"

You don't get conversation of that calibre on a night out in Newcastle.

In addition to my sojourns abroad, I also audited countless companies in the UK, sometimes alone, but often with Les, or one of the other lads on the team. Here the issue of food took on a totally different meaning. It wasn't unusual, for instance, to be interviewing all morning, find you were starving and wondering whether you were ever going to be offered something to eat. Les felt this particularly badly, as it was counter to his philosophy regarding opportunity.

What generally happened was the guy being interviewed would look at his watch and say, "Sorry lads, I've got to nip out for my lunch, I'll be back at about half past one. I'll get one of the girls in the office to see to you." And with that, the sod would meander off.

A girl would then appear and say, "I believe you want something to eat, I can get you some sandwiches from the Alldays shop across the road, there's tea or coffee in the machine in the corridor, you'll just need ten pence for each cup." No problem with bribery there then.

At the other extreme Les and I went to audit a company who were striving to join a consortium of four other companies. Part way through the morning, the general manager who, because he knew their set-up was patently rubbish, stared at his genuine Hong Kong Rolex and said, "Oh look, it's a quarter to twelve. I thought you'd like a bite of lunch; we can take my car."

We arrived at what I can only describe as a building bearing a close resemblance to Disney Gothic, a view confirmed when we saw a pair of genuine plastic suits of armour in the entrance hall. A man dressed in a Burtons' evening suit took our coats, while another man, similarly attired, showed us to our table. A third person then appeared, a lady this time, dressed in widows' black and clutching a number of giant ledgers, which turned out to be the menus.

"Let's start with drinks, shall we?" said Mine Host, who for some reason, kept rubbing his hands.

I won't bore you with the awful details, but the meal went on interminably as each course was preceded by the arrival of the black widow with the ledgers. Unfortunately, despite the grandiose descriptions written in a sort of pidgin French, the food was crap—in keeping I suppose—with the medieval image. And then to cap it all, Mine Host got drunk.

As he was now taking no further interest in the proceedings, Les ordered a taxi on his behalf and at about three in the afternoon we finally got him and us back to the works, at which point I decided to abort the audit. Sadly, for him at least, I'd already mentally come to this conclusion about ten minutes into his pathetic attempt to woo us with rotten pretentious food and thereby reduce the time available to carry out the audit. So, while he was imbibing and talking rubbish, I roughed out a relevant but incomprehensive question to ask him on our return.

As I recall, my 'starter for ten' went something like this:

"As there are four companies within this consortium, there is a need to understand how an integrated management system will be created which is cohesive and amalgamates the appropriate segments of the individual work practices. Who will undertake this task and how will the new system be implemented? What is the schedule for completion in relation to the mobilisation period?"

There was a prolonged silence, as it became increasingly obvious he'd no idea what I was on about (neither, incidentally, did Les,) before he said, "Bloody hell, I'll have to think about that—does this mean we've failed?"

I confirmed his worst fears and I must say he took the disappointing news rather well—or perhaps he already knew he'd wasted his money on what he thought would be a sumptuous meal.

So there you have it, a snapshot of the Auditor at work, making enormous personal sacrifices, lying through the teeth when necessary and being wise (hopefully) to devious practices. All in the noble cause of ensuring that you, Dear Reader, can depend on a steady flow of very costly fuel to your homes.

Section 3

Foreign Parts

1. In the Footsteps of the Great Explorers

There comes a time when one day you find that no one calls you 'young Bri' any more and pretty soon after that blow to the ego, they tell you it's time to retire. This comes as something of a shock, particularly when you've always considered yourself to be a sort of Peter Pan figure.

So, as is the way with these things, we went on a Retirement Course where some unfeeling sod kept referring to us as 'middle-aged.' This was followed by my leaving 'do,' during the course of which I was roundly insulted, given a wholly inaccurate account of past failings, presented with a belt sander (don't ask) and my wife was given a huge bunch of flowers. There was much hilarity, hand-shaking, back-patting (a lovely change from back-stabbing) and copious amounts of drink. All in all, it went well and I was touched by the whole affair.

I was reminded of my retirement party sometime later when working in Kazakhstan. We were housed in a camp and I was sharing a room with an American who was out for a special drilling job. As entertainment was almost non-existent, I'd managed to scrounge a couple of videos and one evening we sat down to watch. The first one was a programme taken off the television and showed a birthday tribute to Bruce Forsyth. As is usually the case with such events, several of his best friends were called on to speak. As I recall, it featured Sean Connery, Jimmy Tarbuck, Ronnie Corbett and several others. A common theme throughout each of the eulogies was that Bruce was roundly insulted. His lack of ability to play golf, dance, sing and act, was the subject of considerable hilarity—and were all taken apart and severely criticised, coupled with comments about his meanness, age and dress-sense.

It was then I noticed my American friend staring at the TV and looking extremely puzzled. "Mike, aren't you enjoying the programme? Is something wrong?"

"Well Brian, I'm a bit puzzled; I thought they said this was a tribute to the man with the moustache."

"It is."

"Yes, but hold on, these guys have done nothing but throw terrible insults. I don't know who the others are, but I recognise Sean Connery and I'm surprised that the guy doesn't just get up and walk out."

"But Mike, that's the way we show our affection in the UK; if you really like someone, you find out all you can about their embarrassing moments and you make jokes out of it. As you can see, Bruce is laughing at everything."

"I know, that's what's been puzzling me—if you did that to anyone famous in the States, they'd have their lawyers draw up massive claims for defamation of character."

"Ah well Mike, it just goes to show, it's not only the language that separates us."

"Too goddam right it isn't, Brian."

Then on the following three nights we watched six hours of 'Smiley's People' and throughout it all Mike was spellbound. At the finish I asked if he'd enjoyed it, as I was conscious it was very much set in a British environment.

Mike said, "I've been amazed at the acting and the story. Who wrote a thing as long as that and all without adverts in between?"

I said, "It was written by a chap called John le Carre and there is another epic which actually precedes this, called 'Tinker, Tailor, Soldier, Spy. It's just a pity you couldn't have seen that one first."

"That's okay Brian, I'll be sure to get a copy when I get back home. But do you know what the most impressive thing was in my view?"

"No," I said.

"Well, it's the fact that you Brits could make a film six hours long about a serious subject like spies and traitors and not once did anybody swear. Just wait till I tell the folks back home — yes sir."

The foreign parts escapade started about three days after I'd put away my retirement gear and sanded everything in sight, when I received a call from Alex, a Consultant who had worked for me on and off for a number of years.

The gist of the call went as follows:

"How would you like to do a small job for me now that you've retired?"

"Yes I could do, where is it?"

At this point there was a fairly lengthy silence, so much so I thought he'd hung up.

"Well, it's a bit out of the way, but sounds as though it could be interesting." This of course, is consultant-speak for 'I'd really like you to agree before I tell you.'

"Where the hell is it?" Me—loudly this time.

"Er, Kazakhstan."

"Are you mad?"

"It's a big project and I've been asked if I know someone who can help out with the development of their management systems. The other thing is, you'd be working for the Italians; they're the Operators of the field. I reckon you'd enjoy it." This is more consultant-speak for 'I've no idea whether you will or not, but it might help to persuade you to go.' So, falling once more for the three-card trick, I said,

"Okay, I'll give it a whirl, how long is it for and how the do I get to Kazakhstan, wherever the hell that is?"

"No problem, it's a two week trip and you go by charter flight from Stanstead."

As soon as he hung up, I consulted my Schoolboy Atlas and learned that Kazakhstan occupied a land mass of one million square miles (for comparison, the UK occupies about eighty one thousand square miles, which means we could fit into Kazakhstan twelve times.) It was where the silk route originated, it had the biggest fresh water lake in the world, called the Aral Sea, the Russians used a place called Baikonor to send rockets into space and the Caspian Sea is at the south end — quite a lot really.

So began my great Asian adventure. I turned up as instructed at Stanstead Airport and waited for the charter flight scheduled to land at nine fifteen pm. It's always rather strange joining a new outfit and, when I checked in, I found there were about twenty other guys all waiting as well. The difference being they obviously all knew one another and kept giving me surreptitious glances as if to say, 'Who the hell is he; and why's he on our flight?' Of course, being British, no one actually asked me; the best I got was a sort of half nod now and again. I suppose this was by way of acknowledgement in case I turned out to be someone important. The plane, which was owned by Malev, a Hungarian airline, finally arrived on time at ten-thirty pm and I was ushered on board. Interestingly, I then found a number of the seats to be already occupied by Italians, who had claimed all the window seats and didn't look best pleased to be disturbed by a bunch of hairy Brits. I found out later that the plane actually started from Malpensa Airport on the outskirts of Milan, where it picked up the Italian contingent, flew to Stanstead, picked us up and then flew on to an airport called Uralsk in West Kazakhstan.

Now, as everyone knows, if you fly in an easterly direction, time moves forward according to international time zones. In my case, the time shift was four hours and, as the flight took four hours, suddenly it was eight o'clock in the morning when we landed. I was already knackered and we hadn't even got off the plane. Although the fun, as they say, was just about to start.

The plane taxied to a standstill and nothing happened, nobody leaped up, grabbed a case, put on a coat or made any sort of move. It was as though everyone had been overcome by a terrible lethargy. Glancing out of the window I saw a completely empty airport, no evident signs of life and sitting on one end of the apron I could see a number of aircraft parked in a herring bone pattern. The funny thing was they didn't look as though they had flown in a long time; they were a sort of matt grey, about the same size as our Hawker jets and could have been early versions of Russian Migs. However, as I had forgotten to pack my copy of 'Janes —All the Worlds Military Aircraft,' I had no way of confirming my suspicions.

Just then I noticed a number of official looking chaps coming towards the plane. They were dressed in what looked like military uniforms and wore those hats with giant rims so beloved of Russian generals. At their signal the door was opened, steps were rolled into place and we came alive. Descending onto the concrete, we were ushered swiftly by the hat brigade into the terminal building. I say terminal, but it looked like a badly maintained two storey hut, of the type you see used for offices on a building site. Once inside, I joined a queue which slowly shuffled forward towards a kind of sentry box, within which was seated another large-hatted individual examining our passports.

Finally it was my turn; I offered my passport, open at the correct page and enclosing my visa, sanctioned by their embassy in London for a limited stay in Kazakhstan. He took my passport, stared at it, stared at me, turned it upside down, stared again, passed it through an ultra-violet light, flicked through the pages, stared at me again, opened it at my photograph, stared some more and with a flick of his finger, motioned for me to stand to one side. What made this exchange a bit disconcerting was that it had been conducted in total silence and he still had my passport. In the meantime, others in the queue were having their passports stamped, and being ushered through to collect their luggage.

At last the queue disappeared and I began to feel like one of John le Carre's characters where he's in East Berlin and the Stasi are holding him at Checkpoint Charlie. (I really should start reading more books by Jilly Cooper.) It was a growing worry that no one knew (or cared) about my being held up and I was also aware that having obtained our luggage, there was a coach to catch. Obviously, I reasoned, if nobody knows I'm trapped, the coach might go without me and I hadn't seen any signs of a taxi rank, or the Kazakh equivalent of the Gatwick Express.

Just as I was about to make a run for it (no, not really, I was too petrified,) my hat man approached and this time he had another hat man with him, the only difference being was that the new arrival's hat sported a larger, shinier badge. The same finger beckoned me forward.

However, in order for them to both fit into the little hut, both hats had to be removed and stacked one on top of the other, which rather spoiled the illusion of absolute supremacy. Senior hat man then went through the same routine, flicking, staring, turning, staring, ultra-violet lighting, more staring and then, finally with a glance at one another, a stamp appeared and was smashed down on my passport. The finger signalled again, I retrieved my passport and scooted through to catch the bus. What amazed me, on looking back from the relative safety of my seat, was the fact that not a word was spoken and I still had no idea what on earth they were looking for. One thing was for sure, I was going to give spy novels a rest and, if I ever got back home, I would kill Alex. All of these pathetic intentions were, however, somewhat premature, as my adventures with our hatted friends hadn't really started.

A word about the coach—this turned out to be a description of the vehicle in its loosest possible sense. In my ignorance, when they said we would be going the rest of the way by coach, I had a picture in my mind of a Shearings' type vehicle. You know—the ones with reclining seats, a toilet, tea and coffee, big panoramic windows, springs, upholstery, tyres with treads, a big engine and matching gear-box.

The vehicle that confronted me was mainly acid yellow, about half the length of a normal coach, had seats which I thought had been abolished with the last of Liverpool's trams and was very high off the ground. By now it's ten o'clock and the temperature is climbing. I also began to understand why it was that seasoned travellers had been carrying bottles of water when they got on the plane. Still, I reasoned, it won't be long now until we reach our destination. Risking a rebuff, I asked one of the lads how long we'd be and he said, "About two hours, depending," he said, "On whether any parts of the road had been washed away. That's why," he added, "The wheels are big and we're so high off the ground." And with that piece of reassuring information, he curled up in a sort of ball and went to sleep.

Then with the noise of an engine about to go into terminal decline and a crash of gears which sounded as though the synchro-mesh parts had fallen off—we were on our way.

When I say on our way, it was with a sort of lurching motion, accompanied by a series of thumps as the driver negotiated whole sections of missing tarmac. Nonetheless, I was determined to keep awake in order, or so I thought, to take in the view. So, peering out of the window, fighting to stay in my seat and realising vaguely that I had at least two more hours in which to sustain my excitement—I viewed.

When I was seven, I was given a lovely book, which I think was called 'Wonders of the World.' It was a large book with a dark blue cover and the contents were divided into different areas of the world. There were numerous sections including Africa, Europe, Asia and The Arctic. I remember repeatedly coming back to one particular photograph which depicted a huge expanse of nothing at all. What didn't help was the fact that it was a miserable sepia colour, but what really baffled me was the caption beneath, which read, 'Tundra in Eurasia.' Now when you're seven, you don't like to let your parents know how little you understand of anything, so I used to stare at the photo thinking perhaps 'Tundra' is a place, but if it is, where are the houses? Then I thought, perhaps Eurasia is a town and Tundra is in it. You can begin to see just what a detrimental effect all this learning had on a young brain (and to this day—I haven't really recovered.) Anyway, I had completely forgotten about this early conundrum until one day, some fifty-four years later, I saw Tundra in all its glory. The funny thing was that it looked just like the picture in my childhood book and to cap it all, was still sepia. So I stared and stared at absolutely nothing, until I was bored out of my skull and a full ten minutes had passed. So I too curled up into a ball and went to sleep.

Finally, after what seemed to be about ten hours of lurching, grinding, bouncing, yawning and tundra-ing, we arrived at our destination—a town called Aksai.

But what on earth, I hear you ask, was I doing there?

Hands up all those who remember the USSR and Mikhail Gorbachev; well it's all his fault really. In the 1980's he came up with a 'good idea;'

Executive Coach—sadly there's no plasma TV, leather seats, satellite dish or bar.

Aksai, a town of grace and distinction, Russian style.

The Czech Camp, not to be confused with Stalag 17

this was to allow the fifteen Republics to seek and declare independence. (This is not a history lesson, I'm neither qualified nor sufficiently interested enough to bore you with more details.) However, Kazakhstan, the biggest of the 'Stans' also decided to become an Independent Republic, which meant that they suddenly owned Karachaganak, a 'supergiant' oil and gas condensate field, which was discovered in 1979. (For the uninitiated, condensate is a hydrocarbon liquid which condenses out of gas when the temperature is reduced to a certain level. It's a bit like oil really.) Obviously, as the USSR went into meltdown, the field fell into disrepair and because of the type of geological structure and past Soviet practises, it had suffered from two unique historical events —a thing called the gryphon and the creation of massive underground storage caverns. These events happened in 1987 when a condensate well suffered a mechanical failure that resulted in a blow-out. (A blow-out is the uncontrolled release of fluid from a well being drilled and is the sort of thing Red Adair was born to sort out.) In this case the uncontrolled fluid at high pressure travelled laterally before emerging at the surface several kilometres away. This unfortunate event contaminated an area of some five hundred and twenty hectares with a surface crater of five hundred square metres which, for some strange reason, is called a 'gryphon.' During the blow-out, which incidentally lasted for some two years, substantial quantities of condensate and gas were emitted as well as underground water with a high brine concentration. You have to agree, the Soviets could really pull out all the stops when it came to minor set-backs.

They then came up with another good idea. The plan was to detonate six underground (peaceful) nuclear explosions in salt domes—as you do —to create caverns for storing the condensate. This was known as the 'Lira Test Site,' which, as a result of the explosions, created underground cavities with a volume of about sixty thousand cubic metres (About two thirds the size of the volume of the Royal Albert Hall.) Unfortunately, in what might be called another small setback, two of the underground explosions came to the surface. However and perhaps fortunately for the Soviets, the liability, along with the monitoring, care and maintenance of the underground storage caverns were fortuitously transferred to the Republic of Kazakhstan on obtaining independence. I guess it's all about timing.

Enter the Italians who, on forming a consortium with a number of British, Russian and American oil companies, made a successful bid to develop and operate the field. So, gearing up to drag the field into the twentieth century, they needed lots of people with oilfield experience. Not surprisingly, they contacted Alex, who in turn, contacted me and after a surreal journey, I arrived knackered and bemused (nothing new there then,) ready to meet my new masters.

But first, I had to live somewhere. This turned out to be what was euphemistically known as the Czech Camp, probably because it was built by the Czechs to house the USSR oilfield workers (you can't beat the Soviets for imagination.) As the bus reached the entrance, we were met by a substantial barrier and two uniformed guards. The bus stopped, the guards came aboard and peered at us, the barrier was lifted and we were waved through. I was now faced with what looked like an exact replica of the set from Stalag 17 (starring William Holden,) The Wooden Horse (starring Leo Genn) and The Great Escape (starring just about everyone else and a fictional bloke on a motorbike.) As far as the eye could see there were lines of wooden barrack-like buildings, all in a tasteful dusty brown but which, in a departure from the Stalag norm, were two storeys high. Not a plant or flower disturbed the symmetry, although there were lamp-posts located at regular intervals. We dismounted and queued outside the Camp Boss's office to be allocated a room. (Remember, the word 'Camp' in this context is a noun.) It was now twelve noon, it was searingly hot, I hadn't slept in a bed for some thirty six hours or eaten any proper food for twenty four. Then someone said, "If I were you, I should just dump your stuff in your room and get to the canteen quickly, as it shuts in about fifteen minutes." And so—as I half raced to find my room, got lost among the maze of buildings (all of which were cleverly identical,) found my room, dropped my gear and staggered back to find the canteen—I thought, what the hell was I doing here and why did I turn down that offer to join the retired gentlefolk's bowls club?

2. Buongiorno — I Think

I was at last tucking into a rather nice meal when my erstwhile informant approached and said, "Don't take too long, the bus for the office leaves in about ten minutes." Oh good, time to move off again, back on the blasted bus and yet more excitement. This time however, the journey was relatively short; our route took us through the town of Aksai, which looked as though it had been designed by Stalin in one of his less endearing moods.

I don't know what I expected, but the office building turned out to be rather modern with a rather nice foyer, a marble floor, more uniformed guards and a reception desk. Finally, I was able to ask for my new employer, a gentleman named Paulo, who turned out to be tall, fair haired, and extremely polite, with a sort of George Clooney look about him. He spoke excellent English (fortunately for me) and from the moment we met, I could see we were going to get on well together. I also noticed that while we were chatting, there was another person present at a desk near the door. Paulo introduced us and said he was Mr Prandi, another member of the team. I also noticed that Paulo treated Mr Prandi with some deference. Possibly because, as I found out later, he used to be Paulo's boss and had, at the time, a fearsome reputation. I also was struck by Mr Prandi's stature, he was obviously in his sixties, quite slender and looked a little like an older version of Al Pacino, with the same sinister aura that he often displayed on screen. Having been introduced, Mr Prandi spoke little, but I did notice that at fairly regular intervals, he reached into his desk drawer and extracted a piece of chocolate which, in one smooth movement, he popped into his mouth. As we were destined to work closely together, he courteously indicated that I might call him Sandro.

So, introductions over, Paulo and I reviewed the work to be done and he then said two things which endeared me to him forever.

"Brian, would you like a cup of tea?"

"Oh yes, please."

"Good, we go now and I make you one."

I followed him upstairs, along a corridor to a room with a sort of rough hewn stable door, closed at the bottom and open at the top. Inside was a lady who, I found out, was the dispenser of all things liquid. Paulo gave her an Italian smile and said, "Chai puzhalsta."

The lady smiled back and produced two cups of tea.

"Spasiba," said Paulo. And immediately I had three very important Russian words at my disposal—tea, please and thank you. Having drunk our tea and returned to the office, Paulo then said the second wonderful thing.

"Brian, we have had a long enough day. I also was on the flight, we cannot give of our best without sleep. I will call a car to take us back to the Camp and we will be fresh in the morning. Do you agree?"

As it was only four o'clock and we should have worked until six, I said, "Certainly, if it's alright with you."

"Good, we go now."

Mr Prandi looked up, said nothing, and popped another piece of chocolate into his mouth.

My accommodation was spacious and in fact, because these were early days in the life of the project, I had two rooms—a lounge and a bedroom where I gratefully collapsed onto the bed—which turned out to be a mistake. For a start, it was like lying on a length of corrugated iron and then, having stretched out and closed my eyes for the first time in several years, I became conscious of a terrible noise. It sounded as though a light aircraft was coming across the rooftops with severe fuel problems and then at about thirty second intervals there was an additional ear-grating sound reminiscent of someone standing on a cat's tail. I shot up and realised the noise was coming from a unit mounted in a space where the topmost window would normally have been. This, I discovered, was Kazakhstan's answer to the need for air conditioning and, as the outside temperature was still in the high thirty's, was most welcome. The only problem was that, as the unit had obviously been manufactured many years ago by people in a forced labour camp and presumably to Soviet military standards, the need for silent running hadn't been a high priority. I then had a brainwave—as it would be cooler at night, I would switch the damn thing off when I went to bed. So, by now working largely on auto-pilot, I had some dinner and then, joy of joy, a good night's sleep beckoned.

Ah—the sheer bliss of bed, especially when you can't remember when you were last there, clean sheets, a light cover, curtains drawn, ablutions rapidly completed, shoes cleaned, a good book discarded, your alarm set for ten hours hence and the blasted air conditioner switched off. And then you find that sleep just won't come, you relax, you think of nice things (but not involving Sophia Loren,) you close your eyes—and absolutely nothing happens. You open your eyes, stare at the ceiling, realise that the corrugated iron bed is beginning to adversely affect your spine, then glancing at your watch, you realise that a precious hour has passed and you're still awake.

And now another small problem is beginning to emerge, the room is taking on all the attributes of a Turkish bath. What you had failed to realise is that the climate in Kazakhstan isn't quite the same as that in the north east of Scotland. There, the climate can be summed up in a short, but accurate sentence—it's plus forty degrees in summer and it's minus forty degrees in winter. So, translating this appallingly simple statement into my situation, we find that the phrase 'in the cool of the evening' is a very relative term. In fact it's still bloody hot. This meant that switching off the air conditioner was not one of my better decisions, borne out by the fact that beads of sweat were forming all over my body, breathing was akin to being too close to a blow-lamp, the sheet was fast losing its crispness and my back was stuck to what was laughingly referred to as the mattress. So, I slid out of bed and switched the infernal thing on again and, soon after it reached mach one speed, the air began to cool and I, being wet, began to freeze. I guess I finally fell asleep some three hours later and so passed my first night in Western Kazakhstan.

The following morning I mentioned the noise to Paulo, who reassured me by saying, "Don't worry Brian, at the end of the first month you'll be used to the heat and then you can switch it off and still sleep." I thought, 'Oh great, just another twenty nine days to go and then I can sleep.'

He then said, "Are you on the ground or the second floor?"

"I'm on the ground floor, why what does it matter?"

"Oh nothing really, but you could start hearing another strange noise, that's all."

He was correct. Later that night, just as I was sort of drifting off, a metronomic tapping sound percolated through to the brain. I lay there thinking how unfair it all was and how the hell did I get into this mess (again, killing Alex seemed to be the answer.) I sat up—where was the noise coming from and what was it? I arose and started a search of the room, was it mice? Was it a cunning torture leftover from the Soviet era? Was it my overwrought imagination? Was it hell—the noise, as it continued to tap with incredible regularity, ensured I was now fully awake. I searched in vain, I couldn't even figure out exactly where it was coming from, only that it filled the room, without being overly loud.

I lay back down on the bed, trying to remember which of John le Carre's books dealt with the favourite interrogation methods as used by the KGB, but to no avail.

Get over it, I thought, you couldn't imagine Dick Barton cracking so soon under such pressure, but one thing was for sure, I needed to sort this out in the morning, or I might never sleep again.

Tentatively, I explained the problem to Paulo.

"Ah yes, Brian, do you remember I mentioned that if you were on the ground floor, you might hear another noise?"

"Yes."

"Well what you're hearing is a drip of condensed water from the air conditioner in the room above; it comes out of an exhaust pipe in small droplets and hits the top of the metal casing of your conditioner. That's what you can hear and there is no way to stop it. What you should remember in order to avoid the water torture, is always to ask for an upstairs room in the summer and a downstairs room in the winter, as you will find that the heating pipes work more efficiently on the ground floor."

Another bit of vital information not to be found in the brochure — not that there was one.

Did I mention the bed? Even if the room was silent, cool, carpeted, modern, comfortable and featured concealed lighting, it would make no difference to my ability to ensure the mandatory eight hours of unconscious bliss. Apparently the bed had been fashioned out of badly seasoned birch obtained at minimal cost from a forest somewhere north of Moscow. The manufacturer, ever mindful of potential contracts for the odd gulag, had erred on the side of structural integrity over comfort. Thus, the base was fashioned out of six inch planks bound together by a series of cross braces on the underside. The unit was then furnished with a mattress made out of material left over from old World War 2 uniforms and filled to a depth of some two inches with kapok. Lying on it was akin to stretching out on the concrete section of a dual carriageway — only not quite as comfortable. Within about ten minutes my hips, back and shoulders were all in a state of severe agony and this, coupled with the ongoing water torture, did nothing to promote slumber. Something had to be done.

On returning home, I nipped smartly into one of those strange shops whose main purpose in life is to persuade you that camping—as a way of life—is extremely desirable. So much so, they stock a vast collection of tackle necessary for survival in the great outdoors. In my case, a rubberised canvas mattress of the blow-up variety was the object of desire. This was duly purchased, together with a strange looking half dome rubber ball, necessary for inflating the damned thing on arrival.

What bliss when, having exposed the Kazakh version of a mattress, I inflated my new purchase, laid it on top, re-made the covers and sank onto my airbed. All I then needed to do was adjust the air pressure to optimum softness and hey-presto—pain free sleep at last. Although quite what the lady who came in each day to clean and make the bed, thought about the new arrangement, I never liked to enquire. I did however, notice she had a tendency to giggle, and then look away rather sharply, whenever we met in the corridor. Yet more confirmation in her mind of the softness of the western male and another dent in my carefully prepared macho image, I suppose.

Incidentally, I never mentioned my sleeping arrangements to the Italian lads; after all, I reasoned, I was the one from northern climes and as such was supposed to feel no pain. The Italians, on the other hand were sensitive, emotional, well mannered and civilised. Or a combination of all four, as I was about to find out.

Obviously I had to ensure that I'd sufficient money with me to take care of essentials such as beer and the odd ethnic souvenir. The currency of Kazakhstan is the Tenge; the only trouble is that it isn't traded outside the country. The answer, as is often the case when travelling to foreign parts, is to take lots of good old US dollars. This wasn't quite as straightforward as it seemed because, when we were waiting to pass (or not) through customs, we were given a miserable looking declaration form to fill in. The document was a tasteful crappy colour and made from thrice renewed paper. But the really clever thing as far as communication was concerned was that it was written in Cyrillic, without any translation. Being given one for the first time was apt to cause a degree of panic, especially as one of the big hat brigade would soon be perusing your declarations. I remember staring at mine for the first time and being unable to understand a letter never mind a word, when a kind colleague, seeing my rising panic, gave me a translated copy. Unfortunately, the translated version didn't match the original in a number of areas, but I did my best and hoped it wouldn't lead to my being incarcerated. The major bits centred on the currency you were bringing in—merchandise, camera, mobile phone, etc. There were also declarations to be made regarding your importation of useful things such as drugs or psychotropic substances, antiques or objects of art and wildlife objects, parts and products thereof. On presenting the duly completed form, it would be perused, scanned, checked, stared at and finally your statements would be ringed in biro and stamped. You then needed to guard the bit of paper with your life, as it would be re-perused (and stamped) before you were allowed out of the country. Finally, with paperwork all complete and still clutching your dollars, you emerged mentally unscathed and left for the office. The Government had also issued a decree that although there was an official dollar-tenge exchange rate, the use of the dollar in purchase transactions was not to be countenanced. Therefore, as we needed to buy the odd round or two, dollars had to be changed. I broached the subject with Paolo, saying I hadn't noticed a bank of any kind either at the airport or in Aksai.

He said, "It's not a problem. What you do is go and see Lyudmila, she is the Production Manager's Secretary; she will change dollars for you, but my advice is not to change too much at a time." I thought this last statement to be somewhat cryptic, but agreed to do as he said.

I found Lyudmila in her office and tentatively asked if she could arrange for some currency exchange for me. She smiled and in excellent English said it would be no problem and how much did I want.

I said, "Oh about twenty dollars and as I'm just downstairs, I can call back for it at any time."

Again the smile and producing a calculator from her desk drawer, said, "No problem, you have the dollars?"

I duly fished twenty out of my pocket and passed them across. At which she opened another drawer and fishing out a huge bundle of tenge, counted out the agreed amount and handed them to me. I stared at her for a moment and then remembered to thank her, which provoked yet another smile and she said, "You're welcome."

Although I was consumed with curiosity regarding this excellent but largely unofficial money changing facility, I realised by now there were a number of things you were better off not knowing, and that this might be one of them.

Sitting within the confines of the Czech camp was a long and as I recall, single storey building made of wood with a set of steps up to the entrance. Blending nicely with the rest of the stalag, it went by the name of 'Teskos' and was euphemistically known as a 'night club.' Now we're not talking here about Annabel's, Stringfellows, The Aquarium, The Ministry of Sound, Koko, Herbal or Pacha (not that I've been in any of them, it's simply that I keep a finger on the social pulse, so to speak.) What we are talking about here, is a sort of semi-dark shed, tastefully furnished with Formica topped tables and some odd chairs. There was a bar at one end, partially lit by several left over christmas-tree lights, behind which could be found 'Mine Host' dispensing drink and collecting the money. He was a big guy with lank hair, a gaunt expression which discouraged idle conversation and a tendency to lapse into Russian when taking your order. Ambience, as required of a proper night club, was provided by a CD player set to a level at which the speakers were incapable of accurately reproducing the sound and were, consequently, guaranteed to prevent any form of communication.

It was to this venue that we migrated in the evening in order to enjoy a relaxing lager or two whilst trying gamely to talk to one another. This need to chat was much easier to satisfy in the summer when we could sit outside on a wooden bench and take in a panoramic view of the tundra. The first time I bought a round, Paolo's comment about not changing too many dollars at one time became clear. As mine host handed over the drinks he said in a commanding tone, "dollars." Fooled for a moment into thinking it was an order not a request, I handed over a ten dollar bill. This disappeared immediately into his pocket and then, ringing up the till, he handed me a pile of change in tenge. So much for the dollar being non-negotiable—the sod.

For some reason one morning, I had ventured downstairs into some offices on a wing of the ground floor, Thinking for a minute it was a deserted area I was surprised to find people occupying the offices, as every now and again a door would open and a man clutching a file would stride purposefully down the corridor and disappear into another office. The one thing they seemed to have in common was that they all spoke Russian. Feeling by now that I had strayed into a parallel universe, I nipped back to our office and asked Paulo what was going on.

He said, "Ah, they're the production people who ran the plant before it was taken over by the project."

"Yes, but they don't run it now do they?"

"Oh no, we have our own production team, the guys on the ground floor just get the production output figures every day so they can pretend they're still in charge. We found when we came here, that there were some seven hundred people employed on a plant that was falling apart. This was a prime example of the Soviet philosophy of providing full employment; for example, each valve had a man in charge of it, even if it only opened once a year. One of the decisions we had to make was to reduce the figures to western levels. This meant we had to dismiss about four hundred, but we couldn't fire the top people for political reasons. So they have offices downstairs and we supply them with data, which they analyse and discuss among themselves."

"But they don't have any influence over what is actually going on, do they?"

"None at all, we just pay their salaries."

The other interesting thing I discovered was that all the office doors opened outwards into the corridor. This meant that you could be walking along minding your own business when suddenly; you made forcible contact with a huge lump of wood. To say this was disconcerting would be an understatement, particularly if you were unlucky enough to be passing just as the doors on opposite sides of the corridor opened at the same time. This reduced your available space to about the width of a small boy and required great presence of mind and manual dexterity to avoid injury.

Once again, I consulted Paulo and he explained, "The philosophy is that should there be a fire, it's much easier to escape from an office when the door opens outwards. Mind you, all the time there isn't a fire, people are continually being clobbered by doors, which is why, Brian, you notice that when you and I walk down the corridor, we go in single file down the middle."

Tesko's Night Club, just the place to raise your spirits

3. Is a Style

During the next six years (remember—the contract was for three weeks,) I became very close to my Italian colleagues and enjoyed their company, philosophy and occasional emotional outbursts. I also found that a number of my fellow countrymen (to their cost) tended to underestimate their capabilities, mistakenly believing that because the Italian government was considered to be largely incompetent—they must be the same.

This was a dangerous assumption as I came to understand that, in general, Italians managed to live their lives despite, rather than because of, the machinations of respective governments. Over time, we became a close-knit group with Paulo taking the lead, ably supported by Mr Prandi, yours truly and on occasions, Gianni (more of him later.) Paulo spoke excellent grammatically correct English (and also Russian, French, German and some Spanish.) Mr Prandi spoke English with an accent reminiscent of a man choking on an olive, whilst I took the opportunity to learn at least five or six words of Italian, four words of Russian and three words of Kazakh. The whole team deferred however, to Mr Vancella, the Head of Human Resources, although I had grave suspicions that he also occupied a somewhat more secretive rank, one which was considerably higher than the title nailed on his door. I say this because it wasn't unusual to see him in earnest conversation with the Project Manager, the Operations Director and sundry officials from the Kazakh Government. Whilst he always displayed impeccable manners, I felt there was an air of quiet menace about him, even when he smiled, (actually —especially when he smiled.) Although slimmer and with greying temples, he reminded me of Paul Sorvino when he played the part of Paul Cicero, the mob patriarch, in the film 'Goodfellas.' I'm not jumping to any conclusions you understand, but as one brought up on (and sadly, very much influenced by) such films, the comparison was both compelling and probably defamatory.

We often used to meet Mr Vancella when Paulo and I were about to take our mid-afternoon chai break. He would arrive at the half door, impeccably dressed with a faint aura of some undoubtedly expensive aftershave and, believe it or not, a cashmere wool cardigan slung casually across his shoulders. We would be treated to a 'Buongiorno' and a smile, while at the same time the lady would produce a cup of 'chai' and hand it to him, all of which was accomplished without any verbal communication having taken place. He would take an exploratory sip; smile again and return to his office, leaving behind the faint aroma of Giorgio Armani. Don't get me wrong, I had no idea what the source was until Paolo told me. I did venture to suggest that he probably just smiled at the shop assistant and she handed it over. But Paolo wouldn't commit himself.

After a while, I also noticed there was never any indication that he felt the need to wait his turn to be served and equally, there was never any indication that anyone in the queue objected (I reckon it was the Goodfellas influence again.)

Over the course of the next year or two, I made a number of fatal errors whilst trying to emulate my Latin friends in matters sartorial. The first example of poor judgement involved sunglasses. Each morning we would meet at the bus stop to go to the office and without exception, the lads would all be wearing shades. Then, as the bus pulled up, the shades would be casually moved off the nose to the top of the head and conversation would continue as if nothing had happened.

So, being of sound mind and determined to fit in, I purchased a pair of sunglasses at the airport on my next outward trip. Then on joining the queue the first morning, I removed my own glasses and casually donned my new shades. At this point a significant drawback to this clever scheme immediately became apparent—they weren't prescription lenses. This meant that not only was Kazakhstan now a complete blur, but was blurred in a sort of dark brown colour. Still, I told myself; image is everything, so feeling my way onto the bus and groping for a seat, I sat down. Time for phase two, gripping the shades by the sides, I casually moved them to the top of my head. It was then that another snag emerged—the world was searingly bright and I couldn't see a thing. So, retrieving my everyday glasses, I put them back on, which meant I now had two pairs in situ, as they say. Sadly, just as I was thinking I could now be mistaken for a devil-may-care Italian, the bus went over a huge bump and the shades, which I'd forgotten were still on top of my head, fell forward onto the top of my glasses, which tried to bury themselves into the bridge of my nose.

Meanwhile, Paulo and the gang were chattering away and, alighting from the bus, they simply slipped their sunglasses back in place. Meanwhile, I was left debating whether to continue with my new image and risk missing the office door, while struggling with two pairs of specs, which had somehow become inextricably linked. I was beginning to see (no pun intended) that being mistaken for an Italian wasn't going to be as easy as I thought.

Sadly, this feeling was reinforced later when, on catching sight of myself in the mirror with the new shades perched precariously on the top of my head, I realised I looked like a prat.

It was the same story with the next 'must have' fashion statement for the Italian man on a project. I refer to the strange habit of wearing shoes with no socks which, if seen in Liverpool, would be a sign of extreme poverty. This mode of dress was favoured by Paulo and first came to my notice when he had his feet on the desk one day. His shoes were what looked to be a sort of slip-on moccasin with lots of moth-holes around the sides. Paulo saw me staring at his feet and said, "Brian, what are you staring at?"

I said, "Sorry, didn't mean to stare, but I can't help noticing you've got no socks on."

"Of course not, Brian. You don't wear socks with summer shoes, it's just not fashionable."

Now this was probably the first time in a long and fairly varied career, that another chap had unashamedly used the word 'fashionable' when referring to himself. So, for one silly minute, I thought, well, if it's good enough for Paulo, it's good enough for me. Until, that is, I remembered I was wearing a pair of Clarke's size eleven, guaranteed water resistant shoes with super cushion sole and weighing about forty pounds. Somehow, on reflection, I couldn't visualise a sockless pair of Clarke's having the same fashionable impact. So, yet another chance to be mistaken for an Italian man about town had once again collapsed. The conversation did, however, remind me of a comment made by that late lamented funny lady, Linda Smith, who once remarked that, 'You can tell Jesus wasn't English because, although he wore sandals, he didn't wear socks as well.'

However, not wanting to give in too soon in my wholly futile attempts to fit in, I tried a couple of other fashion statements, but this time in the privacy of my room. The first attempt consisted of casually slinging a jacket over my shoulders, leaving the sleeves hanging free at the sides. As I mentioned, this mode of dress was much favoured by Mr Vancella, who generally appeared wearing the type of cardigan most discerning women would die for. Tentatively, I slung my jacket over the shoulders and, mistakenly, gave a twirl to see the effect. This was immediate and somewhat disastrous, as buoyed by centrifugal force, the jacket flew off, crashed into the bedside table and sent my alarm clock flying across the room. I suppose I should have realised that a Harris Tweed jacket with pockets full of keys, wallet, loose change, assorted pens and a bag of mintoes, would be slightly heavier than a cashmere cardigan.

The second attempt took place in the winter when I noticed my Italian friends had taken to wearing scarves over their coats. What was different, however, was the way they were fastened. They seemed to be folded in half lengthways with the doubled section placed around the neck. The free ends were then passed through the loop leaving them to hang casually down at the front. Once again the chaps were ahead of the fashion game by about eight years. Still fully unable to grasp the fact that I wasn't going to be mistaken for Rossano Brazzi, (you remember —he played the part of Emile du Beque in the film version of South Pacific,) I popped into one of those miniature Rack shops at the airport and purchased a scarf. Hardly daring to wait until I was safe in my room, I folded the scarf, casually wound it around my neck, slipped the ends through the loop, pulled gently to bring the ensemble into perfect alignment and found I couldn't bend my neck. This minor setback meant that as my head was now restricted to a forward looking position, I couldn't see my feet, which made negotiating stairs something of a high risk endeavour. So, doing a bit more tugging, while peering hopefully into the mirror, it finally dawned on me that I looked like one of those pictures of Rupert Bear, just as his mummy had dressed him to go and play with his friends. So I did the only thing possible, I undid the thing and wore it like a muffler, in the manner of a Liverpool docker, circa 1930.

What the hell is it about Italian men regarding the need to demonstrate sartorial and masculine mastery? — I kept asking myself. This exercise in useless introspection reminded me of a puzzling incident that occurred whilst my wife and I were driving on the E35 just south of Firenze. We were en route to a beautiful unspoilt area of Italy known as Casentino. (If you haven't been there, take a look, its well worth a visit.)

Anyway, there we were travelling along the Autostrade in my Subaru Impreza STi (it's known locally as the McRae syndrome) and carefully overtaking slower vehicles, as you do, when we became aware of the most disconcerting noise we'd ever heard. At first we thought there was something terminal happening to our beautiful turbo flat four engine, however, after a moment of panic we realised the noise was coming from outside the car.

How to describe it; imagine if you will, several hundred very angry bees trapped in a large tin can. They are frantically trying to get out but can't and so and as the minutes pass, they are crashing into the sides of the can, the buzzing noise rises to a crescendo, as their anger increases and you realise that should they finally escape, you will need to be some miles away at the time.

Now, multiply the noise to a level as yet undreamed of and you have some indication of the terrible cacophony coming from somewhere in close proximity. Remember, during this time, we are travelling at about 125 kilometres per hour, a comfortable speed for the car and one which leaves a good deal in reserve. And then, two things happen at once, the noise gets even closer and there, in the left hand wing mirror, we can see a Fiat Cinquecento in the outside lane.

This car, bear in mind, is a three-door hatchback, possibly made in Poland, with front wheel drive and an engine capable, on a good day with a following wind, of developing 40 BHP, from a 903cc power unit (I use the word 'power' here in its loosest sense.)

This then, was the source of the noise.

Over the next five kilometres or so, the Fiat drew level, which enabled us to study the occupants in great detail. Father was driving in a posture reminiscent of a man who thinks, if he were to let go of the steering wheel, he would plunge down a lift-shaft; Mother was close enough for us to see the tasteful highlights in her hair and the fact that she favoured lacy undergarments. The rear of the vehicle was occupied by Grandma, dressed in funeral black, and three small children. She seemed to be carrying on a one-sided conversation with the people in front, as no one responded as far as we could see. In the meantime, the children were holding some sort of wrestling match, albeit a very cramped one, due to the fact that Grandma was of what might be termed 'ample proportions.'

You might find it strange that we could identify the family in so much detail, but you have to remember we were now both travelling at virtually the same speed. As they remained in position, it became apparent that a long line of vehicles was beginning to form behind our new-found neighbours. Horns were blaring, headlights were flashing and cars were starting to weave in and out of both lanes. All to no avail, it was as if our driver was oblivious to everything other than a pressing need to overtake us. By now, as we had covered another three or four kilometres, the Fiat's engine was screaming and the whole car had started to shudder in the manner of someone having drunk the wrong medicine. It made no difference; the driver gripped the wheel, crouched even lower and other than an occasional glance at us, remained oblivious to the madness behind.

As we continued southwards, I asked my wife what the hell he thought he was doing and she came up with the only explanation that made any sense.

"Do you remember," she said, "When we came out of the filling station some time back, you overtook a number of vehicles to get away from the congestion?"

"Yes," I said, "But what's that got to do with this lot?"

"Well," she replied, "Our friend at the side was one of the cars you flashed past; I remember because I wondered what a toy car like that was doing on the Autostrade."

Glancing across once again, I could see that by now, even the children had stopped fighting as slowly and inexorably, he began to move past. My dilemma, as far as I could see, was whether I should slow down or not.

On the one hand I was doing nothing wrong, but on the other, if we didn't part soon we would still be leading a packed mass of vehicles when we reached the outskirts of Rome. So, surreptitiously, I eased off the accelerator and finally our friend managed to get past then, with what I took to be a triumphant manoeuvre, he turned sharply to the right immediately in front of my bonnet.

This was now the signal for a sort of Monza GP to take place, as a long line of his frustrated countrymen flashed past, accompanied by a fresh burst on horns and lights—which I could only pray were not directed at me.

In a vague hope that I might understand the guy's thinking, I related the tale to Paulo one day and asked why he'd shown such determination to overtake, even to the extent that blowing up his engine was a real possibility.

He said, "Ah, Brian, you see, the problem is this; the driver had his family with him and you having overtaken him made him look less macho in their eyes. It was worse because you were a foreigner and the Brits are not supposed to be demonstrative like we Italians. So, to preserve his manliness in front of the family, he'd no option but to prove to them that he could speed past you."

"Speed past?" I said, "Paulo, the guy's car was flat out; he couldn't wring another ounce of power out of his engine, while mine still had the capability to double my speed."

"Oh yes, but none of that matters when you have to prove something. The irony for you is that had he been alone, he probably wouldn't have bothered. By the way, what colour was the Cinquecento?"

"Red."

"Ah yes; that explains a lot—in his mind he was driving a Ferrari."

Paolo offered this explanation as though it was the most logical thing in the world and I have to say it seemed to make sense until that is, I remembered the fear on Grandma's face.

Then, as if that example of lunacy wasn't enough to engender masculine demoralisation in us Anglo-Saxons, you should have seen the effect Gianni had on the female population of Kazakhstan. At the risk of re-awakening old wounds, let me set the scene.

We first noticed the phenomenon during meal times. Now remember, at the time, the project was being run by the Italians and, as is their way with clothes, so it was with food. Although the canteen was located in a single-storey wooden building, the layout and organisation was extremely civilised.

As you entered (having showered first, obviously,) there was an outer area where you hung your coats and left your brief cases, etc. Then, on entering the canteen proper, there was a small bar on the right where you could partake of a pre-dinner aperitif and small nibbles. This enabled you to chat and unwind before taking your seat at one of the dining tables, which were laid with a crisp white tablecloth, shiny utensils, condiments, napkins, a menu, wine and water glasses and four chairs. As was the custom, the Italian lads tended to sit together during meals; this wasn't snobbishness, but was simply to allow them to practise their Italian and talk about someone called Berlusconi and the fate of strange sounding football teams.

Then, once we had taken our seats, one of the Kazakh ladies would approach and take your order, including a choice of red or white wine (Italian obviously.)

The ladies were immaculately turned out in black skirts, freshly laundered white blouses, black stockings and shoes with a small heel. (I can't go into more detail as, to tell the truth, I hardly noticed them.) What was very noticeable, however, was that in general, Kazakh women were gorgeous. They had a slight oriental look about them, but with rather more rounded eyes, they had jet-black hair and carried themselves in a manner which would have driven Kate Moss mad with rage and jealousy (whoever she is.) I don't want you to get carried away with the thought that everything about them was perfect—obviously none were in the same league as Sophia Loren.

So, the scene is set, we have nibbled, taken our seats, the ladies are busy serving wine, when Steve, one of the guys sitting with us, who was on permanent contract, looked around and said, "Just watch, any minute now Gianni will come through the door and the women will go to pieces."

I said, "Hang on Steve; are we talking about the same Gianni? He's smaller than Paulo, sports a moustache in the manner of Douglas Fairbanks and looks a bit like Joe Pesci, but without the psychotic tendencies."

"I know," said Steve, "Gianni's a lovely guy, he's always bright and cheerful and I agree, it's difficult to understand, but I've been watching this reaction for a while now and it's uncanny just what an affect he has, without seeming to notice it himself."

I did begin to wonder whether Steve was in the grip of some jealous emotion and was imagining the whole thing, when the door opened and Gianni arrived. The change was immediate and dramatic.

As one, the ladies turned towards our hero, stopped serving, pouring wine, taking orders, clearing plates or filling nibbles dishes. As one, they moved towards him and almost in unison said "Ciao Gianni," with a Kazakh accent. They smiled, fussed around him, tried to hold his attention with various Italian phrases, offered him his favourite aperitif (obviously committed to memory previously) and at least four of them ushered him gently to a seat at one of the Italian tables.

We were spellbound. "See, I told you," said Steve, "I don't know what it is, but if you could bottle what Gianni has, you could sell it for a thousand pounds. Not only does it happen in the canteen, but it's just the same in the sodding office. As soon as Gianni comes in, there's a rush to help him, his telexes always get sent first and any stationery that you've been told is out of stock, will miraculously appear out of one of the secretary's cupboards. I'm convinced they all save bits and pieces of stuff just in case he needs anything."

I thought I could sense a hint of jealousy creeping in, when Steve said, "You know, if it had been anyone else, I think I'd have hit him by now, but you just can't hate Gianni, he's such a nice guy. The thing that really gets to me is the fact that he isn't the least big headed and never acts like he's 'God's gift to women,' he just seems to accept the adulation as perfectly natural, the lucky bastard."

And then, the whole civilised edifice of meal taking fell apart. I had been on holiday and on my return was looking forward to an aperitif, some nibbles, a glass of wine and meeting old friends when, on arriving at the canteen, I found it to be boarded up and in darkness. Thinking for a moment that I was in the wrong camp, I stared around in some confusion. Wondering where the hell the canteen had gone and should I have brought sandwiches. Fortunately, I spotted Paolo and asked him what had happened. He stared wistfully into the distance for a minute and said, "Ah, Brian, while you were away we had a high level visit from the Managing Director of our British partner. Anyway things seemed to be going well and he and his entourage were enjoying a midday meal in the canteen when we all started to drift in for our lunch. The realisation that we shared the same facilities as he was enjoying seemed to nonplus him and he asked our manager if this was the norm. Mario confirmed that indeed this was the case and that we operated on a democratic basis. Anyway, nothing more was said and after a day or two of poking about, he made a presentation, moaned about progress and escalating costs and expressed the belief that his company could run things much better. Then, after these encouraging comments, he shot off back to the UK.

Sadly, a few days later, our Operations Director received a letter from the Managing Director in which he stated that the availability of alcohol within the confines of the project was contrary to their policy. Apparently, this awful document stated that the consumption of alcohol on their premises was forbidden. He would be grateful, therefore, if the project would withdraw all such beverages forthwith."

I stared at Paulo and for a minute I felt a terrible sense of shame and embarrassment. I said, "But Paulo, there's never been any problem with the system we had; why spoil everything for the sake of their pathetic regulations?"

He gave me one of those sad looks, generally reserved for someone who has failed to grasp the obvious and said, "The problem is, he doesn't trust his own countrymen; he realises that given half a chance many Brits become Jekyll and Hyde characters, especially when there's an opportunity to consume free alcoholic drinks. So, in order to ensure his staff behave themselves, we all have to make the sacrifice."

I have to say, he sounded sad rather than critical, but until then, I hadn't fully understood just how we, as a race, are regarded by other European countries.

So, being redirected to the 'new' canteen I entered the all too familiar world of the 'greasy spoon,' there were the usual trestle tables with chipped melamine tops, an absence of white linen, nibbles or aperitifs. Condiments were now provided in the familiar shape of HP and Heinz bottles and even more regrettably, the lovely ladies had disappeared. The new alcohol-free regime required you to grab a tray, queue at a hatch and be served by having your food dropped carefully on your plate from a height of about eighteen inches. Similar in many ways to a scene from *MASH*, where service was also of the basic kind. For a number of weeks, I still couldn't shake off the feeling that my fellow Italians, Americans, Russians, Kazakhs and Spaniards knew all too well that this reduction in living standards was our fault. I think its called being sensitive to the feelings of others—on the other hand, it could just have been paranoia.

So, having accepted the fact that some things would never be the same, life resumed much as before, Paulo and Gianni didn't blame me for the cultural changes and I was invited to take 'chai' as usual. I was, by now, used to bumping into Mr Vancella at the chai station, during which he took a gentle delight in reminding me that, as a race, the Italians cared very much about image, culture, beauty, art, architecture, food, design, education and the Ferrari. I did at times try a rapid riposte citing, Big Ben, Stonehenge, Liverpool's Cathedrals, the Forth Road Bridge and the Mini (In the heat of the debate I forgot that it was designed by a man called Issigonis.) But surprisingly, he remained singularly unimpressed.

Then one morning just as we had gathered as usual, Mr Vancella said, "Eh, Brian, let me show you something." And then, having spoken to the chai lady in rapid Russian, he turned to me and smiled — a la Paul Sorvino again in 'Goodfellas.' Trying to smile back, but still somewhat puzzled, I began to hear a hissing sound followed by the most wonderful aroma of coffee wafting out of the hatch. The hissing stopped and the chai lady handed him a small white cup on a small white saucer, whilst at the same time passing me a polystyrene cup with the usual tea bag lying dormant in the bottom where, fortunately, from the point of view of retrieval, it was still attached to a piece of string,

Mr Vancella's smile became even broader, as he turned to me and said, "Eh Brian, here we are a thousand miles away from civilised Europe and look what we Italians have managed to obtain—a genuine

Espresso machine, fresh ground coffee and the proper cups to drink out of. Is called style—you agree, no?"

It was a case of the sunglasses all over again, but being a coward and hoping to enjoy the fruits of his endeavours, I smiled weakly and agreed that it was indeed—style.

One more word about style before we move on. As winter drew close, I realised that style wasn't the sole province of Italy. This, as I was about to find out, was now greatly influenced by the weather.

4. Officialdom — You Just Need To Be Patient

As a seasoned traveller, I had, by now, become resigned to the Kazakh authorities' little ways with passport examination involving cross-checking, suspicious looks, pursed lips, ultra-violet light, visa review and second opinions. All you did to preserve your sanity, was to go into a sort of mental shutdown, until finally you were released into either the aircraft or the tender care of the bus driver.

Sadly, however, there was one travel experience during the course of which stoicism wasn't enough and it ended up with the Italians causing a riot. We were now in the middle of a fairly severe winter and in order to be on time for the plane home, we had to board the bus at four am. This gave the driver time to negotiate a road liberally sprinkled with snow, ice and potholes and still arrive at the airport by six am. This, in turn, gave officialdom just enough time (four hours) to examine our passports several times, before the plane took off at ten am.

However, things started to go wrong as soon as we pulled in the front of the transit building. We woke up, shook ourselves and prepared to dismount, when a big-hatted man arrived at the door and speaking in rapid Russian, made it clear to the driver that we were to stay put, which, to put it mildly, caused us some disquiet. However, simply by threatening the driver with physical harm, we ascertained that the incoming aircraft was delayed by snow and, as long as this was the case, the Authorities believed there was no need for us to disembark.

This fine example of logical thinking neglected one simple fact —it was about minus twenty degrees outside and, as the engine had been switched off, the bus began to take on some of the less endearing attributes of a fridge. Realising that protest was futile, we fell back into our seats, wrapped our coats around us and began to doze or read books. Within a few minutes the windows had frozen over and there were increasing requests for the driver to 'turn the bloody engine on'—it was now seven am.

By nine am, we were beginning to get restless, there were no signs of the big hat brigade and despite numerous window scraping, the scene outside remained very much as before—an empty runway, flurries of snow, locked doors and the odd bird of prey staring back at us. By ten am, a sort of lethargic silence had descended on the bus, when there was a bang on the door. The banger turned out to be our interpreter, who was ensconced in one of the Toyota Land Cruisers that had accompanied us to pick up senior management off the incoming flight. Apparently, he'd been on the radio to our people back at base and the good news was —the plane was expected to land at mid-day.

Cheered by the news and safe in the knowledge that our hosts would need at least two hours to check passports, we stood up, waited, shuffled about, sat down, scraped again, peered hopefully at the locked door and nothing happened. Except, that is, it became steadily colder and we became more miserable. By now it was twelve o'clock and not only were we in a slough of despond, but the realisation began to dawn that we hadn't eaten since seven pm the night before and despite having nothing to drink, we needed a pee. Our interpreter was persuaded to approach the locked door and attract the attention of the hat men. He must have been successful because, after protracted negotiations, we were shepherded off the bus and led into the real terminal building.

This turned out to be a cross between a mausoleum and somebody's misguided idea of an ancient Greek temple. There was marble everywhere, on the floor, the walls, on giant columns, facing the check-in desks and up and down the stairs. Several of the world's biggest chandeliers hung from the roof and bathed the whole massive expanse in a sort of fifty watt glow. There were also two other significant features; the place was completely deserted and it was freezing cold. Remaining under close supervision in case we made a run for the frozen wastes outside, we were shepherded to the toilets. Access to the facilities was via another grand staircase into the basement. As we ventured downwards, it became increasingly obvious that we were at least heading in the right direction, as a most awful smell became more intense with every step downward. Some of the more sensitive members of our party gave up halfway down but those with a more urgent agenda proceeded gamely into the depths. By now the smell was so intense it started to make your eyes water and you were faced with another miserable decision, which was an overwhelming urge not to breathe. Sadly, the only way to achieve this was to take a deep breath, nip smartly down the stairs, find a urinal, take a much needed pee and dash back into the relatively fresh air. The only drawback to this strategy was in taking the deep breath. If you remembered to breathe in through your mouth, it wasn't so bad. If, however, you forgot and sucked in a great lungful through your nose, your entire olfactory system went into lock-down and your eyes watered to such an extent that you couldn't see the stairs.

By now it was two o'clock and we were starving. Fortunately, our interpreter had been in touch with base once again and a vehicle had arrived stocked with an assortment of filled buns. When I say assortment, I mean there was a choice between ham or cheese, but nonetheless welcome for all that. We were once again shepherded into the terminal and this time led upstairs into a kind of marble ante-room and there, laid out before us were the trays of buns and two giant Samovars dispensing chai. Interestingly, no one said anything fatuous like, 'I don't like ham' and the whole lot was demolished in about ten seconds. Having scraped up any remaining crumbs and cadged a second polystyrene cup of chai, we were ushered back into the bus. Then, with partly filled stomachs and after awakening from a lengthy doze, we found it was five o'clock and beginning to go dark. Fortunately, just as the need for another pee was becoming essential, word came through that the plane had taken off from London and was en route. As we were now frozen, weary, hungry, fed-up and past caring, the news was greeted with deafening silence. Until, that is, the big hat brigade appeared and with loving gestures, indicated we should grab our luggage and make our way to the transit area. Forgetting the need to pee, we queued up outside and slowly shuffled forward so that our bags could be examined before we were ushered into the passport check area and then finally, we arrived upstairs. This rapid progress meant that the lucky first half dozen could occupy the only available benches, while the rest of us were left standing in small groups, making no attempt at conversation. One guy, obviously not believing the impending arrival information, went to a window and drew back the curtain in a vain attempt to see if anything had landed on the runway. This act of deliberate provocation against the Republic had an effect similar to that of those poor East Germans who were seen trying to scale the Berlin Wall. As one, several of our minders arrived at the scene of the crime, pulled him away from the window, re-drew the curtain and made it very clear there was to be no illicit peeping.

Happily, in the stunned silence that followed, we heard the sound of an approaching plane and realised we would soon be on our way, with a nice in-flight meal to look forward to. Pretty soon, we could hear our incoming colleagues being processed on the ground floor, although at no time were we allowed to fraternise. It was now about seven p.m. and most unusually, our pilot and co-pilot appeared in the room and, with the help of our interpreter, began to have a heated discussion with big hat brigade.

Then, just as suddenly, the debate stopped and our interpreter gave us the good news. There was a suspicion that contraband (unspecified) was being smuggled onto the plane, therefore, we were to retrieve our baggage and place it on the floor so that the officials could make their way among us, examine the contents and no doubt, in their minds, pounce on the smuggler and have him summarily executed. There comes a moment when, having left the camp some sixteen hours earlier and in that time travelled absolutely bloody nowhere; this latest example of *entente cordiale* brings on a silent, seething feeling of utter frustration.

However, recognising that protest was futile, we squatted by our bags to await interrogation. Mine arrived in the form of a female big hat who, with brief gestures, indicated I should empty the contents on the floor. She raked through various articles, shaving gear, books and some video tapes when, wrapped in a pair of (clean) underpants, she came across one of those Russian dolls which fit inside one another. I had bought it at the local market for my eldest granddaughter, thinking it would be nice for her to have the genuine article. My interrogator, with what I thought was a great deal of unnecessary caution, lifted it out and indicated I should undo the doll. I stared at her in what I hoped was incomprehension; surely she didn't think I'd stashed the plans for a new Baikonor space rocket inside — did she?

She obviously did, and so I undid the six dolls, until they were neatly spaced along the floor in order of diminishing stature. At which point, she stared at the display for a minute, pronounced herself satisfied that I wasn't a spy and moved onto the next poor sod. I then flung everything back into my bag and returned it to the baggage chute. Finally, having found no contraband, illicit plans, bits of Mig fighters or drugs, we were instructed to board the plane.

And then, by some miracle, we were airborne. Heaving a collective sigh of relief, we settled down to a meal and started to talk to one another again. Such was the feeling of euphoria that Jim and I started to debate the relative merits Peter Mandelson and Jeffery Archer; Jim said he felt that Mandelson had a lot to offer, but couldn't remember what it was. Just as we had exhausted this stimulating topic and were dozing nicely, we noticed the stewardess in conversation with our Production Manager, who then made his way onto the flight deck. After a couple of minutes, he emerged to give us the following news:

"Sorry lads, but due to the number of delays encountered today, the

Pilots will be 'out of hours' before we reach London. The plan, therefore, is to divert to Budapest, land at about ten o'clock, find accommodation for the night and fly on to our destinations in the morning."

I guess it was a measure of our mental state that hardly anyone spoke; there were no protests, voices raised in anger or futile fist shaking—we just sort of sagged back and stared into space.

But why, I hear you ask, are we heading for Budapest? The answer is twofold; the first is to do with the Russians. The most direct route from Uralsk to London takes you across the environs of Moscow but obviously, bearing in mind the history of east-west relations, permission to do this was refused and, as we didn't fancy being shot down, we took another rather less direct route. This involved a dip southward on a flight path which took us over the harmless southern tip of Russia, the Ukraine, Romania, Hungary, Austria, Germany, Switzerland and onto London. Now, as our charter flight was contracted to Malev, the Hungarian airline and we would be flying over Hungary, the choice of Budapest seemed logical—miserable, disappointing, annoying and frustrating—but logical.

We landed at Budapest Airport at about ten thirty and were met by coaches, which deposited us in several hotels across the city. We checked in and were instructed to be ready to depart in the morning at six o'clock —oh good!

As there was no chance of a meal, Jim and I pushed forward in a most un-British fashion and grabbed the key to a twin bedded room. Then, wiping away any stray tears, our brave soldiers were asleep in about ten milliseconds (it could have been fifteen, but we settled for ten.) Then, with only a brief pause, we were up at five thirty, swallowed a bun and a cup of coffee, piled onto the coach and set off to the airport. On arrival at the terminal, we were directed to a check-in desk and as we approached, it became obvious that something was seriously wrong. For a start, all the Brits and Americans were standing in groups some distance from the counter, and having joined one such group, we became aware of a terrible din coming from the vicinity of the counter. Closer inspection revealed an awful sight; the Italian lads were going berserk—and I do mean berserk. They were crushed against the counter, some were halfway across the top, others were trying to rip the access hatch off its hinges, fists were being waved, they were yelling at one another and the din was increasing by the minute. Their behaviour was reminiscent of the Coliseum where an irate crowd, being unimpressed by a gladiator, decides he should be sacrificed. The enigma was that, normally, the Italians were unfailingly peaceful and polite. They didn't arrive at the airport clutching a 'carry-out' of six cans of Newcastle Tennents dark brewed wotsisname, they seldom drank anything other than the odd glass of wine and several espressos and they certainly never raised their voices. In fact, unless you looked carefully, you wouldn't know they were there.

However, on this particular morning all hell had broken loose and the recipient was an increasingly nervous lady in a Malev uniform, who could just be seen cowering behind the counter, whilst trying desperately to grab at a telephone on the wall.

This was so out of character, that I needed to know what was going on, and spotting Gianni in the crowd, I asked him what had upset his countrymen.

"Eh, Brian, is a tragedy, is not right, is more than flesh and blood can stand."

"Gosh, Gianni, has one of the lads been sacked, is that the problem?"

"Sacked, sacked, is not sacked, is worse than sacked, is the Malev people who should be sacked, I tell you, is terrible what they do."

"Yes, but Gianni, what is it they've done?"

"I tell you what they've done, they've announced the new Flight Plan and tell us that we are to fly to London before travelling back to Milano, that's what they've done, I tell you we won't stand for it. In Budapest, we are close to Italia and will fly over Milano en route to London, is crazy, they should take us to Milano first."

And with that final emotional outburst, Gianni left me in order to carry on the good fight for Italian justice.

I have to say it hadn't occurred to me until then, that there was indeed a considerable degree of unfairness in the flight proposal, particularly when you consider the delays we had suffered so far. If, however, you take a look at your Bumper Atlas of the World, you begin understand why the Italians had decided to riot. The route from Budapest to London takes a straight line, crossing a tiny country called Slovenia and then on to Italy. What's even more galling from their point of view is, as Gianni pointed out, you also cross over Milan on the way.

And then, just as we were beginning to get really worried that Airport Security would step in and we would all be arrested, a silence descended, the lads climbed down off the counter, fists were unclenched, threats were rescinded and the lady reappeared.

Apparently, Malev had seen the force of the argument; either that, or they were terrified of losing the contract, and a revised schedule was hurriedly proposed. This confirmed that the plane would land at Milan's Malpensa airport before disgorging the rest of us at Stanstead. I managed to collar Gianni and congratulated him on a sensible victory.

"Eh, Brian, we are so ashamed of our behaviour, but it had to be done. We couldn't just fly over our homes without a protest, but is not in our nature to make such a terrible noise. I hope you will forgive us."

I stared at him and said, "Gianni, I've seen Brits make more fuss at a football match when the caterer ran out of pies at half time."

He said, "Ah yes Brian, but we Italians love melodrama, that's why we are so good at opera."

I nodded in agreement and although he said it so nicely, I hadn't a clue what he meant.

Finally, having disgorged our European friends in Milan and flown over the Alps on a beautiful clear day, we arrived at Stanstead at twelve o'clock, which meant I had only another five hours to wait for my flight to Aberdeen. I think it's called the glamour of international travel, although I had a different name in mind when finally I arrived home some thirty-nine hours after starting out.

Looking back, now the pain and misery has subsided, I suppose it's a good job global warming hadn't started and we didn't have to count our carbon trees or plant a footprint when we arrived home.

5. I Blame John le Carre

My latest case of paranoia started when I received a call from Paulo mid way through my home leave. Apparently, they had arranged a number of important meetings with prospective power generation contractors and, as I was instrumental in developing the technical work scope, could I please attend.

The problem was timing, as unfortunately, the request didn't coincide with the fortnightly charter flight. However, being in charge of everything, Paulo had made arrangements for me to travel by various scheduled flights to the nearest airport and then to be picked up by car for the remainder of the journey. He also informed me I was to be given VIP status and would be provided with a Travel Guide whilst en route. Fame at last and a taste of the life as lived by film stars and David Beckham. Obviously, and I should have known better, this flight of fantasy turned out to be wrong in just about every way.

Although I have to say it started off in grand style, travelling club class on a British Airways flight from Heathrow to Moscow's Sheremetyevo Airport, I arrived refreshed and replete at eleven thirty am. However, on entering the concourse, it began to dawn on me that I was now in Russia, with no onward tickets, no idea where to go next and conscious that being restricted to saying 'chai puzhalsta' wasn't going to be an awful lot of use, especially if I didn't want a cup of tea. But, being a seasoned traveller, I managed to retrieve by bag by the simple expedient of following everyone else, after which I stood at the end of the carousel looking lost — which I was.

Just then I noticed a chap coming my way, who bore an uncanny resemblance to Oskar Homolka when he played KGB Colonel Stok in 'Funeral in Berlin.' Oskar was famous for playing sinister parts and from where I stood, this chap looked equally sinister. I tried, rather nervously, to ignore him but, as he came closer, he suddenly brought his arm from behind his back and flashed a piece of white cardboard in my direction. Having been convinced that I was about to be shot and just about resisting the temptation to dive on the floor, it was a minute or two before I looked again at the card and realised my surname was spelled out in black capitals. The only thing was that the letter 'P' faced the other way, a small point, but one which nevertheless made instant recognition difficult. I now realised that 'Oskar' was to be my guide, so I nodded, waved and gave a sort of half smile. At this display of overt gratitude, he said 'passport' and held out his hand.

I thought, "What if it's a trap, what if he runs off with it, how far away is the Lubyanka from here?" But then sanity returned and I handed over my passport. Gesturing that I was to follow, he marched off, passed the queue for entry control and took me into an office. Once there, my passport was examined, I was closely scrutinised and a stamp was added to one of the empty pages. After which, Oskar gestured again and I was led through a number of corridors until we came to a door which, on opening, revealed a small room decorated in Russian Vogue circa 1945. Another gesture and I was invited to sit down on a huge leather couch, help myself to a selection of drinks consisting of orange juice or tea. He then said, "You wait here," and disappeared out into the corridor. Looking around, I realised I was in the Russian version of a VIP lounge, with the rather unsettling prospect that I was the only occupant. And what did he mean by 'wait here,' where did he think I would go, and when would I get my passport back?

Time passed and eventually, at about four o'clock, Oskar reappeared and continuing in his chatty mode said, "You come." So I came and we ended up outside the concourse where a car was waiting. Gesturing for me to get in the back, Oskar took the front passenger seat and with a nod to the driver, we set of into the gloom of an autumn afternoon in Moscow. Belatedly, I realised we were heading for Domodedovo Airport, which was somewhere on the other side of the City and from where I would take the next exciting leg to my destination.

So, it's going dark, I'm sitting in a black Zil (the car of choice for discerning Soviet Presidents,) being transported to god knows where, by two guys who don't talk to one another, let alone me. And it was about this time that paranoia began to kick in. You see it's all the fault of my favourite authors. Sadly, I've never read any books by Thackeray, Tolstoy, Kafka, Koestler, Hugo, Hardy, Galsworthy, Flaubert, Conrad, Trollope, Socrates, Herodotus or anyone who's won the Booker prize.

No—my reading is of a wholly different genre (whatever that means.) I've read, and still treasure, every spy story written by Len Deighton, including his trilogies—*Game, Set & Match; Hook, Line & Sinker* and *Faith, Hope & Charity*. Then, of course, there's *Tinker, Tailor, Soldier, Spy* and *Smiley's People*, by the master himself—John le Carre. I guess that anyone like me who was influenced by Dennis Wheatley, from an early age, is bound to gravitate towards the murky world of spies and spying sooner or later.

Anyway, be that as it may—as I say, I'm being driven across Moscow in the dusk by two suspicious looking characters; we're passing mile after mile of grim tower blocks, as described in the aforesaid books, I can't read the road signs and I'm trying hard not to think of what happened to Alec Leamas who sets out to pose as a double agent in The Spy Who Came in from the Cold. Will I ever see home again, how can I contact the British Embassy, should I swallow my contract notes, what if I were to leap out of the car and escape in the dark, would I be exchanged for anybody? Fortunately, just at that moment, boredom set in and I dozed off.

I awoke and realised we had arrived at Domodedovo airport. We pulled up in front of the entrance and the pattern was repeated; Oskar leaped out, motioned me to follow and made off through the doors. We bypassed the queue, went into another annex, my passport was scrutinised, stamped and returned to Oskar.

Chatty as ever, he said, "You come," and we ended up in yet another VIP lounge where, motioning for me to sit down, he disappeared once again. Being rather more blasé this time, I risked a glance around and discovered there were two other passengers, both males. One was smoking a cigarette and because he coughed every time he took a drag, he emitted a foul smelling cloud of smoke at some speed. Surreptitiously studying my colleagues, as practised by one of Smiley's undercover agents, I decided they were both Russians. This conclusion lacked a certain credibility as I had no real idea what Russians looked like; still, it whiled away the time, but I couldn't help wondering whether they had been put there on purpose to watch me.

Fortunately, the next two hours passed without incident, food, drink, conversation or passport, until the door opened and Oskar reappeared. By now I was used to the routine, he said, "Come," I came, and off we went, a silent duo negotiating corridors and Customs until we arrived at the check-in desk. At this point, Oskar handed me my flight ticket and thank goodness, my passport and I realised his job was done. Thinking back on the day, I realised I'd been looked after very well, I'd met no snags, bureaucratic nightmares or uncalled for delays.

Suddenly and far too late, I warmed to Oskar and realising he might think me to be an ill-mannered swine; I tapped him on the shoulder and said, 'Bal'shoye Spasiba,' which I think (hoped) meant 'Thank you very much.' On hearing my pathetic attempt to speak Russian, his face lit up, a number of gold fillings were flashed in my direction and he replied, "Pazhalooyasta," which I knew meant, "You're welcome." So we parted and all of a sudden he didn't look at all like Oskar Homolka, but more like a nice, middle aged uncle.

And then it was eight o'clock and time to board the Tupolev to Orenburg, a town close to the border with Kazakhstan. Still in VIP mode, I was ushered to my seat by one of the cabin crew before the ordinary passengers were allowed to embark. And rightly so I thought. To say the plane then filled up would be an understatement; it was packed to the gills, as they say. The major challenge turned out to be just how much luggage could be stuffed, forced, manhandled, crushed, jammed and pressed into the overhead lockers. However, as is the way with cabin staff everywhere, the locker doors were forced shut, a safety briefing was given and the seat belt sign lit up.

I say safety briefing, but in my case, there were two fairly crucial drawbacks to its effectiveness. One was the fact that it was given in Russian with minimal demonstration; and the other was the fact that the pilot decided to try and achieve maximum revs from the engines at the same time. I tried to pretend I didn't care, which by now was largely true, as I was completely knackered. So, as we taxied to the end of the runway ready for take-off, I shut my eyes and started a blissful doze. I was vaguely aware of the engines being revved against the brakes when there was a series of sharp bangs. I was instantly awake, this is it, it's just as I feared—the terrorists are on board and they're shooting to gain attention, I knew coming to Russia was a mistake; I'm too old for this sort of thing. Then suddenly we were airborne and on glancing round I could see no sign of masked gunmen, hostages or demands to be taken to the Seychelles.

What I did become aware of was there was luggage everywhere; it was in the aisle, on the floor, across the seats and on top of the passengers. As the cabin staff fought their way along the aisle, it became apparent where the source of the gunshots had come from, as most of the overhead locker doors were swinging gently in the breeze, so to speak. Apparently, as the plane lurched into the air, accompanied by the most awful engine vibrations, the door catches couldn't stand the strain any longer and had snapped violently open, giving me the distinct impression that numerous Kalashnikovs had opened fire. Once again I vowed never to read any more John le Carre novels, especially if foreign travel is likely.

Meanwhile, luggage was being stuffed back in the lockers, after which the cabin staff arrived with refreshments. I use the word 'refreshment' in its loosest sense, as what I actually received was a polystyrene cup, a tea bag on a string and a splash of relatively hot water from a battered jug. I waited for the sugar and milk to arrive but, as the staff had all disappeared, I realised there wasn't going to be any. So, stirring what was, by now, half a cup of lukewarm, brownish water with my pen, I gulped it down, stuffed the cup into the seat pocket and dozed off, thinking I would never again criticise British Airways.

To my relief there were no more sudden noises and we finally landed at Tsentrainy airport in Orenburg. It was now ten o'clock and everyone on the plane knew exactly where they were going except me. So much so, that within about five minutes, luggage had been retrieved and the place was empty. Empty that is, with the exception of a tired, fed-up idiot standing near the exit, clutching a bag and briefcase and hoping that someone, anyone, would take me by the hand. In the meantime, just to reassure me, the lights began to go out and there was every sign that the airport was closing down. I was now plotting various lingering deaths for Alex if I should I ever see home again, when a friendly Kazakh face appeared. It was Santov, one of our drivers and, apologising for being late, he picked up my bag and we departed just before being locked in. Sadly, he hadn't brought the air-conditioned luxury that was the Land Cruiser. He reckoned that as there was only one passenger, the Lada would do just as well, but by now I was past caring and fell gratefully into the back seat. Seeing me in a state of semi-consciousness, Santov found one of the gears and off we went into the night.

A word about the Lada; for many years under Soviet rule the ubiquitous Lada had been the car of choice for getting about in Kazakhstan. In fact, it was the only car of choice, having been made by a Russian car manufacturer called AvtoVaz The name replaced the original Zhiguli brand, because of phonetic resemblance of Zhiguli to Gigolo, which hampered exports. Though in Sweden, the early models were sold under the name "VAZ" because 'lada' is the Swedish word for barn.

Lada made its name in Western Europe selling a Fiat based car and its many derivatives as an economy vehicle in large quantities during the 1980s. The common Lada sedan/estate, sometimes known as the Classic in the west, was partly based on the 1966 Fiat 124 sedan, and has become one of the most successful cars in history. The keys to its success were: competitive price as an export, simple, DIY friendly mechanics, unpretentious functionality, and lack of competition in its USSR home market. Over 18 million Ladas have been made over the years and being exported worldwide in the 1980s and '90s, the Lada was a big earner of foreign currency for the hard pressed Soviet economy. It was also used in barter arrangements in some countries (the mind boggles!) Over half of Lada production was exported, (the US was the only large market not to have imported Ladas, probably for political reasons and anyway, they were much too small to fit the average American.) The Lada is unique in being the only car brand found on every other continent of the world, including Antarctica. The rugged design of the Lada Classic, built with heavier steel bodywork, was able to cope with the extreme Siberian climate, poor roads and few service facilities. This meant that high mileages (300,000 miles) were possible under less extreme operating conditions. Because of their very competitive pricing and ease of service, Ladas are common as police cars, taxis, and a range of public service/civil defence vehicles in many parts of Europe, Africa, and the Caribbean.

In March 2008, Renault announced that they were purchasing 25% of Lada's assets, in a one billion dollar deal which will result in new Lada models being developed on existing Russian assembly lines. Lada is the third largest automotive group after General Motors and Toyota (although due to the recent failure of GM to sell any cars, this league-table might have changed). Despite much ridicule these small, old fashioned cars provide cheap and reliable transport for many people around the world, many whom would never have been able to afford a new car otherwise.

I do recall that we motor enthusiasts were equally sniffy about Skoda, until we found they were Volkswagens by another name and they started to produce a lean and mean rally car.

Enough of the transport history, back to the plot. Here I am fast asleep in the back of one of the most popular cars in the world, it's eleven o'clock at night, it's pitch black and we've a four hour journey in front of us. I don't know how long we'd been travelling, when the car stopped and Santov turned to me, uttering that immortal word, "Passport." Apparently, in my stupefied state, I'd forgotten we had to cross the border from Russia into Kazakhstan at some point and this was obviously it. Peering out of the window, I could see no razor wire, floodlights, machine gun towers, armed guards or attack dogs. In fact all I could see was a sort of cottage with one light in the window, a dirt path and an emaciated looking lurcher, sniffing at the wheels. Motioning me to stay put, Santov meandered over to the house and after about ten minutes, during which I remembered this was where spies were exchanged, he reappeared, handed me my passport and off we went. I'm free; I told myself and promptly fell asleep again.

We arrived at the camp at four in the morning, except that it wasn't, as I now had to move my watch forward by four hours. Oh good, it's now eight o'clock, I've missed breakfast, I'm exhausted, my nerves are in tatters and six hours from now, I have to interrogate a bunch of worldly-wise contractors on their proposals for a perfect partnership. I'd no idea that being a VIP was so exciting; no wonder Wayne Rooney looks permanently bewildered.

Later on, I mentioned my paranoid tendencies to Jim, blaming it on my choice of reading material. He said, "If I were you, I'd take a couple of Mills & Boon novels with you next time you travel." He could be right. And then, as they say in all the best novels, two incidents were brought to my attention, which led me to believe I wasn't so paranoid after all.

Paulo and I were chatting about the perennial delays at the airport when he told me what had recently happened to Mr Prandi. Apparently, they had arrived at the airport ready to go home when one of the hat men, on checking Sandro's passport, did the usual wave to one side. He waited, as the rest of the crew filed past, until everyone had gone and as he said later, began to get worried. After some time, a couple of senior hat men approached and in broken English one of them told him to, "Come with us." Still baffled and by now even more worried, he was led out of the airport and taken to an office where a very senior hat man was seated behind a desk with Sandro's passport in front of him. Having alternately stared at the passport and then at Sandro for some minutes, he said, "Passport is out of date."

This rather alarming news took Sandro by surprise and he asked what the problem was. "Problem is passport is out of date, you have no right to enter the Republic of Kazakhstan with illegal papers, is very serious breach of law."

"Can I please see my passport? I don't understand what's happened, as my company looks after this sort of thing."

With some reluctance, the Interrogator passed the offending document across. Sandro examined the dates and said, "Yes, it is out of date, but only by two days. It's obviously an oversight for which I apologise, but you will see that my visa is stamped by your embassy for the correct period," said Sandro, somewhat nervously.

"Is out of date, you have committed a serious crime against my country, you will be detained until we decide what is best to do."

Sandro tried one more time to defuse the situation, which, as he said later, made things worse. "I don't understand, but after all I'm leaving the country, not coming in."

"You will be held until we see what has to be done. Take him away."

By now, Sandro was obviously extremely worried, what was to happen, how could he get in touch with his people, and where were they taking him?

Meanwhile, the outgoing crew had boarded the plane and due mainly to the fact that it wasn't unusual for guys to be delayed, no one had missed Sandro until they were airborne and Paulo realised he wasn't on board.

In the meantime, Sandro was taken to a small hotel some distance from the airport and was there locked in a room. Food was provided, but he was given no further information. Fortunately, behind the scenes, word had been sent from the plane to Mr Vancella at the office. Enquiries were made and they were able to contact Sandro by phone, he assured them he was okay but had no money. Mr Vancella, in his role as Mr Fixit, sent an envelope full of dollars to Sandro, who was then able to offer about two hundred to his captors, by way of an apology. This noble gesture seemed to work as, after about forty-eight hours of incarceration, he was reunited with his passport and escorted back to the camp. I asked Sandro later on how he felt when it happened and he said he couldn't understand why they were making such a fuss. Until, that is, he realised it was money they were after and he'd inadvertently presented them with a golden opportunity to acquire some. He also confessed to being terrified—and why not? The other thing that now began to make sense was that perhaps this was the reason they spent so long examining each passport, in the hope that an anomaly might be discovered. But maybe we were just being cynical.

The second incident involved Jim who, being required to travel routinely from the office to the construction site, used to borrow a Lada from the car pool, which, on this occasion, turned out to be a mistake. As he was driving along the road out of Aksai in a car normally used by the locals, he was stopped by two policemen who demanded to see his papers. Realising that cooperation was probably the best option; he handed over his passport and driving licence. Sadly, these documents appeared to be insufficient to satisfy the local guardians of the law, as they both became increasingly upset, at least as far as Jim was concerned. Realising belatedly that what they really wanted was cash of the American variety; he turned out his pockets to convince them he hadn't got any. Jim told me, "This further effort to convince them they'd got the wrong man caused a good deal of arm waving, finger pointing, and a heated discussion between them, which seemed to be centred on their contention that I was to blame for this unsatisfactory state of affairs.

"After some further minutes of wrangling, one of the policemen spat forcibly on the ground and turned towards their vehicle, whilst the other one stared at me for a while longer, then with a sudden thrust of his arm, returned my passport, but not my driving licence. I tried remonstrating but to no avail, they simply waved me away, and climbing in their own car, shot off down the road."

Worried about the loss of his driving licence and thinking — if I'm ever stopped for speeding on the M6, It'll be no bloody use telling them I can't produce my licence because its been stolen by the police in Kazakhstan - Jim went back to the office.

Realising this was a job for someone with more clout than he, Jim told Mr Vancella the story. Having listened impassively, he gave Jim a half-smile in the best tradition of a 'Godfather' about to bestow a favour and said, "I know someone who can sort this out."

With that, he rose, straightened his cardigan and strode off down the corridor with Jim in tow. He knocked on the door of another office marked Human Resources, which turned out to be occupied by a Kazakh person who was apparently 'twinned' with Mr Vancella. She was a formidable looking lady who bore an uncanny resemblance to Ethel Merman but who, fortunately, spoke excellent English.

She listened to Jim's story and then leapt to her feet saying, "You will come with me please."

Jim then said he felt as though he'd entered a parallel universe, as she marched out of the office, into a Landcruiser and down to the local Police Station. Sweeping, literally, past the reception desk, with Jim trailing in her wake, she entered a briefing room where a number of very startled policemen were gathered. Stopping in the centre, she stared silently at each of the occupants in turn, which, in itself, seemed to have a disconcerting effect on the occupants. Then, having given everyone the baleful eye, she turned to Jim and said, "Point out the two who have taken your licence."

Jim, trying gamely to stand behind her, said, "It's those two over there."

As if fired from a gun, she moved towards the hapless duo and proceeded to carry out the most incredible bollocking Jim said he'd ever seen. Although it was in Russian, there was no need for an interpreter; she lashed into them and under the onslaught, the unfortunate pair visibly wilted, quaked, shuffled and generally wished they were somewhere else. While this tirade was taking place, Jim said he noticed, out of the corner of his eye, a mass exodus of the other occupants, which was carried out in complete silence.

Finally the verbal onslaught stopped, which seemed to be the signal for one of them to open a desk and, still visibly shaking, hand over the licence. This admission of guilt brought on another tirade, accompanied by yet more finger pointing, after which she turned to Jim and said, "My apologies, it won't happen again."

Jim said he thought, "I bet it won't."

As they drove back to the office in silence, he said it was evident she was still in the grip of some strong inner turmoil and was terrified she might blame him for not being as macho as she evidently was.

On returning to the office and after having had a restorative cup of chai, Jim met Mr Vancella in the corridor and relayed to him the incredible scene he had just witnessed.

"What really baffled me," said Jim, "was how she could strike such terror in the police; after all, they didn't work for her and yet it was patently obvious that she had them by the balls, so to speak."

"Ah," said Mr Vancella, "What you have to understand is that in a previous existence, prior to the break-up of the USSR, she was a Major in the KGB, and as such, old habits die hard. As far as the local police are concerned, she is still someone that you don't mess with. You have to admit, her ability to achieve quick results can come in handy at times."

Jim said, "And with that, he gave one of his sinister smiles, you know the one where the mouth turns up slightly, but the eyes bore clean into your brain. Then, having carefully readjusted his cashmere cardigan, he disappeared back into his office."

I think I said something eloquent like 'bloody hell' and Jim said. "I know what you mean. I stood there for a minute trying to decide who, ultimately, was the scariest figure, but after some deliberation, I reckoned it was too close to call."

Not long afterwards, I also came into close contact with our Major (retired.) Paulo and I were deliberating on the relative merits of Sophia Loren and Gina Lollabrigida (no contest as far as I was concerned,) when there was a knock on the door and our friend entered. Nodding briefly to Paolo, she said. "Brian Page?"

"Yes, I'm Brian Page."

"HIV AIDS."

"What?"

"HIV AIDS. We need proof that you don't have the disease."

I was starting to become increasingly nervous and in growing panic tried to reassure both she and Paolo that there'd been some mistake.

"I don't have AIDS, I've been happily married for forty odd years, I have three children, there's never been any question regarding my preference for the female of the species, anyone will vouch for my loyalty, besides I missed out entirely on the swinging sixties. Oh no, I think you've been given inaccurate information."

And with that outpouring of absolute rubbish, I sagged back against the desk.

Throughout my increasingly high pitched attempts to deny all knowledge of any illicit relationships which might lead to my acquiring a socially unacceptable disease, I noticed that Paolo was staring at the wall, while the Major (retired) was staring at me as though she'd just bumped into a demented halfwit.

"You are not being accused, what the Republic needs is proof that you don't have HIV AIDS, this means that on your next trip you will have to provide documentation from a reputable laboratory that a blood test is shown to be negative."

I said, "Oh," which although lacking in erudition, was about the best I could manage under the circumstances, as all I wanted was for her to stop saying 'HIV AIDS' in such a commanding tone.

Having now believed she'd conveyed a perfectly reasonable message to a panic stricken idiot, she turned to Paolo and said, "Good afternoon Paolo, you will please make sure your colleague complies with my request? Thank you." And with that she left us.

Trying desperately to regain some composure, I said, "Bloody hell, Paolo, now I know just what those policemen felt like when she went to retrieve Jim's driving licence."

"Brian, with respect you don't; with you she was being friendly. Just imagine what it might be like if she discovers you really do have AIDS.

Time for an espresso, I think."

The next totally embarrassing scene was played out in our doctor's surgery.

"Hello Brian, what's wrong with you?"

"Er, there's nothing wrong, it's just that I have to have proof that I don't have HIV AIDS."

"Why, do you think you might have?" I may be wrong, but as he said this, I couldn't help feeling that he was becoming rather more interested than usual.

"No, (going red in the face) but I have to have a certificate to say I don't, or they won't let me back into Kazakhstan."

He stared at me and I thought, "He doesn't believe a word of this. He thinks this is just me trying to lead up to some terrible confession about having become drunk and inadvertently spent time in a foreign house of ill-repute and finding that crucial bits of my anatomy were now dropping off."

You can see that when in the hands of any kind of officialdom, I suffer from an overwrought imagination.

However, after scribbling some notes, he came to my rescue and said, "No problem. I'll have to take a blood sample and send it off to the laboratory in Aberdeen. We should have the results back in a few days."

Unfortunately, there was some sort of delay, which is unusual in the health service, and I ended up at the laboratory on the evening before I was due to fly back. Finally, having rung lots of bells, travelled along numerous corridors and asked several porters where the hell the lab was, a technician found my results and in a fairly loud voice assured both me and several people within earshot that, "You'll be pleased to know Mr Page, you don't have AIDS." The bastard.

6. So this is Winter

I've probably mentioned already that the weather in Kazakhstan was different to that in Knotty Ash. For a start Knotty Ash was famous for its azure blue sky, balmy westerly breezes, dappled sunlight playing on the water, a constantly warm temperature and long scented evenings. Or is that Barbados I'm thinking of? Anyway, I now lived inland from Aberdeen where, if you are really lucky, you can experience all four seasons in one day. Not so in Kazakhstan however, here the weather was reduced to a simple equation — plus and minus forty degrees. So, throughout the summer it was hot, but as the humidity was low, it was dry and, if you weren't careful, tended to burn your skin off. Then, as winter began to take hold, I had a visible early warning that things were about to get serious when the five ladies in the office changed their outer apparel.

I arrived one morning to find, as if by some telepathy, the ladies had all turned up in fur coats and hats. Now don't get me wrong, we're not talking here about coats with a fur collar and cuffs made of some artificial nylon type material. These coats consisted of fur in epic proportions. For a start, they almost touched the floor, they had huge collars, the fur itself was beautifully soft and each garment must have meant a large sacrifice on the part of many animals. I was informed they were made of silver or brown fox or mink and I have never seen a group of women who looked so cosy and yet still so feminine in my life. The piece de resistance, however, was the fact that all five were wearing a matching fur hat. The whole ensemble was a vision of utter luxury as far as my untrained eye was concerned.

I was obviously staring, because Irina, our secretary, said "Brian, do you like our coats?"

"Yes I do, you all look splendid and what's more they look nice and warm."

I realised this wasn't exactly sparkling conversation (as practiced by George Clooney) on my part and I was trying to think of something sophisticated to say, when she said, "I am told that women in the West don't like to wear real fur."

I agreed this was so, saying, "There was some kind of protest in the seventies, led largely by a group of people who, while waiting for global warming to start, decided they didn't like the idea of killing animals for their fur. They picketed a number of fur shops, accused the wearers' of unspeakable cruelty and therefore not fit to live in a civilised society. I think they've now extended their hit list to include leather belts and rabbits, but I'm not sure of the details."

Irina said, "So you're not allowed to kill fox and mink for fur coats?"

"That's right," I said.

I could see the ladies staring at me with growing incomprehension, when Zjanna said, "But Brian, that's what they're for."

I've noticed that on certain occasions, women can say something which has the benefit of unerring logic—and this was one of those times. I found myself unable (and unwilling) to counter her statement and anyway, who was I to criticise the age old customs of a country about which I knew very little? And besides—I still thought they all looked gorgeous. Just the same, every time I admired a coat or hat, I was reminded of the film 'Gorky Park' where Lee Marvin plays a man smuggling mink out of Russia into the USA (so I guess there must have been a secret market for real fur, even in the land of the free.) I also realised the coats were the Kazakh equivalent of a long range weather forecast, predicting severe weather to come and, as far as I was concerned, the ladies beat Michael Fish every time.

And so, as the weeks went by, the temperature dropped steadily from a playful minus twenty to a rather more hairy-chested minus thirty. Prior to this latest dip, it had stopped snowing and the air now became very dry. After a while I became used to moving around in temperatures of about minus thirty, although visits to the construction site brought home the difficulties of working outdoors in such conditions. One thing that did cheer me up however, was the fact that the Italian lads hated the cold far more than I did. I guess it was a fine example of the inherent hardiness of the true Anglo-Saxon when compared to the Latin types. Or, maybe I just lacked their sensitivity.

And then one evening, we were warned that a further drop in temperature was expected but, having become somewhat blasé about minus thirty, I didn't take too much notice. Until, that is, I stepped out of the accommodation to go to the canteen for my evening meal. Bear in mind I was wrapped up in a big insulated coat, gloves, insulated socks, trousers and underwear and a thick woolly hat. However, on stepping out of the door, it seemed at first glance to be colder and crisper underfoot than usual. And then I made a terrible mistake — I breathed in.

The immediate effect was that I thought the end of the world had come. There was a searing pain up my nostrils which travelled from there to my brain; I then coughed, which brought about an involuntary intake of air, this time, through my mouth. Again, there was a sharp pain in every tooth, down my throat and into my lungs. This latest turn of events caused my eyes to water, which also turned out to be a mistake, as the water immediately froze and I couldn't see anything. While all this was happening, it became apparent that I hadn't gone more than a couple of steps and it also became apparent that I couldn't stay where I was if, that is, I didn't want to freeze to death in the next couple of minutes. I dimly recognised it wasn't so much the cold that would kill me as the fact that I was now reluctant to breathe. Thinking quickly, as you do on realising that you would starve to death if you didn't get to the canteen fairly soon, I wrapped my scarf around my mouth and nose and breathing as shallowly as possible, I staggered forth.

Fortunately the canteen was only about a quarter of a mile away and even in that short distance I could feel the cold eating away at my insulated gear, fingers, toes, nose, eyebrows, ears and knee-caps. I thought, 'bloody hell, what kind of a place is this, how long does it go on for, why am I here and will there be lots of hot soup on the menu?'

Having arrived and slowly divested the outer gear, I was just about to order when Paolo appeared at the table.

"Hey, Brian, what do you think? I told you it would get cold."

"Oh very clever Paolo, I can see and feel its bloody cold—incidentally, what's the outside temperature?"

"It's minus forty degrees."

All I could think of was how I could manage to stay in the canteen until Spring arrived.

During the course of the following extremely cold weeks, I found there was another way to defeat the cold, or at least diminish the symptoms. This miracle product was known as vodka, which until then was not a substance I was what you might call 'familiar with.' Like most people, I'd dabbled with the stuff, generally adding copious amounts of coke or orange juice to the mix, in order to defeat the appalling taste and provide some kind of flavour. This experimentation with strange liquors took place during a brief period when I was about nineteen and my mates and I decided that in order to be considered 'men about town' we ought to specialise in cocktails.

This involved us finding a dubious pub in the centre of Liverpool whose claim to fame was that it boasted of a cocktail bar. We would then meet and order the most awful mixtures, which seemed to feature either gin or vodka as a base, into which numerous strange sounding bottles were added and the whole mess topped off with a slice of orange or wilted cucumber. Laughing heartily and marvelling at our sophistication, we imbibed all sorts of ghastly rubbish. Sadly, after about three weeks of such high living, we realised that a pint of Guinness was far superior and, more importantly, was a hell of a lot cheaper. So ended my only foray into the world of 'shaken not stirred,' as portrayed by James Bond—the prat.

Fast forward some forty odd years and I'm once again presented with the strange grainy spirit. We are at another of a series of meetings with potential Kazakh contractors and obviously, in order to demonstrate their appreciation and to show the proper degree of hospitality, both food and vodka are in plentiful supply. Sadly, as far as I was concerned, there were one or two differences to my last attempt at drinking the same spirit. For a start, there was a complete absence of orange juice or coke with which to dilute the stuff and even if there was, it would have been useless, as the drink was served in what are commonly known as 'shot' glasses and, as frugal measurement wasn't our hosts' strong point, there was no room for anything else. Watching our hosts carefully, as you do, we noticed there was no 'namby-pamby' sipping, chatting and sipping; instead a toast was proposed and the contents were hurled to the back of the throat in one fell swoop.

We followed suit and then, trying gamely to continue breathing, stop coughing, prevent our eyes watering and answer technical questions, we slowly recovered and put down our glasses. To our horror, they were promptly filled again, another toast was proposed and the flinging motion repeated. This brought about a round of back-slapping and much laughter from the Kazakh contingent. The call went out for more food and once again the glasses were refilled. Another incomprehensible toast was proposed, the stuff was flung down the throat and slowly we began to feel no pain. There was more laughter and back-slapping and then our host suggested we start the meeting. Somehow, by now, I'd completely forgotten we hadn't actually held the meeting and thought, through the haze: we could go back to the camp and lie down.

The really clever thing was the toast. Once, many years ago, I was invited to a cocktail party, which consisted mainly of standing around in groups and chatting to people with whom you had absolutely nothing in common. Every now and then, the so-called host would appear, ask some damn fool question like, "Have you met so and so?" and then answer his own question by saying, "Oh, but you really must." He would then do nothing about it and shoot off to harass another group, with the same intellectual refrain. At first, I rather foolishly believed it would be made bearable by copious amounts of drink. However, alcoholic beverage as far as mine host was concerned, consisted of white or red wine of the most appalling vintage. So, in order to avoid being poisoned by illicit additives, I learned to nurse the same glass throughout the entire ghastly proceedings. All of which led me to believe I still hadn't experienced the sophistication of cocktail consumption as demonstrated, for instance, by Audrey Hepburn in Breakfast at Tiffany's.

Back to the toast; unfortunately, there is no nursing of drink or taking small sips from your glass if your host proclaims "I drink to your Queen." This requires you to empty your glass in one speedy move. Then, just as you start to relax, the glass is re-filled and the host says, "To our beloved Republic." Again you consume the glassful. This toasting seemed to me to be a cunning way to put the softy Westerners at a disadvantage when it came to detailed negotiations. Our hosts had been brought up on vodka, they never diluted the stuff and it was generally kept in a fridge, so there was no need even for the addition of ice cubes. What was even more demanding, with regard to the unwritten laws of this game, was that we were also expected to propose a toast in reply. The inability to give a proper toast is a terrible social (and business) shortcoming. As we discovered, Kazakhs believe western parties are terribly boring. Parties, in their view, should be filled with food, alcohol, music and dancing. Standing around holding a drink and talking about business is definitely not a party. Unfortunately, the same rules applied to contract negotiations —but possibly without the dancing—thank god.

I was chatting to Jim about the need to become expert at vodka consumption if, that was, we were ever to complete a negotiation to our advantage. He said, "I'd a personal example the other week regarding the anaesthetic effect of vodka on the brain. Harry and I were invited to our secretary's birthday party and so we bought a wee present and arrived at the apartment in good time. It was bloody freezing that evening, probably about minus thirty five degrees or so and when we'd been welcomed by her folks, the usual glass of vodka was pressed into our hands and all in all, it was a great party. Irina's family were very hospitable, there was plenty to eat and, just as you found in your meeting, lots of toasts were proposed both during and in between the dancing. Toasting was endless, there must have been about a dozen to Irina, her mother, her father, her sister, her aunts, uncles, grandparents, us and sundry other guests. Well, by the time it came for us to depart, I could feel nothing, but was still able to walk. We said our goodbyes and ventured out into the freezing night. We were staggering along, saying what a lovely family they were, how they had made us welcome and how gorgeous Irina looked, when Harry stopped and said, 'Where's your coat?'

"I said, 'What?' and he replied, 'Where's your bloody coat? You're not wearing your coat; you'll freeze to death, you daft sod.'

"It then dawned on me that I was stood in the road in my shirt sleeves in minus thirty odd degrees and could feel no pain, so I said, 'Bloody hell Harry, why didn't you tell me? I'll freeze to death any minute. I must have left my coat in the hallway, we'll need to go back before I get hypothermia.'

"Harry said, 'There's not much chance of that, with the vodka you consumed tonight. It'll act like anti-freeze in your blood stream. Besides, if I hadn't noticed, you'd have been back at the camp by now, although I have to admit, you might be a little bit stiff with a tendency to crack if you bent over.'

"I said, 'Oh, very funny Harry, now let's get back and retrieve my coat.'"

Jim commented, on recounting his tale, it wasn't until the following morning that the seriousness of the situation dawned on him and he vowed that the next time he was invited to a party, he would either keep his coat on, or ask whether they'd any beer.

On another occasion, concerning the cold, Paolo and I had just returned from lunch when he said, "Brian, will you look after the office for a couple of hours this afternoon?"

"Yes," I said, "But where will you be if anyone asks?"

"I'm going with Angelika; she is being baptised and I want to be there, while the immersion in the river is taking place."

"Hang on Paolo, did you say the river?"

"Yes, the river."

"Paolo, it's January, it's about minus twenty outside and the river is frozen over; how can you baptise anyone like this?"

"Angelika is a member of the Russian Orthodox Church and on the Feast of the Epiphany, she can renew her vows by being baptised again."

"You mean she'll be in the open air and immersed in the river?"

"Oh yes; the assistants will break a hole in the ice, the participants will undress to a bathing costume and she will have two assistants to hold her arms while the ceremony is performed. They'll lower her into the water while the priest carries out the baptism ceremony. Is it okay for me to leave you for a while?"

"Of course; I hope it all goes well for her."

After about thee hours they both returned and I must say Angelika looked radiant.

"So everything went alright?" I asked.

"Oh yes," said Paolo, "And I joined Angelika in the ceremony and was also baptised."

I stared at him; to volunteer to undress and be lowered into freezing water with the temperature so low—this was true love indeed. Although I could see that Paolo was unsure whether or not I believed him.

And then, just before we finished for the day, I returned to the office and found some black and white prints on my desk, showing Angelika and Paolo standing in the snow in their bathing costumes. As if that wasn't proof enough you could see, in the foreground, a hole cut into the ice in the shape of a crucifix. What's more I still have the pictures. Who was it said Italians can't bear the cold? (Just about everybody I guess—but only if you ignore the love factor.)

In a moment of weakness (later rescinded) the company decided we could have Sundays off and, as there was absolutely nothing else to do, it became a sort of tradition for three of us, Harry, Jim and me, to stroll to the local market in Aksai. The market was housed in a stark two storey building, similar to the architectural monstrosities seen in most UK town centres—but without the graffiti.

Once inside the market, we saw various stalls selling things to wear, play with, decorate, eat and drink from, carry in, wash with and read. There were numerous stalls offering a frightening number of varieties of vodka, from Poland, Russia, Finland and of course, Kazakhstan. However, it was the scene outside the building which drew our attention. This was the fresh meat section and the quality of the display was very much dependant on the type of animal available. For instance, there were trestle tables for some products, while others were restricted to large dishes or buckets placed on the floor. They all had one thing in common; all were filled with what, to us, were unidentifiable chunks of meat. Closer inspection, however, revealed a number of clues as, by way of advertising, various animal heads were displayed next to the butchered offerings. We spotted a sheep, a goat, what looked like a yak and on one stall something that looked suspiciously like the remains of a horse. I guess you could view the whole area as either a carnivore's dream or a vegetarian's nightmare. The meat itself wasn't cut into nice wee chops or steaks; it was rather a case of having the stall owner chop and hack the meat into roughly the desired size—or so we observed with a growing sense of unease, and from a reasonable distance. Funnily enough the same system prevailed during the heat of the summer, but with the addition of flies. I think it was Jim who ventured the theory that, 'It was probably better to eat vegetables you didn't recognise, rather than meat that you did.'

One of the most popular meat dishes was horse and Jim said he had been given it once at a dinner to which he had been invited. He said it tasted meaty, and I said something clever like, "Well there's a surprise." In defence of my sarcasm, he said what he meant was it wasn't tough or gristly, but throughout the meal, he couldn't help thinking it's what cowboys rode and, as horses generally had a name, would come when you called them.

I guess it's another cultural thing and definitely not confined to the East. In fact, once when working in Milan, I was asked if I would like to go to a restaurant which specialised in horse-meat. I politely declined and said I would prefer to go to a sea-food restaurant. But, as my son keeps reminding me, most shellfish are what he calls 'bottom feeders'—whereas horses eat grass.

Having satiated our morbid curiosity regarding meat, we ventured out onto the open area on the top floor, there to be confronted by the delightful sight of a group of small children at play. Remember, the temperature was about minus twenty, the snow lay crisp underfoot, the air was crystal clear and most of the locals were enjoying a day at the market. Enjoyment as far as the children were concerned, involved their participation in a death defying home-made ice slide. In fact, it was the screaming that drew our attention to the source of the noise. Their 'slide' was simply the outside stairs leading from the open area to the ground. As is generally the case, they were designed to go down in several sections, so the first set of steps led down to a landing, the next set turned at one hundred and eighty degrees down to another landing, and so on. Being exposed to the elements, each individual step had filled with snow which had frozen into solid blocks, rendering the stairs far too dangerous to use. Except, that is, by a host of small children who found they had a ready made, steep, dangerous and incredibly slippery ice slide at their disposal.

We watched the carnage in amazement and waited for serious injuries to emerge, but what we'd underestimated was the inherent ability of small children to bounce off hard surfaces. This was helped, to a considerable extent, by the fact that they were all encased in big padded jackets to keep out the cold which acted in a similar way to the protective gear worn by American football players. The game they had devised went as follows:

Without any interference from adults, the children, whose ages ranged from about three to twelve, formed an orderly queue at the top and then, without any warning, they would launch themselves bottom first onto the steps. Being sheet ice, it caused the child to accelerate rapidly downwards, accompanied by shrieks of either fear or delight—or both. Then came the clever part; stopping at the bottom of the flight was accomplished by simply smashing into the wall on the landing. Now, as each child arrived at the wall, another would hurl themselves downwards, crash into the brickwork and, if things were going really well, knock an earlier arrival off its feet. After about five minutes, the landing was full of wee kids, lying in a jumbled heap, screaming with delight as their mates came hurling down, hitting the wall and landing on top of the growing mass of bodies. As those at the bottom were struggling to regain their feet and drag themselves back up the slope, they would be skittled back down again by another carefully aimed body. The noise was incredible; we had never seen so much enjoyment in one place at one time. But perhaps best of all, were the reactions of the parents, who wisely elected not to interfere, mollycoddle, invoke 'elf & safety, remonstrate or try in any way to curtail their death-defying adventures.

Such was the noise that we were soon joined by a couple of our American colleagues, who, like us, had been whiling away their off-duty time in the market. As we watched the children, Mark, one of the Petroleum Engineers, said, "Wow, that looks really cool, I'm going to have a go."

We stared at him in horror, "Mark don't be a bloody fool, you'll kill yourself; besides, it's only little kids who can bounce like that and not get severely injured." We were, however, wasting our time; apparently the need to prove to the world that whatever a Kazakh three year-old can do—well so can a goddamn American—or so we imagined his warped

Genuine fur coats and hats—after all it is minus twenty.

Baptism on the Feast of the Epiphany. That's Paulo on the right giving Angelika a helping hand.

brain was telling him.

Be that as it may, Mark moved to the top of the steps and as soon as his mad intention became clear, the children moved smartly out of the way. What they did do, however, was to stare at him in amazement while at the same time, crowding round to see what they must have thought was a suicide attempt by a foreign idiot. As the crowd fell silent, I think Mark was now beginning to regret his macho stance, but realised it was too late to back out if the pride of the good old US of A was to be retained.

Taking a deep breath, he launched himself onto the frozen stairs and within a milli-second was hurtling downwards. For a very brief period, we are now considering the effect of a mysterious thing called momentum. Consider a super-tanker moving through the water; relatively speaking it's not going very fast, however, due to its enormous weight, it takes about five miles to stop.

In Mark's case, we had a classic example of the opposite distribution of weight and speed; he was now under the influence of gravity, a very low coefficient of friction and a relatively light weight, a combination of which meant that bringing Mark's momentum to a safe stop would require considerable distance, an absence of ice and a gentle braking system. Sadly, he had none of these. What he did have within about two seconds was a brick wall. Now they say that energy can neither be created nor destroyed (well Newton did anyway.) However, in Mark's case, hitting the wall revealed two things, (a) the wall hadn't been destroyed and (b) Mark's body certainly had. As he lay there, the children, erroneously as it turned out, thought that his arrival at the wall, together with a marked reluctance to move, was a signal to join him in the game. As one, about fifteen kids, shrieking with delight, hurled themselves onto the stairs intent on joining in the fun. Regrettably, it was at about this point that Mark, on finding he was still alive, decided to try and stand up. Unfortunately, this gallant attempt to pretend that all was well coincided with the arrival of the airborne kids, who promptly skittled him off his feet and back into the wall.

We were now witnessing a scene similar to those popular but bizarre nature programmes where a group of worker ants, finding an unwary beetle, climb all over the unsuspecting creature and within seconds it disappears from view. As more and more kids launched themselves into space, Mark also began to disappear and for some time he was lost to us. Finally, as the nippers dispersed, he reappeared and still pretending that all was well, discovered the next fatal flaw in the ice-slide system—

Kazakh style. This was the inability of a severely winded adult to clamber back up the icy steps, compared to that of a lightweight child. Whereas the nippers clung to the side wall, and fought their way to the top with considerable slipping and sliding, Mark found that as soon as he clung onto the top of the wall and tried to move upward, his feet decided to adopt a horizontal aspect. The upshot was that he was now clinging onto the wall with gritted teeth as if his life depended on it, while his feet took on lives of their own, the result of which was, he made no upward progress.

By now, quite a crowd had gathered to see what on earth a grown man was doing at the bottom of a set of very slippery steps, making no apparent effort to climb up them. Even the children had stopped their game and were also looking extremely puzzled at his lack of progress. After a minute or two some of the older children started to shout advice but unfortunately, as it was in Kazakh, most of it was lost on Mark. It was just after this latest bout of incoherent advice that his hands gave way and he found himself back down on the landing. We were now faced with yet another problem—one of distinct embarrassment. Not so much on Mark's part, as by now he was past caring about anything. No, it was the rest of us; standing helplessly at the top and glancing round at the crowd, we began to sense they felt we were responsible for spoiling their children's innocent game.

It was time to do something—and quick. I shouted down to Mark, "Get your bloody self out of there, you're spoiling the kids' game, you daft sod." At least that was the gist of the message I was trying to get across. Whatever it was, it didn't sit too well with Mark, who stared up at us and said, "I am bloody well trying to get up! What the hell do you think I'm doing?"

"I don't know what the hell you're doing, but if you don't do something quickly, there's going to be a riot up here."

And then, in desperation Mark said, "Well, I sure as hell can't come up. So I'll just have to go down." And with that, he slithered to the top of the next flight and slid down out of view. For a moment, there was absolute silence and then, the kids, who hadn't understood a word of our exchange, thought that Mark was upping the slide stakes and, to a nipper, they launched themselves down the first flight, crashed into the wall, recovered and disappeared down the stairwell in pursuit of the western madman.

The adults, not quite believing that a grown man could be so stupid, also recovered and we all charged back into the market and plunged down the inside stairs to the ground floor. It was just as though a hundred Rangers supporters had been told that Ronaldo was outside the ground, as to a man (and woman) we surged out into the open air to find that once again Mark was lying at the bottom of the last flight of stairs, buried under a dozen shrieking children. This time, anxious to be away from the awful scene, we helped him to his feet and, holding an arm each, began to move him away. Unfortunately, we failed to understand that, in the eyes of the children, Mark was now some kind of hero. They clung to his legs, jumped on his back, danced around us and, worst of all, made pulling motions for him to repeat the daredevil enterprise all over again. Gently shaking them off and trying gamely to smile, Mark indicated we must get back to the camp and slowly the kids, realising their hero wasn't about to make a return appearance, raced back inside, no doubt to savour the new-found delights of negotiating three flights of death-defying stairs.

Jim said, "I hope you've learned a lesson, you daft sod; at least now you know that little children bounce off walls, whereas big, daft Americans just crash into them."

"All goddamn right," said Mark, "Enough of the lectures already! I feel as though every bone in my body is broken, I just want a hot shower and bed."

"Never mind," said Jim, "Just think, to us you're a sodding idiot, but in the eyes of a six-year-old Kazakh kid, you're a bloody hero."

7. The Railwaymen

Whilst we were busy developing major contracts for such exciting things as power generation, gas compression and chemical injection, we also undertook a number of what might be called social improvements. These were things like building a medical centre, a primary school and improving the electricity and water supply to the town. I remember being amazed when I realised that the electricity supply regularly failed during the winter months. On a number of occasions, during the coldest spells, Marina said, apologetically, that she was a bit late because the supply had failed once more. In an idiot moment I told to her that had it happened in the UK to the extent that they had to put up with, the populace would march on the council offices, threaten the occupants, wave banners, sing 'why are we waiting?' and demand action. At this catalogue of UK style direct action, she stared at me and I should have realised I was guilty of assuming everyone had the same degree of freedom as we had. She simply shrugged and said, "We can't do that in my country." I then learned two more important things; one was the meaning of stoicism and the other was that I was guilty of being an arrogant fool.

And then one day Paolo said we were to develop a contract for the supply and operation of a railway. As a throwaway line this took some beating and I thought I'd better mention the fact that the sum total of my technical know-how regarding railways was restricted to travelling, at the tender age of fifteen, to one of Billy Butlin's holiday camps at Clacton-on-Sea. Sadly, on reaching London, we were required to change trains and having travelled through a strange place called Essex, we found, after about two hours, that the train had stopped at a terminus which turned out to be nowhere near Clacton. Having hopped off the train in some panic, we dashed along the line until we came to a station, when I remembered I'd left my suitcase behind. I really can't go on; it's still just too embarrassing.

Paolo said, "Not to worry, we can find a railway consultant to help out and between us we'll sort it out, besides, it'll make a nice change from gas compressors." I wasn't so sure, but I have to say I was already thinking—it can't be bad, here I am, in deepest Kazakhstan, walking in the footsteps of Isambard Kingdom Brunel.

The line was to be a single-track rail link between Aksai and the production complex some thirty kilometres away. The scope also included the provision of two new stations, with passenger and freight marshalling facilities. We would need signalling systems, manned and unmanned crossings, bridges, power, drainage, ballast, a shunting loop and a link to the existing main line railway at Aksai. The need was somewhat urgent as the main project was gearing up and we estimated that about a thousand workers would need to be transported at the start and finish of each shift, as well as massive amounts of goods and materials. As the scale of this undertaking was revealed, I began to wonder how on earth Brunel had built the Great Western Railway without a computer. In one way, the contract was straightforward, due to the fact that in Kazakhstan, there was only one company capable of carrying out the work. They already ran the national railway system and so had all the necessary manpower and skills. The downside, as far as we were concerned, was the fact that they knew full well they had us over a barrel—as they say in books on contract negotiation.

Suddenly, I was becoming acquainted with the language of Thomas the Tank Engine; there was talk of sidings, marshalling, wagons, signals, passengers, footbridges, freight, points and inevitably, the Dispatcher. I also learned that Russian track gauge was four feet eleven and seven eighths inches, whereas the UK's was four feet eight and a half inches. I don't know why this seemed important at the time unless, that is, we tried to sell them some of our old rolling stock (see—the jargon's creeping in already.)

After some early skirmishes regarding capital expenditure, compensation, penalty payment, percentage retention, confidentiality obligations of the Republic and the Kazakh definition of 'force majeure'—the railway line and associated gubbins was duly built. In fact, the only thing missing was an engine, which had been promised for some time, but for reasons which we never quite understood, had failed to materialise.

Which is why I was quite surprised when, on a fine sunny day, Paolo said, "Brian, we should go and inspect the railway, it is our duty to see that everything is in good order and there are no problems."

I said, naively, "But Paolo, we haven't got an engine. All there is to see is thirty kilometres of shiny track and two stations with no one on them."

"Ah yes, but we can look at the earthworks, track, turnarounds, sleepers points ballast and transmission lines. Besides, I'm fed up being in here and it's a lovely day outside. What do you think?"

Slowly, it began to dawn on me that a 'little trip' was in order and anyway, who was I to quarrel with the man who paid my salary?

So, looking suitably thoughtful I said, "I agree Paolo; a thorough inspection, that's just what's needed."

And so, at about two o'clock on a lovely late spring afternoon we were bowling along out into the tundra in a borrowed Land Cruiser, chatting happily on a matter of major importance regarding the state of the Italian film industry. The road, such as it was, ran parallel to the line and we had travelled about fifteen kilometres without actually having checked anything, when Paolo pulled up beside a level crossing and we clambered out. The view, if that's what it was, could be summed up in a short sentence—a lot of nothing much to see, with a railway line running down the middle. This apparent lack of stimulus seemed to be lost on Paolo however, as he leaned against the side of the vehicle, adjusted his sun-glasses, stared around and said, "Eh Brian, what do you think? Here we are on a lovely day, nobody to bother us, in peaceful surroundings and going about the company's business."

This latter statement was actually somewhat at odds with our efforts so far, but, hey, who was I to quarrel—and it was a very nice day. Sometimes just being where you were at the time was enough, if you see what I mean. But just in case, I made a note that the rails were nice and straight, the ballast was very neatly arranged and the overhead line poles were perfectly upright. As I remarked to Paolo on the way back, "You know, when you think about it, we didn't take long to become railway experts." He agreed, and so, having fooled ourselves once more, we went back to the office and Paolo made us both a well earned espresso.

And then, with brain cells no doubt overly stimulated by an influx of caffeine, I said, "What's next on the agenda?"

Paolo said, "We need to develop and negotiate a contract for a company to run the railway."

"Oh bloody hell," I thought, this means more toasts, more vodka, more translations, more negotiations, more explanations, more late nights and more headaches. Although we were by now reasonably well aware of the pitfalls of negotiating major contracts Kazakh style, it still required a great deal of patience and stamina. Our last marathon session had begun in Italy, when we were putting together a five year contract for the provision and management of power generation and distribution.

At first it was reasonably straightforward; Paolo and I had short listed three potential contractors, all of whom had good track records in Italy. The complication, as far as we were concerned, was the edict from the authorities that any such contract should be in an equal partnership with a Kazakh company. In principle, you couldn't argue with the demand; in practise, it complicated matters to some degree. On the one hand, the Italian generating companies were sophisticated, competent, modern, innovative, competitive and efficient, while the local company, by comparison wasn't. However, recognising the futility of protest, we set to.

As I mentioned earlier, we visited the Italian power plants, asked lots of questions, undertook guided tours, examined documents, records, plant uptime statistics, improvement projects and were taken to a number of lovely restaurants. Although there was little to choose between the companies, we conferred, cross-checked, developed a 'weighting' table, analysed the results, drank more espresso, just missed seeing Sophia Loren and, despite this setback, informed the successful bidder. We then put the company in touch with the Kazakh bidders to enable them to agree protocols, allocation of roles, responsibilities and operating costs.

Having understood that there was only one Kazakh company who could realistically form a viable railway partnership, the scene was set for a joint contractor — project meeting. Our Kazakh friends decided it would be a good idea to hold the negotiations in the headquarters of a bank rather than in our offices, a ploy which puzzled us at first until we were given to understand that a major director of the bank was a close relative of the President (of the country, not the bank) and had more than a passing interest in the railway company. So, the scene was set for a lively debate, even though we realised that our options were somewhat limited. And, just to prove this was probably the case, we (the Italian company and us) were beamed at, congratulated, offered loyal toasts and presented with modified work scopes, revised time-scales and cost estimates. Unfortunately, from the point of view of healthy debate, the aforementioned documents were all in Russian and, as they were no doubt well aware, would need to be translated later. Throughout these proceedings the bank director said nothing to us, drank vodka, smiled a good deal and occasionally conferred with his colleagues in a low voice. During the course of one such clandestine debate, I said to Irinka, our interpreter, "What the hell are they saying?" She said, "They're not speaking Russian; most of what they're saying is in Kazakh and they're

The railway—now, if only we had a train to play with

mainly discussing whether we can be persuaded to accept their changes." I thought, 'It's John le Carre all over again, where the Stasi smile a lot and promise to set you free if you just sign a confession.'

And so the afternoon wore on, more vodka was offered (and by now, reluctantly accepted,) the evening arrived, snacks appeared, more vodka was produced, smiles became more fixed and Irinka showed distinct signs of exhaustion. It was, however, becoming increasingly obvious that if we wanted the railway to operate at all, we were well and truly 'stuffed,' as they say. And so we promised to amend the contract, finalise the terms and conditions and create a successful working partnership between both parties. Irinka duly conveyed the good news to our hosts, we all stood up, hands were shaken, toasts were declared, lifelong promises were made, smiles turned to beams and our backs were slapped.

Settling back into our seats on the way back, we thanked Irinka for her efforts and she said, "It could have been much easier though."

Failing to understand what she meant, I asked her to explain, "Well," she said, "I was on duty at an official reception last week and I noticed that the bank director was speaking perfect English to one of the British Embassy staff. I asked my friend about it and she told me he was educated in America, which is why he spoke English so well."

"But Irinka, why didn't you tell us this at the meeting?"

"Because I have to live here and you don't."

I think it's called a highly developed sense of self preservation—and in one so young, too.

When I returned to the office, I remembered a book to which I occasionally referred when contemplating contractual arrangements. I turned to the page entitled 'An Organisational Strategy for Developing Relationships.' This gave advice on such worthy topics as 'Recognising the consistent need to enhance or, at the minimum, maintain the other party's self-esteem.' Followed by 'Using negotiation as a tool to develop the relationship, not as an autonomous activity.'

So I threw it in the bin.

8. More Sinister Goings-on

We were graced with a visit one day from a number of executive (and non-executive) directors from one of the Partners. I guess they felt it wise to see for themselves what on earth we were spending their money on. So, we polished things, laid on food, arranged for some local entertainment (school children in national costume singing incomprehensible songs—always a winner,) polished our fleet of Landcruisers, re-arranged sleeping quarters, prepared wildly optimistic presentations (with lots of pictures) and prayed that we wouldn't be called on to explain anything technical.

Our honoured guests duly arrived (but not by bus) and after some time, curiosity got the better of me and I asked Paulo who they were.

He said, "Is very interesting Brian, one of the Non-Executive Directors is the lady who used to be the Head of your MI5, what do you think about that?"

My mind raced. Why was she here? Did it have anything to do with my having been in Russia? Will I be recruited? Will she use a code to identify me? How will I know what it is? Are we being watched? Who can I trust? Again, I was cursed by having read 'The Quest for Karla,' where Smiley finally uncovers the double agent. How would Smiley play this? How can I stop living in a dream world?

You may well scoff, but there was no denying we were about to meet someone who had worked in all three branches of the Security Service; counter-espionage, counter-subversion and counter-terrorism. She had visited Russia to negotiate with the KGB and on her return had been promoted to Director-General. This was serious business and quite a change from the usual run of non-executive bods one generally met, most of whom wouldn't know a Third-stage Separator if it fell on them.

It's not for me to betray confidences or name names, so I'll just refer to her as 'Stella'—obviously to afford her some degree of protection, should this book fall into the wrong hands.

A word about Non-Executive Directors. The official version is that they act independently to ensure integrity and the highest standards of corporate governance in order to safeguard the interests of the shareholders. Unofficially, until recently at least, the post was seen as a sinecure for both active (in the passive sense) and retired (in the passive sense) politicians looking to obtain imposing headed notepaper and a free bash at Christmas. Non-executives were generally chosen on the basis of their 'city' expertise, political contacts, networking potential, complicity and club membership. In general, they were seen as the acceptable face of unacceptable practises.

In this case though, we were faced with a totally different scenario. With your average non-executive, there was a mutual recognition that they would stick to asking innocuous questions such as, "Does it get very cold in the winter" and "How do you like working here?" Bill said he was once cornered by one of our retired politicians and asked whether he had any idea how many expats voted Conservative in the last general election.

Overcome by mild curiosity, I asked, "What did you tell him?"

"I told him there was no doubt that just about everyone out here voted Conservative."

"Did he believe you?"

"He must have done, because the thanked me very much and went off muttering about him being right and how he couldn't wait to tell the Party Chairman when he got back. The bloody idiot."

However, in this case, we were in a totally different situation; foolishness of this kind obviously wouldn't work with 'Stella.' Here, we were dealing with a woman who had battled with the problem of advanced encryption and due to her intellectual prowess, the codes had always been cracked the in the end. Not only that, but she was on record as saying that keeping suspects for three months without charge is outrageous to some people but, she added, it may also be essential. The other issue she embraced was the tracking and locating of mobile phone calls. Of terrorists she said, "These people do have to talk to each other and they have to communicate and that makes them vulnerable." What a pity it is that the civil liberties contingent can't grasp essentials as readily as 'Stella.'

One thing was for certain, if 'Stella' asked me a question, I would answer very carefully. I know she may have retired, but as far as I was concerned, she could just be a 'sleeper' (as we security buffs say.) Besides, I've watched every episode of 'Spooks' and I know that MI5 have ways of getting at the truth.

A couple of days later I happened to pass 'Stella' in the corridor and thinking quickly, I gave what I thought was a discreet nod. It must have been so discreet that she didn't notice or, what I thought to be more likely, she felt it was too dangerous to acknowledge.

Realising I could well compromise her position; I decided to keep out of the way until she'd departed.

Ironically, we could have done with her know-how when, on the following day, I bumped into Len, our Camp Boss. He was livid; apparently he'd been waiting for an overdue and increasingly urgent delivery of food for the whole camp. The lorries had finally arrived; having crossed several European borders, with customs seals still intact, and been escorted for the last six miles, by a refurbished Lada estate containing four members of the local police force.

Len, who closely resembled Robbie Coltrane both in stature and accent, then recounted the events leading up to his having suffered a serious rise in blood pressure.

"The lorries had parked-up close to my storage units and the drivers passed me their manifests. Everything was in order, so we went to the back of the first lorry and I cut off the customs seal. Funnily enough, the noise of the snips coincided with the sound of the Lada doors being opened and four sets of footsteps approaching at some speed. In the meantime, one of my Kazakh guys moved forward with the fork-lift and began removing the pallets from inside the lorry. Things were moving along okay and, by now, we had just about emptied the load, when one of the sodding police who'd been silently watching, moved swiftly in front of the forklift and shouted for us to stop."

Len said, "I thought, 'What now?' I couldn't see anything wrong, so I asked my guy, who spoke reasonable English, to find out what the matter was."

"And what was it?" I asked, by now overcome with curiosity.

"Bloody cheese," said Len.

"Cheese?"

"Aye, what they wanted was four blocks of cheese and without further ado; they sliced through the shrink wrap and loaded the blocks into the boot of the Lada."

"Still, I don't suppose a few bits of cheese will make much difference, will it?"

Too late, I realised I'd said the wrong thing.

"Bits of cheese? What the bloody hell are you on about, bits of cheese? These blocks have travelled several thousand miles, they're about a foot long and weigh five kilogrammes each and now, thanks to the thieving sods, I'm still short of Mature Cheddar, Red Leicester and Double

Gloucester."

"But how could they justify nicking so much in one go," I asked.

"Oh, they had the answer off pat; they said the cheese had to be taken to their laboratory for testing. Apparently, it's another of those little-known regulations that says incoming food has to be examined to see if it's fit for human consumption."

I said, "Len, have you seen the stuff they sell in the local market? You can smell the festering cheese stall from thirty yards away. Not only that but on a hot day viewing the stall from a distance is similar to seeing a mirage—the whole lot shimmers. Anyway, if it's for testing, why didn't they just take a sample slice off each end?"

"That's what I asked them and the lying swines said it was necessary to take samples from random parts of the block, they were sorry, they said, but had no option other than to take the whole cheese."

I thought, this was just the thing that 'Stella' would be able to sort out, knowing her past contacts, but then it occurred to me that perhaps this was really a case for our ex-KGB lady, the one who so effectively recovered Jim's passport. And then I thought, sod it, It's none of my business and besides—I can manage without cheese for a week.

I bumped into Len about three days later and asked if he'd recovered from the great cheese heist. He said he had, but was just about to order four extra Land Cruiser tyres, as word had come back that the authorities would need to take samples from the next delivery for testing.

9. Back and Forth

Paulo rang me up at home one day and rather diffidently asked whether I could join him for three weeks at the Project Offices in London. My task (should I choose to accept it) was to assist with the development of some major contracts. In the event, he was right to be diffident, as the three weeks ended up as three years. This new regime meant I had, for the first time in my life, become a commuter, travelling down on the 'red eye' flight on Monday mornings and back in the late afternoon on Fridays. The offices were based in Hammersmith, which was adjacent to a building belonging to L'Oreal, a company famous for the development, manufacture and sale of beauty products catering to every female fantasy. (I shudder to report that they have now extended the range to cater for those men who are unfortunate enough to believe they suffer from fatigued skin.)

As far as we were concerned, they were also famous for the considerable number of nubile young women they employed, the vast majority of whom, on exiting the building, immediately lit up fags. We reckoned this was to relieve the stress of having to dream up scientifically sounding but, as far as the general public were concerned, meaningless product descriptions. They offered numerous miracle sounding potions such as a Collagen Re-Plumper to give 'bouncier looking skin,' or Derma Genesis for 'dewy, plumped up, younger-looking skin.' I guess if you were really clever, you could use both products and end up with skin that was not only plumper, but bounced as well. Then, if all that failed, you could always turn to the ReFinish Micro-Dermabrasion Kit, and scrub it all off. Because—as it said in their advert—you're worth it.

So, for the next three years I stayed on the seventh floor of the Novotel in Hammersmith. It was a massive, fairly soul-less place with some six hundred and thirty rooms but, as far as I was concerned, it had two major advantages. It was literally next door to the office and about two hundred yards away was the Underground station, which could take me into central London and Heathrow, just as long as I didn't mind sharing a rapidly depleting oxygen supply in a carriage with about two hundred other lucky travellers.

As we were pretty busy during the day, it was unusual for me to finish work before six o'clock; which meant that in all of my three years in

London, I didn't get to the Science Museum, the Natural History Museum, the V&A Museum, Greenwich, the Tower of London or Madam Tussauds. I did, however, get to the National Portrait Gallery, which turned out to be full of paintings of people and the Imperial War Museum, which turned out to be a salutary experience and not to be missed. The other thing I discovered, as a means of breaking the monotony, was my ability to get very good single seats to West End Theatres. This enabled me to see a considerable number of excellent plays and events, albeit on a sort of ad-hoc basis. The funny thing was that the chaps in the office, who lived in and around London, were somewhat envious of my theatrical leanings. Apparently, such was the need to join the mad commute in order to get home within two to three hours—they hadn't the will or the strength to come back in again. Sadly, in all of that time, there was only one act which evaded me. Billy Connolly was appearing for two weeks at the Hammersmith Odeon and try as I might, I couldn't get a ticket. This was doubly frustrating as the venue was within walking distance of the hotel and I even resorted to queuing for returns, but sadly, there were none. I did, however, get to see Victoria Wood at the Royal Albert Hall. What a funny, talented lady she is, standing alone on a stage facing an audience of some two thousand people and wowing them with her humour, some of which I laughed a little nervously over, as I reckon she was aiming her comments at the female section of the audience.

The hotel was always busy, due largely to the fact that it catered for what I suppose you would call the 'package' tourist trade. This was made evident by the fact that the first four floors were not available to business people and the open basement area was in many ways similar to that of a major coach depot. Throughout the day, transport belonging to numerous tour operators could be seen disgorging passengers at one end, while at the other, queues could be seen waiting to be picked up and whisked off elsewhere.

For a time, I became fascinated with this hitherto unknown trafficking in human kind and, as an ardent watcher, began to appreciate the sheer scale of the tourist industry in the capital. The regimented holidaymakers fell into two main categories, those from the USA and those from the East—either China or Japan. You could always tell the Japanese from the Chinese, as the Japanese would check in and immediately pour out of the front entrance to begin taking photographs. This compulsion to snap at anything in sight was fascinating, as it has to be said that the photogenic properties of Hammersmith posed no threat to the Grand

Canyon. Then, having exhausted the scenic qualities of the immediate area, they started snapping each other, passers-by, school children, traffic wardens, nuns, bus drivers, taxis, rain, policemen and anyone else who stood still long enough.

By contrast, the Chinese would venture out some time later and stare rather bemusedly at the main road, after which they would chatter a lot and move back inside. I often wondered what they thought—did they perhaps come to the conclusion that well, London's not all its cracked up to be, we've come all this way and there's no dog or snake on the menu? Although there've been times, when delving into a dubious looking curry—I've not been too sure.

The Americans, on the other hand, were generally very old and couldn't wait to get into their rooms and have a kip. After which, they would change into something befitting of a mad octogenarian and venture into the restaurant, ready to sample the delights of mass produced English food.

As a casual, but increasingly fascinated observer of our foreign visitors (well, it was better than re-reading the menu, which hadn't changed for a year) I noticed a couple of fairly common themes regarding the meals taken by the various parties. The first group, generally consisting of Americans, were obviously governed by severe budgetary constraints. This involved them in considerable debate as they stared longingly at the wide choice of food on offer and then being forced into a decision based on the cost of individual dishes. It was quite common to see a line of elderly Americans moving slowly along the service counters, finding a desirable item, stopping to consult the menu, realising it was too expensive and shuffling on to the next dish of goodies. Then, having finally chosen a meal, they would find a table, sit down, devour the contents and begin to hold an in-depth re-evaluation of the selection. Unbelievably, in some cases, this involved the use of a pocket calculator, comparisons with fellow tourists on adjacent tables, close scrutiny of the bill, animated discussion, waitress interrogation, head-shaking, checking of exchange rates and criticism of portion size.

The second group had no such worrisome decisions to make. They were our Chinese friends, who were led to a long line of tables set cunningly out of sight of the normal dining area. Then, having been allocated seats by their minder, a number of waitresses appeared from somewhere in the dark recesses of the restaurant and proceeded to give everyone a bowl of soup. Six minutes later they reappeared, scooped up the bowls and in rapid succession, replaced them with a plate of something or other. This done, the dishes were once again whisked away and the smallest desert I've ever seen was plonked down. The whole thing took less than thirty minutes and was organised on SAS lines.

Occasionally, one or two of the braver members of the group would make a break for freedom and wonder over to the main dining area; soon they could be seen animatedly discussing the real food selection until, that is, they were spotted by their minder who, moving swiftly and with stern gestures, rounded up the escapees.

But what of the Japanese, I hear you ask; well I never saw them at all during dining hours and can only suppose that stopping to eat would radically interfere with the need to take yet more photographs of Hammersmith—this time in darkness.

As time went by I became endlessly fascinated by these arrangements for the continual flow of mass tourism. Coaches would arrive and depart at the strangest hours and just to avoid (or create) confusion, each coach would have the appropriate tour logo displayed on the front window. The tour guides, resplendent in uniforms reminiscent of a Gilbert and Sullivan production, would pin up notices itemising the fun to be had the following day. After which they would retire to a hidden bunker for much needed rest and recuperation.

Studying these itineraries always left me feeling quite tired; some were so onerous they'd have brought Steve Redgrave to his knees. A typical notice might say—'Breakfast at 0730hrs, coach leaves at 0815 stopping at the Tower of London for 40 minutes, Buckingham Palace for 30 minutes, then on to Ann Hathaway's Cottage for lunch. Afternoon trip to Winchester Cathedral for 35 minutes, then on to the London Dungeon for 25 minutes, before returning to the hotel in time for dinner.'

Another fairly common notice which stuck in my mind went roughly as follows:

'Morning call 0600hrs, Breakfast at 0630 hrs, Coach departs for airport at 0715 hrs. Luggage to be left outside room for overnight collection. Note: coach must depart on time, latecomers will be left behind.'

I couldn't help but wonder just how many of the poor souls sat up all night for fear of being trapped in a country where food was still rationed.

It also became my habit when entering the lift on the ground floor, to say hello to our weary friends. They had obviously been the lucky recipients of yet another sightseeing marathon and I was returning from a hard day at the office (would I lie?) They staggered in, leaned on the lift walls, most of them with evident hip, knee or heart problems. There was one guy who, before we set off, shared with me with the news that he'd recently had major heart-by-pass surgery and was supposed to take it easy. Which is why, his wife said, they'd decided to come 'across the pond' to give him a complete rest. I ventured to suggest that the type of holiday to which they were being subjected, was not perhaps what his surgeon would have recommended.

"Too damn right he wouldn't," said the guy. "He only gave me permission to go on a promise that I would take it easy, have a nap in the afternoon and be in bed by eight o'clock. When we booked, nobody said anything about us having to leap on and off a goddamn coach every thirty minutes, race around yet another castle, swallow down some god-awful things called sandwiches, before being thrown around these twisty little things you limeys call roads."

I was beginning to feel sorry I'd opened the conversation and was relieved when we reached his floor and they staggered out. The other thing was, I somehow felt he blamed me for the apparent shortcomings of his package holiday.

However, this little episode paled into insignificance when next I was fortunate to share the lift with two elderly American couples who, once again, had just been released from coach captivity.

I realised something was wrong when, on entering the lift, they sagged back against the sides and made no attempt to press the requisite floor button. As it was evident I was now in a lift with four people in some form of extremis, I waited quietly in the corner, where, despite my size, I don't think they'd noticed me. After a minute or two, the wheezing noises had subsided and the conversation went as follows:

The lady on my left, who was tastefully dressed in some sort of loose pink and blue striped top with canary yellow pants, said, "Oh my, I'm really bushed; I don't think I could walk another step."

Her husband, who sported a Hawaiian shirt and a pair of three-quarter length chequered pants, of the type worn by teen-agers on the beach in Acapulco, which were partially held up by a money belt, said, "Too damn right Edna, I ain't walked so goddamn far since I was in the army. I don't even remember where the hell we've been. We just need to get to the room and lie down before dinner."

The lady on my right who, in some nightmarish moment, had decided that a bright orange shell suit with white trainers would be just the job for visiting stately homes, had until then, been staring straight ahead, whilst taking great gulping intakes of air; she gasped, "Heavens to Betsy, Ah'm just the same, ah cain't hardly lift ma feet of the ground. Ah'm soo tired."

And then, focussing with some difficulty on her compatriots, she uttered the immortal words:

"Say, are you all going on the trip down the Rhine after dinner?"

There was a lengthy silence and then her husband, who sported a pair of golfing trousers and a bright blue windcheater with an eagle having outstretched wings tastefully embroidered on the back, said. "Uh, honey, Ah think you mean the Thames."

However, although he was geographically correct, his pronunciation was not. He pronounced the word phonetically, so instead of saying 'TEMS' he said 'THAMES.' Once again there was an embarrassed silence, while we all digested this new information.

And then they all turned towards me, as though realising for the first time I was present, and the lady who thought she was somewhere in Germany said, "Oh my, what will you think of us, the trouble is, Ah gets sort of confused."

Thinking—wrongly as it turned out—that I might make a small joke to relieve her embarrassment, I said, "It's like they say on these tours —if it's Wednesday— it must be Paris." This was followed by complete silence, as all four pair of eyes turned towards me in what can only be described as utter incomprehension.

Then our chequered pants chap said, "That ain't right, we did Paris last Saturday."

At which they all nodded in agreement and I pressed the lift button.

10. In and Out of Africa

There was a bit of a lull in all things Kazakh and rather than have me sitting festering at home, Alex rang and said, "We've got a nice little job in Africa—what do you think?"

I've noticed that whenever Alex has an 'iffy' job for me he speaks quickly as though, in ensuring I have no chance to interrupt, he already has my tacit agreement. I am, however, on to his devious ways and in the perceptive manner for which I'm renowned, said, "What do you mean, Africa?"

"What do you mean, 'what do I mean?' it's Africa, that big continent just below Europe. What more do you need to know?"

These negotiations with Alex can take some time, and the less he reveals, the more suspicious I become. "Whereabouts in Africa?" I said, "And don't tell me it's Nigeria, because I'd rather go to Uzbekistan than Nigeria." This wasn't quite true, but there's no use me sounding even remotely keen because, as far as Alex is concerned, anything other than a flat denial is a sign of acquiescence.

"Well?"

"It's Gabon."

"Where?"

"I've just told you, Gabon, you'll love it."

"No I bloody won't—it'll be just like your three week job in Kazakhstan, and I'll never see home or family again." I also find that some sort of emotional appeal is the only way to get through in these circumstances.

"It's just for a couple of weeks, and anyway I'm coming with you."

Now over the years I'd learned two things about Alex's attempts to 'sell' me a good idea. One was a tendency to speak fast, which would render any attempt to interrupt impossible; hence his pronouncement sounded like:

'It'sjustforacoupleofweeksandanywayI'mcomingwithyou.'

The second 'giveaway' was a marked reluctance to provide information regarding minor details such as, scope, whereabouts, duration, salary, travel arrangements, hardship, language barriers, currency, visa requirements and communications.

However, with considerable pressing, threatening, cajoling,

persuading, ignoring and blank refusals on both sides, some details finally emerged. We were to travel from Paris Charles de Gaulle to Libreville International Airport, transfer to Air Service Gabon and fly to Gamba via Port Gentil. This all sounded very straightforward, but having been to Africa previously, I wasn't too sanguine, besides, wasn't Libreville the scene of some so called peace negotiations to bring an end to the massacres in neighbouring Congo. Why can't we go to somewhere nice like the Bahamas?

Inevitably, I agreed, just as Alex knew I would, so preparations were made and at least this time, I could provide evidence that I didn't have AIDS. There were the usual requirements for a visa (accompanied by a cheque for £70,) some local currency, vaccination certificates designed to prevent, among other things, a delightful disease known as Meningococcal Infection.

I was also to find out that Gabon has a moist, hot climate and other than in December and January, rainfall is heavy, which as far as I was concerned was a criminal understatement. Forget words like downpour, heavy, stormy or cloudburst—this was serious vertical water, which laughed in the face of windscreen wipers, umbrellas or waterproofs. I watched a gutter in the building opposite one morning fill to the brim in about six seconds and then pour over the edge in what looked like one continuous sheet of water. A bit like Niagara Falls, only bigger.

A by-product of all this damp was the fact that the humidity was awesome. So much so, that stepping out of the office or accommodation caused your glasses to completely steam up, the result of which was that you moved cautiously, in the manner of 'Poor Blind Pugh,' and with a tendency to stumble over fallen leaves.

However, after a few days of sweating, soaking, boiling and re-hydrating, we began to see that Gabon was indeed a beautiful country. It was still heavily forested and realised it was one of the last great sanctuaries for wild animals. On one occasion I had to travel inland to the main Production Facility, which meant taking a forty-minute trip in a small aircraft before landing at an airstrip in the middle of the rainforest. I was given the usual guarded welcome and having, in my own inimitable style, messed up a complete morning for the Production Supervisor (consultants are prone to do this to innocent hardworking people) I expressed an interest over lunch in seeing some wildlife. The Supervisor's eyes lit up and before I could change my mind, a trusty landcruiser had been allocated, Terry, an Inspection Engineer had, without the option, been delegated to accompany me on safari and off we went along a series of red clay roads cut into the forest. Within a couple of kilometres, Terry, who had by now realised that taking a consultant for a joy-ride, was better than inspecting, pulled up and we trekked a short distance into the undergrowth. This little detour was taken very much in the manner of David Attenborough; we went in single file, Terry kept shushing me and started to use some incomprehensible hand signals. However, he seemed to know what he was doing as, on reaching a natural clearing by a small lake, we spotted a herd of elephants doing elephant type things with water. I have to say it was much better than asking damn-fool questions of largely reluctant production staff.

From there, we followed more tracks, in an effort, said Terry, to spot some monkeys—which we did, but I can't for the life of me remember what type (or should that be species?) they were. As I said to Terry, "Well there's one thing I'm fairly sure of, they weren't gorillas." I laughed knowingly at both my wit and in-depth knowledge of wild-life, until Terry said, "It's a bloody good job they weren't; they don't generally venture this far towards the production area, but there have been times at night when you could hear them calling."

"Are there many then?" I asked.

"It's reckoned there are some thirty five thousand gorillas in Gabon with about sixty thousand elephants."

I said, "Oh, shouldn't we be getting back to camp?"

Interestingly, if that's the word, I was waiting in the open air queue to check in for my flight back to the coast, when somebody said, "Bloody hell, there's a great big elephant coming our way." We crowded to the edge of the tarmac and sure enough, there it was and having emerged from the trees, was about to meander across the runway. Two thoughts crossed my mind, one—it was bigger than our plane; and two—it had the longest tusks I'd ever seen. At this point, a couple of airport baggage handlers rushed (somewhat tentatively in my opinion) across the loading area in a suicidal attempt to frighten the beast. We were now transfixed; what would the elephant do? As they got closer, the two lads slowed down as they presumably realised, in terms of muscle power, the tusker had a distinct advantage. However, apparently noticing for the first time that he was about to be surrounded from a discreet distance, the elephant raised his trunk and gave out an ear-splitting roar. This, for some reason, brought about a change of plan on the part of the lads, who stopped, stared at one another, turned as though on ice and raced back to the edge of the loading bay. The elephant, having lost interest in the now departed clearance team, continued on a meandering path along the centre of the runway. Just then we heard the sound of our incoming plane making a tight turn to line up for a landing. I thought; let's just hope the pilot sees the tusker in time to abort his landing, or there's going to be an almighty crash as animal and metal collide at speed.

And then, just as the erstwhile elephant removers reached safety, the plane came into sight over the top of the trees with the wings waggling up and down as the pilot fought the cross-wind—a bit like Biggles who, having shaken off the Hun, is limping back to base with a plane full of bullet holes. I could see the headlines—*Disaster in the jungle as plane hits bull elephant*, but fortunately, it wasn't to be, the elephant, on hearing the terrible noise of twin aero engines being retarded, decided to amble off back into the trees.

And to think, at Aberdeen Airport they get all tense over a few seagulls.

What I most enjoyed, on return to base that evening, was telling Alex in graphic and exaggerated detail just what he'd missed in the way of wild-life, Africa style. I felt this to be a reasonable revenge for him having sent me 'up-country'—as we explorers say—without any thought for my safety. I also regaled him with stories about the proliferation of the Gaboon Viper, the need to check your bedclothes and boots for deadly spiders and the risk of meeting a stray crocodile. I must confess that I made most of it up, but when you're on a terror strike, it's best to capitalise, I find.

Our office was close to the sea and we often drove the short distance to the beach after a quick lunch. I couldn't fail to be impressed the first time we saw the South Atlantic from close quarters, a pristine area of sand stretched away into the distance on both sides; there was a complete absence of people and the jungle came right down to the edge of the beach, just like it does in films. The most startling thing, however, was the sight of dozens of huge (and I do mean huge) logs lying along the beach. We clambered down for a better look and found they had obviously been washed ashore, as most of them were aligned just above the high water mark. They were enormous; many them were some thirty to forty feet long and three to four feet in diameter. I foolishly tried to move one of the smaller logs, without any success, but with the distinct possibility of a hernia. They were a deep red colour and I thought they must be teak. Being curious, I asked one of the Gabonese guys whether it was, in fact, teak and he said, "Yes, they're most likely to be the result of logging operations where they float the logs down to the port. However, if there's a storm, many break away and are later washed ashore." He also told me that Gabon is home to the okoumé, a hard, reddish-brown type of mahogany, and another tropical hardwood known as padouk is also found here. Then there are rare dyewoods with names such as bubinga, moabi and beli as well as ebony. I remembered many of the names from my days as an amateur wood turner and knew how expensive even a small piece could be; I now began to understand why.

I couldn't help thinking that had the logs been washed up within striking distance of the average Scouser, the beach would have been full of blokes sawing, chiseling, drilling and assembling the logs into bespoke house and garden furniture. In fact, I could foresee the beach being completely cleared in about six months, while the self-styled craftsmen prayed for bad weather as a means of ensuring a regular supply of raw material.

Meeting the Gabonese staff for the first time was a pleasant experience. They were unfailingly polite, anxious to please, spoke French, were interested in Manchester United (nobody's perfect) and proud of their country. We set to and did our thing on matters managerial and after several days of interviews, meetings, document searches, statistical analysis and coffee, we made our recommendations. As is the way with these things, our conclusions were met with stunned silence, partly because, as one of the Maintenance chaps observed,

"We already knew what was wrong, but hated having it confirmed by outsiders."

However, as it was they who'd asked us along, implementation of our recommendations was placed in the hands of a lad by the name of Aniset; he had been very helpful throughout our investigations and was extremely keen to please. He was of medium height, wore spectacles which made him look uncannily like a dark-skinned version of Harry Potter, and had received a traditional education under the tender mercies of nuns, before breaking free and obtaining a degree in Statistics.

Delighted to be the focal point of such an important venture; Aniset worked tirelessly to develop a game-plan, schedules of meetings, Gantt-charts, critical-path analyses, implementation goals and coffee. Agreeing we were extremely lucky to have such a capable assistant, we decided to return home for a couple of weeks. From our point of view, it's called 'delegation' and 'retained ownership,' from the recipient's point of view it's called 'bloody typical' and reinforces the definition of a consultant as 'someone who borrows your watch to tell you the time.' We of course disagreed with this awful calumny.

On our return, we met Aniset in his office, there to be confronted by a wall full of charts, graphs, critical path diagrams, colour-coded meeting schedules and progress reports. We were visibly shaken—dedication of this nature was, to say the least, rare. Aniset was delighted to see us and keen to show off his efforts; we in turn, were full of praise and ordered coffees all round. When I say 'ordered' this actually meant me going into a sort of lean-to next to the Inspection office, rinsing some disgusting mugs, finding the instant sachets and boiling water in a dangerous looking electric kettle. Still, this was no time for nit-picking; here was real progress and all apparently without threats, pleas or bribery.

Becoming dangerously excited, I suggested it would be a good idea to carry out a random sample of progress so far; peoples' opinions of the changes and what benefits might accrue. So, armed with a copy of Aniset's game plan, off I went. After about an hour, during which I had questioned a number of recipients, I became increasingly puzzled. In each case, the answer was the same—no one had approached them with the revised operating regime—in fact, they were equally puzzled, as they thought the changes would be initiated by Alex and me on our return. My showing them Aniset's document only caused head-shaking, and a denial of ever having set eyes on the thing. Time to retreat, make a cup of coffee and find out what had gone wrong.

I nipped in to see the George, the operations supervisor and explained my dilemma: on the one hand, a wall full of progress charts and job schedules, on the other hand, no sign that the agreed improvements had been introduced.

George, who bore an uncanny resemblance to Henry Fonda, said, "Who is it that's handling the job for us?"

"Aniset," I said.

"Ah."

"What do you mean, ah?"

"Well, it's not that he's not a good lad—he is. However, he's incredibly shy and we've found in the past that implementation isn't his strong point."

"Yes, but what about the progress charts all over his wall?"

"It's just another example of what I'm saying; he's full of good intentions and rather than let you think he hadn't been busy, he's probably created a sort of dream world where he knows what needs to be done and by whom, but he's failed to apprise them of his plan."

"Yes, but he seemed so pleased when running through the detailed charts; we were very impressed and told him such initiative was rare and what a grand job he'd done."

"I should have warned you, but I didn't think for a moment he would prepare a wall full of highly imaginative rubbish. I'll need to talk to him; in the meantime, I'm afraid the implementation programme is up to you guys."

I thought, 'If he smiles at me when I get back, I'll swing for the little sod.'

As it happened, he did and I didn't, but I did sit down with him and try to get him to distinguish between fact and fiction. I even quoted from one of my favourite films, *The Secret Life of Walter Mitty,* starring the genius that was Danny Kaye, where he also lives in a sort of dream world. But all he did was smile and agree; even though I was convinced he hadn't understood a bloody word I'd said.

So, overcoming our disappointment and deciding not to kill Aniset for raising our hopes of a swift conclusion, we conferred all over again, held more meetings and with a promise from George that he would oversee Aniset overseeing progress, we departed for home.

Then, just as we were due to return—and as if we hadn't had enough excitement—the roof in Terminal 2E in Charles de Gaulle airport collapsed. A thirty-metre by twenty-metre section of the vaulted roof of the departure building—a futuristic, curving structure supported by stilts and hailed as a technological masterpiece when the terminal opened—fell into the passenger lounge. This caused the concave, glass-and-steel walls to give way in turn and crush airport service vehicles and a passenger gangway below.

Terminal 2E was the partially completed jewel in the crown of Charles de Gaulle airport. It's reserved for the national flag carrier, Air France, and its partner airlines. If the building, which was capable of receiving 10,000 passengers at a time, had collapsed at a busier period than early on a Sunday morning, there could have been scores of victims.

The provisional casualty list was five dead (all believed to be passengers) one person critically injured and three police officers slightly hurt.

Questions were asked in France about how such a recently completed building—symbolic of the engineering panache and aviation prowess dear to the country's heart—should have collapsed after only eleven months in service. Apparently, there'd been controversy before its opening, including union complaints that the work was being pushed forward too quickly.

Interestingly, we heard that the Government inspection team refused to grant a safety certificate at first, delaying the opening for one week, after a chandelier plunged to the ground while the team was in the building. Which, I suppose, just goes to show that timing is everything.

However, a contract was a contract so, staring cautiously at the ceiling, we boarded France's finest and travelled south once more, where were met again by a smiling Aniset. Clutching a coffee apiece, we re-convened in his office to find that the wall charts had all been updated, re-coloured, annotated and revised. The only trouble was, we didn't like to ask him whether anyone else on site was aware of the progress he'd so painstakingly identified. So, adopting my well known 'kindly old uncle' mode, I suggested we take copies of his output and pop along to the key players to see how they were doing. He beamed at this proposal and copied everything in sight, provided me with a document folder to carry them in and marked it with the project name, my name, Alex's name, George's name, his name and the date. I hadn't the heart to stop him.

So, armed with freshly named documentation, we set up a series of appointments with the relevant supervisors with whom, by now, we had become relatively at ease. Then, after a fresh cup of coffee, Alex and I set off to talk to each one in turn. We knocked on the first door and entered only to find it was empty—strange. However, as we moved along the corridors we were met with the same absence of occupants. By now, word was percolating through to us that all the supervisors and section heads had been called to an urgent meeting and as such, it was unlikely we would be able to conduct our interviews in the foreseeable future—very strange we thought—which called for a restorative cup of coffee.

Hoping to solve the puzzle, we went across to the second office block in an effort to see Leroy, our contract sponsor and find out from him just what was going on. This was the guy who had asked us to carry out the study and, more importantly, was the chap who paid our invoices. Obviously, we thought, he was the best person to throw some light on the missing interviewees.

Consider our surprise therefore, when, on reaching his office, we found it was locked. The whole enterprise was taking on all the attributes of an onshore Marie Celeste. By then, we were becoming more and more baffled and beginning to wonder whether it was something we'd said, so we nipped into the General Office to find at last, signs of humanity. Again, on reaching the first row of desks, a feeling of paranoia descended as, on seeing us, a hush fell on the populace, heads were bent steeply downwards, people began to peer into drawers and cupboards, making it patently clear that, as far as they were concerned—we weren't there and they hadn't seen us.

However, being consultants and used to being ignored, we waited for a sign of weakness and when finally, one of the chaps glanced up to see whether we'd gone.

I pounced, "Where is everyone?"

There was a long pause as he digested the fact that he'd been conned and very reluctantly, he said, "Ah, I believe there's some kind of a problem and everyone's been called into the Operations Manager's office."

"I can see there's a problem, but what is it?"

He stared at the ceiling, and then at his colleagues, who in turn, were careful not to meet his gaze. Then, realising we weren't about to go away, he said, "I believe there's been a bit of trouble regarding contracts, but that's all I know."

It was now clear we would get no further in solving the mystery of the missing staff, so I thanked him and we went off for a coffee. I said to Alex, "I've seen this before; I'll bet someone's been dipping into the till and has been found out. I wonder who it is."

The morning wore on, nobody appeared, we went to lunch, onto the beach, back to the office and still we were on our own. By now, it was patently clear there was something serious happening—or in our case —not happening. We trooped back to Aniset's office to find that even he'd disappeared. There seemed to be nothing for it but to go back to our place and nod off until we found out what was going on. We must have nodded for a while, because at about five pm, Aniset appeared and said the Operations Manager wanted to see us in his inner sanctum. We trooped across, knocked and entered. The great man bade us sit down and came out with one of those classic understatements.

"I expect you've been wondering what's been going on."

"Well yes, we were a bit puzzled." This was me being understated as well.

"I can't take you completely into my confidence, but we've discovered a member of staff has been behaving unethically and as a consequence, I've had to call on Internal Audit to carry out a thorough investigation."

Alex said, "Oh well, thank you for telling us. We understand your need for confidentiality, so we'll come back in the morning and re-convene with Leroy to set up a new game-plan."

There was a sort of choking cough from the manager and he said, "I'm afraid that won't be possible—he's been sacked."

As there didn't seem to be anything else to say, we thanked him and beat a retreat. We were pondering on the ramifications of the news on our way back to the Camp when Alex, with an unerring sense of priorities, said, "It's all very well them sacking Leroy, but what I want to know is who'll pay our invoices now."

I said, "Let's just hope that Leroy, in his quest for financial independence, hasn't sold our contract to some sinister organisation." I guess I must have been thinking of the troubles in Libreville again. Still, things began to look better over a meal of langoustines and cold beer and there was always Aniset who, come what may, could always be relied on to give us one of his encouraging smiles in the morning.

So we pondered for a while, ordered more beer, looked at one another, ordered more beer, then decided that a smile, however gleaming, wasn't enough to sustain us and it was time for us to go back to the relative sanity of Aberdeen.

However, as is usual when consulting, you need a promise of further work. This involved us in finding out where Leroy's deputy was hidden and seeking a promise that he would let us know when it was safe to return. Having, as we naively thought, done so, we said goodbye to Aniset (who smiled) and came home. Then, over the next few weeks we waited in vain to hear from anybody, but to no avail. This was somewhat puzzling as we hadn't finished our assignment and yet, despite sending numerous emails, we heard no word back.

Having amused ourselves by blaming one another for the prolonged silence from the heart of Africa, Alex finally obtained a likely explanation from one of our colleagues who'd just returned from a project in the same area. Apparently, our friends had been the victim of what is known in the business as 'downsizing in order to better realign resources with changing market conditions'. This is a well known euphemism for the elimination of jobs and the inevitable consequence of which is a reduction of budget allocated for important things like consultants.

Here I was once again out of a job and I have to say I was quite beginning to miss the company of my Italian friends. So, I thought, let's go back to Kazakhstan, where being harassed by morose people wearing big hats, in a two storey wooden terminal, probably built by slave labour and with a distinct absence of chandeliers, seemed very attractive. As usual, this exercise in logical thinking turned out to be wrong.

Oh, I nearly forgot, we did get paid—eventually.

Washed-up teak log—make a nice set of patio furniture, that would.

My first return trip fell into the usual pattern of queuing, checking, stamping, waiting and being stared at for minutes at a time, whilst they compared me to my passport photograph. Finally we boarded our bus and with the reassuring crash of gears being randomly engaged, we set off. I was quietly dozing when the bus turned sharp left, plunged down an embankment at the side of the road and I was thrown forward, only to be stopped abruptly when my head hit the back of the seat in front. As I tried to regain both my seat and composure, the bus ploughed on, bouncing over rutted tracks alongside a field. We were running parallel to the road which could be seen from the window on my right and I thought 'we're being attacked by bandits and the driver's trying to get away—we're all going to be killed, I should have stayed in Africa.'

You may notice here a tendency to leap to the most awful conclusions without a scrap of evidence in support. It's not my fault; if anything unexpected happens, I'm once again mentally transported into the realms of fantasy created by John le Carre. This time it's the one where the double agent is trying to get across the East German border in a stolen Trabant when he spots a road block ahead and with great presence of mind and dodgy steering, drives off the side of the road and into the forest. (If you want to know more—read the book.) Funnily enough, I soon found we weren't about to be chased—it was simply that the real road had been washed away and rather than spend money on repairs, the Authorities encouraged drivers to take their own evasive action. This required you to plunge down a one in three embankment and drive alongside the road for about half a mile before hurling the bus back up the slope to rejoin the carriageway. In some strange way, I was kind of reassured by all this mayhem; nothing had changed, lunacy ruled as usual and nobody thought that what had happened was in any way out of the ordinary.

It was good to be back and reminded me of a conversation I'd had a year or two previously, when I was annoyed and frustrated at the meaningless behaviour of the airport customs brigade. We were chatting over lunch one day and I let rip with a degree of pent-up emotion at the useless delays we suffered every time we entered or left the country. Ron, one of our drilling engineers, heard my outburst and said, "Brian, why would they hurry?"

"Why?" I said, "Because they know we're only going to a secure camp a hundred miles away and while we're there, we simply go to work for a minimum of twelve hours, before staggering back for a meal and bed.

We pose no threat to anyone and it's even more futile when we're going home. We're locked in the airport, we're escorted to the plane and we're not allowed to look out of the windows. That's why."

You can perhaps see that I was in the grip of some strong emotion and the more I thought about it the worse I felt.

Ron listened to all this in silence and said, "You need to put yourself in their position and ask—why would they hurry? We're the sole foreign flight in to their airport and we only arrive and depart once a fortnight. In between time they have absolutely bugger all to do. Our arrival is the highpoint of their day, uniforms are pressed, hats are brushed, medals are worn and for a couple of hours they can pretend it's a return to the good old days. It's their chance once more to inspect, check, confer, re-check, examine, refuse, stamp, search, stare, strut and generally re-enact the glorious past, when they could send suspicious characters like us to a Gulag.

"That's why they don't hurry; it's a moment for them to savour and convince themselves that their ability to strike terror is alive and well—at least that is, in a remote empty airport in the middle of bloody nowhere."

Then, for some unaccountable reason, I felt ashamed. Who was I to deny a perfectly nice group of people their moment of glory? And that's how from then on, when arriving or departing, I perfected the art of suspended animation.

It seemed as though I'd just settled back into a well-loved routine of chai, espresso, contract negotiations, vodka, debates with Paulo regarding the astonishing beauty of Sophia and the reassuring sight of Mr Prandi eating chocolate, when my routine changed once again.

I travelled out on my next rota only to find that Paulo had sort of disappeared and that the project was being subjected to a mass attack by a very expensive Business Consultancy.

Apparently, as is the way with consortia, one of the partners, being convinced that they could run the project better than the present incumbent, had engaged the services of said consultants. And they, being firmly in Mckinsey type mode, had descended *en masse* on the project and began to make a nuisance of themselves by asking hundreds of carefully prepared and mostly useless questions.

Now, in order to be considered for a job with these people you had to fulfil certain criteria. You would be in your early twenties (but look about sixteen). You would have perfect teeth, shiny hair, no acne scars, play squash, have absolutely no experience of the real world, call everyone sir and, most important of all, carry a pre-programmed lap-top.

This machine was the Bible; it contained all the essential elements needed for the perfect project and could spit out copious amounts of coloured pie-charts, cause-effect diagrams, stratification trends, scatter diagrams, stress in organisational change pointers and high-velocity culture norms—to name but a few. Over the weeks I was there, they pointedly ignored me, but inflicted endless presentations, recommendations, workshops, seminars, brainstorming sessions and dozens of coloured wall-charts, on everyone else.

I did manage to hold a conversation one evening with one of these wizz-kids (no—I'm not being cynical, well—maybe just a little) and he confessed, in an unguarded moment, that his parent company had pre-ordained what they should look for, how they should make the information fit their programmes and how to present the results to an organisation, prior to leaving as soon as possible thereafter. I asked him whether they ever stayed around to help a company with implementing their recommendations and I must say he looked appalled at the very idea. This is where, I told myself, that Alex and I went wrong in Africa, we should have given our plans to Anicet in a sealed envelope and beat a hasty retreat.

One unfortunate result of this incredibly costly (and as I found out later —entirely futile) exercise, was that my presence was seen to conflict with the findings of the child geniuses and therefore my contribution was no longer required. So once again, I found myself back in Aberdeen, with no leaving party, and still not having solved the mysterious disappearance of Paulo.

I hadn't long to wait, as one morning the phone rang and the dulcet tones I'd been used to hearing when partaking our daily espresso said, "How are you Brian?"

"I'm fine, but what happened to you, nobody seemed to know where you'd gone?" This was about the best I could manage before overcoming my surprise.

"Ah, Brian, that's why I'm calling, I've joined a new project being developed for the Caspian Sea, how would you like to join me?"

This was Paolo at his devious best, so I said, "Yes, but are we going back to Kazakhstan?"

"No, Brian, the project is located at present in an office in The Hague; could you come over for a week to help out?

"No problem," I replied, and so that's how the next great adventure began.

I travelled to Schiphol, took a train to Den Haag, found the office—which was designed by some madman with a fetish for the shape of ships bows—and waited at reception for Paulo.

We greeted one another warmly and he escorted me to my new domain, there to find Mr Prandi at a desk in the corner, Gianni in an office one floor above and to cap it all, when we went to have a celebratory espresso, a fleeting glimpse of cashmere cardigan, a whiff of Armani and a sinister smile. It then became obvious that my friends had gained advance notice of the impending descent of the child consultants and had moved smartly to pastures new. Brilliant!

As usual, my 'week' turned out to be six months, during which I stayed at the Carlton Beach Hotel at Scheveningen, I became a seasoned tram traveller, I discovered Henning Mankell's books and had my briefcase stolen at the railway station. All before we moved to new offices in London—but that's another story and one which I don't intend to bore you with. Enough already.

11. And Finally...

Well, here we are at the end of another saga of selfless devotion in the cause of bringing fuel to the masses and making the company's shareholders happy. Although the likelihood of the book being used in the future as a work of impeccable reference on the oil and gas industry is perhaps remote, it's worth reflecting on the fact that the anecdotes are true. Okay, some names and dates have been changed and on occasions my imagination has run riot when describing things. I worked on the premise that anything I might have made up couldn't possibly compete with the lunacy of the actual events—or maybe it's just that I was incapable of understanding the seriousness of the situation.

This book, I'm sure you'll be relieved to hear, is the last in the oil related series; there's a limit to the number of situations one can recall in a career spanning some thirty five years.

I have to say that I'm enjoying being a member of the literary fraternity, especially as I only started writing when I realised that waiting much longer for inspiration wasn't perhaps a sensible option. This need to get a move on was brought home to me when I came across a comment from Sylvester Stallone. He said, "I'm astounded by people who take eighteen years to write something. That's how long it took that guy to write Madame Bovary, and when was that ever on the best-seller list?"

I was puzzled by the comment until I realised he was referring to the fact that he wrote the script to 'Rocky' in three days. (Some may say 'you can tell' but nevertheless you have to agree he didn't exactly hang around).

The good thing about jotting down personal reminiscences is that you don't have to stare at a blank sheet of paper waiting for a complex murder plot to emerge. Although I have to say putting pen to paper is not as easy as some people think. Again, while we're on the subject of quotes, I like the one made by Raymond Chandler, who said, "When in doubt, have a man come through the door with a gun in his hand." Unfortunately this advice wasn't of much use to me—although there were times when having come up against the occasional toe-rag, being able to produce a gun would have been quite useful.

You may be astonished to know that never in my entire career did I get to meet Red Adair, Tony Benn, Harold Wilson, Jimmy Young,

Silvio Berlusconi or Zoltan Nazurbyev. But then again, sadly, I never met Sophia Loren either. Sometimes I find you can just be in the wrong place at the wrong time. Still, I mustn't sound too bitter; I did once bump into Rolf Harris at the airport, but he didn't appear to notice me.

It was, however, a privilege to meet and work with a super bunch of people both on and offshore and I wouldn't have missed being involved in the never ending quest for oil and gas for anything.

So where are we now, I hear you ask? Well, the infamous buoy was taken away in 1989 and contrary to Liam's fond hope that a depleted uranium guided missile would accidentally blow it to smithereens; it was towed to Loch Kishorn for a major refit. This inspired exercise in cost-saving required a complete replacement of the topsides, and in 1990 it was towed to another platform where it served as the crude oil export route until 2005, when it was finally taken ashore and broken up. As Bert remarked, "The sodding thing nearly outlasted the lot of us."

Our first platform, ably managed by Sid, was bought in 2006 by a Canadian company and continues to produce crude oil to this day. I hear that the estimated reserves are something in the region of 88 million barrels, which is interesting, especially when I remember what happened when we first went into production in 1976. We were all quite excited, until our esteemed Director came out to tell us that had they known the platform was going to cost £54 million to develop—they probably wouldn't have built it. It's a good job he isn't involved with the new Olympic Stadium, otherwise the athletes would find themselves running around the local park. To cap it all, our big concrete platform was sold in 2008 to a company from Abu Dhabi, I shudder to think what Vince would have made of that.

And just to dispel any doubts my loyal readers might have regarding their continued wellbeing, I'm pleased to report that only a short time ago, I enjoyed an excellent lunch with Liam and Bert and it seems only fitting that, as they opened the proceedings in Book One, they should close out Book Two.

You'll be glad to hear that both are still in good spirits, a little wider around the waist, somewhat greyer and like me, they move rather more slowly. However, their zest for life remains undimmed and during the meal they announced that a joint summer holiday was to be taken boating on the Norfolk Broads. As Bert remarked to me later, "It'll be great just as long as Liam isn't allowed to get his hands on the crane in the boatyard."

And then, a couple of months later I was chatting to Liam on the telephone and remembering they were soon to go on holiday, I said I hoped they would have a good time. Liam thanked me and replied, "It'll be great just as long as Bert doesn't start messing about with the engine." I suppose that French chap put it best when he said:

"Plus ça change, plus c'est la meme chose,"

THE END